THE ANSWER
IS WITHIN YOU

THE ANSWER
IS WITHIN YOU

Psychology, Women's Connections, and Breast Cancer

LAUREN K. AYERS, Ph.D.

CROSSROAD • NEW YORK

1994

The Crossroad Publishing Company
370 Lexington Avenue, New York, NY 10017

Copyright © 1994 by Lauren K. Ayers

Printed in the United States of America

Library of Congress Cataloging-in-Publication Data

Ayers, Lauren K.
    The answer is within you : psychology, women's connections, and
breast cancer / Lauren K. Ayers.
        p.   cm.
    Includes bibliographical references (p.).
    ISBN 0-8245-1431-9
    1. Breast—Cancer—Psychological aspects. 2. Breast—Cancer—
Prognosis. 3. Women—Psychology. 4. Interpersonal relations.
I. Title
RC280.B8A97   1994
616.99'449'019—dc20   94-34810
                                                              CIP

For Wilford Kurz
with Love

Breathe through the pulses of desire,
thy coolness and thy balm;
Let sense be dumb, let flesh retire,
Speak through the earthquake, wind, and fire,
O still, small voice of calm.

—John Greenleaf Whittier

Contents

Preface

What keeps us from falling out of bed at night? Far beyond our ability to reason and plan, forces within operate to protect us, day and night. These parts of the brain are much older than the thinking consciousness that is our constant companion, and they have operated down the eons to insure a future for the species. These drives do far more than to save us from injury while we sleep. For women, they have safeguarded health and, in so doing, have insured the survival of the next generation. For without mothers, reproduction fails and the human species dies out.

A host of inclinations, preferences, and patterns, all called "feminine," serve to enhance women's health and to maximize chances for survival, even in the face of serious illness. These are not magical powers, but rather the outward evidence of internal chemical balances that together strain toward health. These patterns have operated throughout human life on this planet, and they have kept us robust and powerful. The body is not a fragile organism and does not easily do itself in. But the vortex of social convention can overpower our own species wisdom.

The predispositions of women represent potent sources of healing and produce a measurable difference in health outcomes with breast cancer. For women dealing with this disease, the issue is therefore learning to speak with one's own voice and to trust internal capacities as sources of healing. It is a matter of giving our body and psyche what they need, including strong medical treatment and a good emotional climate, and having faith that the body will do the rest.

Modern medicine offers a great deal in cancer treatment, but this is only a part of a woman's resources. All of the internal female ways must be utilized, for they are powerful in the face of illness. They boost the power of medical treatments, multi-

13

plying their effectiveness, and they make the whole process more tolerable.

This book is not a new set of tricks for dealing with breast cancer, nor does it present miraculous findings or cures. Its purpose is to explore why some women do well with breast cancer and to identify the forces at work that can be utilized by other women.

Much of the research data described here may seem elementary to women, but it represents a hesitant revolution that is occurring in the great centers of psychological research. There are new understandings of the chemical connections between what we feel, as coded in the neurological and endocrine systems, and our other systems, particularly the immune system and the cardiovascular system. An emerging unitary view of body and mind is beginning to explain why, when a friend holds your hand, there is a change in pulse and an accompanying surge of internal chemical messengers.

But the research findings in this area are so far only academic curiosities, and rarely are they available to patients in clinical treatment. Taken together, they reveal potent human capacities for dealing with breast cancer. Largely for this reason, I wrote this book to make new information available to the women who can benefit most from it. It has been a constant frustration to see these findings beyond the reach of breast cancer patients.

Information-seeking is characteristic of women who deal successfully with breast cancer, for this type of behavior appears to correlate with physical disease resistance. Psychological research can be difficult to interpret, however, and so the material presented here has been summarized and explained as an aid to information seekers.

For women, health is not a solitary or individual issue, for it depends on the relationships they form with others. The life-enhancing need to connect is everywhere apparent in females, in the chatting that occurs on a restroom waiting line or in the agreeable head-bobbing characteristic of women's conversations. It is not something that needs to be relearned or instilled, but only expressed and supported. The psychological research demonstrates that these behavioral tendencies have a clear impact on health, and that women are most healthy when they act like women.

Femininity takes many forms and appears as a unique expression of each woman's inner voice. There is no one way to be female, but all require being one's own woman and speaking for oneself. Acting for others' approval, suppressing feelings, needs, and values, is not only stifling to the spirit, but detrimental to health.

This book has three things to tell women: first, that they can change the experience of breast cancer treatment; second, that they have a good chance at affecting the outcome; and third, that friendships are crucial to this process.

To maximize health, women need to understand the way that they are put together, in particular the critical and life-saving role of relationships. This is no casual matter. Women fight breast cancer best when they act like women and listen to the internal pilot that guides their behavior and choices. When they become like stereotypical males, they risk losing the gender wisdom that is essential in dealing with disease.

Women know what is good for them, and they have always known. They have had to know in order to take care of another generation's needs, which first requires knowing one's own. The knowledge is carried in the genes and the culture and comes forth anew in every generation. It explains why women rarely abandon, exploit, or abuse their children, and why most children can grow into healthy adults. But somehow as women came to look for power and equality in society, they began to turn away from the basic truths of femininity in service of the values of the larger culture, which has often seen "feminine" as a derogatory term. This book tells women what they already know but have ceased to believe or have come to ignore: that it is connections that maintain and restore health and that healing cannot be a solitary activity.

Acknowledgments

This book has been a long time coming, and many people have helped to produce it. First and foremost is Michael Leach at Crossroad Publishing Company, who has been willing to support a new perspective and to make available his dedication, his time, and his energy.

Jenilu Schoolman and Kate McLaughlin have been most generous in sharing their insights and experiences. Many other women with breast cancer, as well as women with concern for their friends and relatives with breast cancer, offered their ideas and their suggestions. We have learned from them that breast cancer survival is not some random trick of fate, but rather an orderly process that involves sometimes obscure rules of physiology and psychology.

Dr. Albert Ellman has been a strong supporter of this work, his primary interest being the welfare of women who might benefit from this material.

The Voorheesville Public Library and its director, Gail Alter Sacco, have been a wonderful source of information and help over the years, and their support has been invaluable. Dr. Joe Sacco's help has also been appreciated.

Dr. Fred Storm read and commented on this manuscript, and his insights were very useful. Yale Sussman, a writer by profession, spent a good deal of time helping to insure that this manuscript was readable, and his assistance is greatly appreciated.

My husband, Phil Roberts, has been a source of strength and support, and without his help this book could not have been written. My children's enthusiasm and encouragement in sharing the puzzle and excitement of these research findings has been a source of inspiration as well.

Chapter One

Marylu's Battle

When Marylu talks, it's not hard to listen. She is talking now, over lunch, and her sparkling blue eyes always seem about to laugh. A tall woman in her mid-fifties, she wears little makeup, the sunshine giving a rosiness to her cheeks and brightening the freckles that sprinkle across the bridge of her nose. She looks younger than her age and radiates a delight in life that most people lose after the teen years. She is more fundamentally alive than most other people you meet in a day, and that's what makes the puzzle even more perplexing. How can somebody with advanced cancer look so healthy?

She is, in fact, supposed to be dead. The doctors who treat her for her breast cancer were clear and said things like, "No hope," and "Short time," and the word spread through our community of psychologists. Terminally ill. So sad. Such a good person, and a fine psychologist. One of the most disturbed by her illness was a brilliant colleague with a national reputation, who was himself killed shortly after we learned the news about Marylu when a drunk driver entered the exit ramp of the thruway and struck him head on. Not much later, another psychologist developed a rare neurological disease and died within months. It was a very bad year for our professional community.

But all this happened a long time ago, and after the initial flurry of distress and concern, people lost interest in Marylu's illness, although when anyone thought of it, they asked her how she was feeling. It was still understood that she was terminally ill, but it had begun to dawn on us that nobody is immortal, and life is not nearly as predictable as we think.

There had been no mistake in the diagnosis. Marylu had metastatic breast cancer, and after treatment it had continued spreading. It had begun dominating major organ systems, so that her whole body was compromised.

But then something happened to the progression of the disease. It stopped. Without any faith healers, magical treatments, or miracle drugs, the cancer stopped advancing. Marylu's body held its own, brought the disease to a standstill, and held it there. The tests every six months show the same result each time: no change. Her cancer is not cured and has not disappeared. It remains metastatic breast cancer, spread to vital organs. But she is not sick, and she lives the life she enjoys.

This was the puzzle that would send me on a long search, a search for answers about why one body can do this, about the internal conditions that are hospitable or hostile to cancer growth. I have a strong faith in scientific causation and believe that there are no miracles in health and illness, only lots of unknown unknowns.

So now Marylu is eating a big lunch of a roast beef sandwich with French fries and potato salad. She says that if she's going to die, she's going to eat whatever she likes, and the natural color to her cheeks as she winks at me makes me wonder why she doesn't have bags under her eyes like most therapists our age.

Marylu first found a breast lump years ago, but since her mother had had breast cancer and was still alive and well, it wasn't very frightening. She had undergone a mastectomy, followed by chemotherapy, and found it a strange experience. The medications had few side effects until one day that her hair fell out during one twenty-four-hour period when she said she felt very much like a shedding dog.

After the treatment, she thought a good deal about life and her dreams and options, and that was when, in her words, she "bought the farm." You may know that in aviation lingo, when a pilot has "bought the farm," it means that his plane has crashed and he has gone down with it. So it seemed a great joke to Marylu that at death's door she bought the farm. But she wasn't talking about airplane accidents. She literally purchased real estate with her friends, and together they have created a pastoral life.

Since childhood she had loved the life and routines of animal keeping, and because caring for others comes spontaneously to her, the farm was a good fit. It was a full family to her, the cows and goats, dogs, rabbits, and, most importantly, the llamas. It was here that she felt most peaceful, and her face reflected it. When she came in from making rounds in the evening, there was serenity and joy in her eyes.

The farm was, more importantly, a gathering place for people. Friends, neighbors, and family all loved to be there and share in the sense of refuge and warmth. They often gathered, sometimes uninvited but always welcome and usually lingering. At the beginning, people thought that Marylu was crazy to buy a farm, particularly since she knew nothing about farming, and that she would be quickly overwhelmed. But people didn't really know Marylu. When her first kangaroo arrived and needed to be nursed around the clock, she bundled him up and took him with her wherever she went, feeding him when he needed it.

The farm was working well when she learned on checkup that her cancer was on the move again. This round of treatment was difficult, and she was often sick, and the news from her doctor was not good. There was now a steadily advancing cancer and treatment would give her a little time, but not much. She needed to "get her affairs in order," make a will, plan a funeral, write good-bye letters — and everything inside her raged.

Chemotherapy exhausted her and made her feel sick and old, but at home there were all the farm animals to keep her company, and the llamas often came and sat with her when she was too ill to move, quietly humming their soundless tune. She complained a lot and got angry and frustrated with all the restrictions and conditions on her life, and the llamas and the loved ones listened and sympathized. Often the only thing that others could do for her, people and animals, was to sit with her and make comforting sounds.

As the effects of the chemotherapy cleared, she began to feel better and got back to her chores. She found herself slipping back into normal activities, like her private practice — where therapy patients treated her like a reincarnation — the weaving on quiet evenings at home, the talking, laughing, and crying whenever she needed to, and getting interested again in her friends' troubles and crises.

An active person, she felt the internal pressure to return to a full work schedule, but instead she chose to live her life as though it were about to end, spending good times with family and friends, working less, and exploring the feelings that go with a powerful life experience.

Good health continued, requiring more decisions. The everyday problems put off during crisis reemerged and demanded solutions. No longer could she put aside her customary frugality and indulge in one final this or that. The choices had to be made, either for a life extended or a life limited.

And life went on, lived a day at a time, and fully. And it still goes on, at this writing. To the pessimist, we begin dying the day we are born. To the optimist, life is to be lived in the current day.

For me, eating lunch with Marylu and sharing the warmth of friendship and conversation, it is painful to know that she still has advanced cancer and that although she lives a healthy life, it is not clear why. But perhaps there is an opportunity here: maybe the better question is to look at her experience, and the field of breast cancer, and ask, *Why not?*

•

Marylu is not the only cancer patient who has survived a gloomy prognosis. When doctors predict how a patient will fare with breast cancer, they predict according to averages, and many patients do far better than expected. Medical treatment for breast cancer offers a great deal of hope for patients, but a woman's power to counter breast cancer does not end when she leaves her doctor's office. Nor need she revamp her personality or develop special powers or learn biochemistry, to expand her body's natural defense system. For women with breast cancer, the answers are already within.

This book is an attempt to explain the forces at work that have restored health to Marylu and others, those variables not yet identified by science, the unknown unknowns that tip the scales in a patient's favor. It is not a miracle story, and it offers no guaranteed methods of beating cancer.

It is instead like a good mystery that attempts to identify those invisible forces that confront a powerful villain intent on doing harm and, against all odds, thwart that villain's course. But there are really two mysteries. The first involves the inner resources that checkmated Marylu's cancer. The second is stranger and more ironic. That is the mystery of why forces that can change the odds in cancer treatment are generally ignored in medicine.

The Spiegel Breakthrough

Advances in electronics and communications have produced a society in which the power to transmit information has outpaced our human ability to understand what we hear. Often messages are sent too quickly for us to comprehend, and we need more time to grasp what is being communicated. It is easy to feel inadequate and ignorant in the face of so much information coming at us.

Science often seems more dependable than our own judgment, and it is easy to assume that progress in cancer treatment will come from technology and medical advances. But the problem with anticipating news from one source is that you may fail to hear news from another, unexpected source. That is why when in 1989 breast cancer study results were published that would change our understanding of cancer completely, they had little impact on medical treatment.

When David Spiegel first began working with breast cancer patients, he already had a very large reputation in psychology and medicine. Although a young man, he was a major figure in the field of medical hypnosis as well as general psychiatry, and the research journals are sprinkled with his publications in psychology and medicine. Together with Irving Yalom, an important voice in the area of group dynamics, Spiegel conducted a research program at Stanford University that involved group psychotherapy to help women with breast cancer deal with the emotional turmoil of the disease.

Spiegel was not the first to use psychological techniques to ease the misery of cancer. Forty years earlier, psychologist Lawrence LeShan had worked with very ill cancer patients to reduce their ordeal. A brilliant and insightful clinician, LeShan suggested in the 1950s that cancer involves despair and loneliness, the result of a sense of estrangement from others. He suggested a connection between the psychological experience of loss and the biochemical process of disease.

LeShan's findings were based upon individual psychotherapy with many cancer patients and led him to make certain predictions. He suggested that a nation's cancer rates would go up during a war if the nation were disrupted and down if the country were united. He also predicted that married people with children would have lower cancer rates than married people without children. The predictions were later borne out by research.[1] He used psychotherapy to help his patients reestablish a sense of belonging and to help them create more satisfying lives.

So when David Spiegel used group psychotherapy for the same purpose, the approach was not a new one. But his research occurred at a time when exorbitant claims were being made for the healing power of psychology. Physicians, writers, and others were contending that thinking the right thoughts and being happy would cure cancer. Those working in legitimate science were understandably dismayed by the disappointment, accusations, and ridicule that resulted from these overblown claims and magical thinking about cancer treatment.

It's frustrating to work hard at a complicated job and have others mess it up out of ignorance. Spiegel, always a man for facts, decided to challenge the "positive-thinking-cures-cancer" advocates. He could refute their claims by reporting results from his group psychotherapy work with women with advanced cancers.

Advanced cancers are challenging to treat because the burden of the tumors on the body systems is so great that there is little medical treatment that can have much effect, and life is considerably shortened under these conditions. When surgery or chemotherapy are done at this point, it is usually to improve the patient's quality of life, because they have little effect on the length of time left. The Stanford program used group psychotherapy in addition to regular medical care to help patients feel better and enjoy life more. But the disease was so powerful that if medical treatment had minimal impact, then, in Spiegel's hypothesis, negligible forces like feelings and thoughts would show no influence at all.

During the 1970s and 1980s, groups of all sorts abounded. There were sensitivity training groups, consciousness-raising groups, and many kinds of groups that served the "let it all hang out" philosophy of the times. Traditional group psychotherapy as done at Stanford, however, was distinctly different, since it followed traditional practice in this form of psychological work. Women learned in group sessions to speak clearly about themselves and their feelings, and in doing so they formed strong and supportive connections with one another. Groups met weekly for ninety minutes for a year and were led by two trained therapists.

In studying psychological influences on advanced cancer, Spiegel was stacking the deck against himself, because statistics showed that the disease was relatively unresponsive to anything at this stage. His experiment seemed destined to demonstrate the obvious, that psychological factors make no difference in the course of the disease. With early breast cancer, the situation is distinctly different, because cancer at this stage responds to many outside interventions.

Most women with primary breast cancer — the mildest and most common form of breast cancer — recover and return to health. It makes sense to predict that they recover faster and stay healthy longer if psychological forces are on their side, so group psychotherapy would be more likely to have an effect with this form of the disease. But this was not the focus of Spiegel's research.

To test his hypothesis, that psychological change can't affect the course of advanced cancers, Spiegel compared disease outcomes in breast cancer patients who had group psychotherapy and those who hadn't. He obtained records of women who had been in his psychotherapy groups years earlier, and compared the disease's course in both over a decade.

His findings were *exactly the opposite* of what he and the field of medicine would have predicted. Breast cancer patients who received group psychotherapy along with standard medical treatment survived an average of *twice as long* with their advanced disease. Women who had only the standard medical treatment survived half as long as the women in the psychological treatment groups. Furthermore, ten years after the group psychotherapy ended, several of the patients who received group treatment were still alive, while in the control group, none had survived.[2]

Spiegel's findings shed light on Marylu's experience. They proved that the course of advanced breast cancer is not unalterable and it can be changed by nonmedical influences, even in its most potent form. But how can this happen?

Women as Health Experts

The idea of special feminine powers is an old one and has its roots in ancient perceptions of woman as sorceress and, sometimes, witch. It is more than mysticism, however, and the practical tasks of soothing and healing babies, children, and family members are usually seen as responsive to a woman's touch.

Women know things that men do not, often without teaching or training, although these can increase a woman's abilities. The differences between male and female go far deeper than acculturation, however, and some of them exist on a biochemical level. The male and female central nervous systems are not the same, for example, and in severe stress, men have higher levels of stress chemicals, specifically catecholamines, than women.

This is strange talk in an age when the equality of men and women is a sacred belief. In a nation where human differences have been used to deny people political and economic power, it may seem risky to point to women as unique. But the differences are real, and they extend throughout the life cycle.

New theories of human development, in particular, those of Jean Baker Miller, Carol Gilligan, and others, have argued that women develop differently than men do. For a male, self-reliance and control are important to develop in childhood and adolescence, and a boy needs to separate from those he depends on to feel his own strength.

For women, the needs are different; girls may not need to draw lines between parent and child since personal identity develops in a different way. Carol Gilligan's research at Harvard finds that attaching, sharing, and relating to others are the primary vehicles for the development of a woman's adult concept of herself. It is in relationships such as those fostered by Marylu that women can feel most individual and free.

Self-worth is different for men and women. For men it depends on the ability to sustain themselves; for women it depends on the ability to sustain relationships and be themselves. Often in this culture, girls experience what Gilligan calls a psychological foot binding, in which they are taught to mask their genuine feelings and thoughts so as to be acceptable in relationships.

This leads to very different beliefs about what makes for personal well-being, and may lead to conflict as well. When a husband says that his wife is too dependent on him and she says he doesn't express his feelings, they are in fact reflecting differences in how they are put together. He is seeking autonomy, while she is seeking a way to be her own person through connecting with others. When women assume that they are the same as men on the inside, they deny their own needs. Women are not necessarily better than men, but they are different in the ways that they support their own well-being.

The Spiegel results involved far more than the success of group psychotherapy in boosting medical treatment for breast cancer. They established that women need to be connected to other women and that their health is enhanced when they act most like women.

Talking, sharing feelings and reactions, exploring ideas in depth, and discussing relationships are powerful forms of therapy for breast cancer. When this sort of talking is expressive and supportive, it has the capacity to sustain life beyond normal limits. On a more daily level, it has the power to enrich the days and to help one to live life well. When we work to strengthen relationships with others, the immune system responds with more activity and gets more powerful, and other body systems work better as well.

Why does connection with others strengthen a woman's health? Talking intimately to others allows the release of feelings and the relief of self-disclosure. It clears away the effects of trauma and introduces new perspectives. Altruistically listening to the feelings of others in reciprocal relationships builds self-esteem and personal power. It provides a chance to make a difference in the lives of others. There are measurable physical effects of these practices, as we shall see in later chapters. They have an impact on the course of breast cancer for an individual woman and on her moods as well. They have a measurable impact on the action of immune cells as they deal with cancer cells.

But some relationships work better than others. Women in psychotherapy groups reach a level of openness and sharing not often available to women in other circumstances. Perhaps the most important part of the group experience is the opportunity to speak in your own voice, to tell what you see, and to listen to the small voice inside you. This is the source of vitality for women, and it is what makes for genuine relationships. It is what we call letting our hair down, being ourselves, and speaking from the soul.

For women, things don't work well in relationships in which it isn't possible to speak with this inner voice. There is instead the terrible feeling of not being heard, the sense that others don't listen or understand. This is the root of depressions and anxiety problems, it saps the days of color and intensity, and it can make a woman feel trapped inside herself.

If a woman can't convey her feelings, perceptions, and experiences to others, it makes it harder for her to absorb them into her personality. She may feel that this is the price of relationships, this abandonment of herself, and it may be preferable to the loss of belonging. But inside it feels like having to choose between your left foot and your right foot.

When a woman is able to speak genuinely with her own voice about what she sees and needs and this is welcomed in her relationships, there is enormous power, as seen in David Spiegel's work. The female body draws on this experience to enhance health and helps a woman to go beyond limits. The Stanford work is not the only research that illustrates the effects of feminine behaviors on health. The same results show up in the data on self-disclosure, expression of feelings, social support, and relaxation training. Women with breast cancer can have faith in their emotional logic, in the impulse to reach for relationships and to share emotions, and know that these are powerful allies.

Health is not controlled solely by medicine, although medical science has done a great deal to reduce human suffering. The human body itself is extremely powerful, and two million years of fighting mammoths, microbes, and each other have produced a remarkably sturdy strain of our species. Medical treatment is relatively new on the historical scene, and it is easy to overlook the forces on which humans have relied through most of their centuries on earth. Our immune cells have evolved over two million years, and the weaker variations of them were left behind long ago. The best the race has produced so far is within you.

This means that restoring health is not a matter of learning new tricks or new ways to use our brains. Instead, it requires using all of the strength and resources within us and noticing what has kept the species going until now. We may have no way to explain, for example, what keeps us from falling out of bed, but we can still depend on it. The voice within you is not an alternative to medical treatment but rather helps to create a setting or a climate in which medical treatment can have maximum impact.

In breast cancer, women's capacity to enhance the healing process is only now beginning to be illuminated by laboratory research. In the Stanford psychotherapy groups, women were not taught new and exotic skills. Instead, they were offered a format where they could use the powers within — the ability to express, support, and relate — most optimally. Without ever spelling out the capabilities they brought to the experience, the women were able to draw on them.

This was a surprise to cancer treatment researchers, who assumed only that they were disproving the old ideas of magical mental cures of cancer, the belief that peace of mind can cure disease. They planned to put to rest the idea that psychological state affects biological outcomes.

In fact, this turned out to be a simplistic conceptualization of a very complex phenomenon. Group psychotherapy is not a matter of mind curing illness, but of a woman taking care of herself in the ways that she inherently knows will heal, and thus creating a context hospitable to medical interventions.

So Spiegel had been wrong and had stumbled upon the find of the century. Psychological factors, those invisible, predictable forces, have a powerful impact on breast cancer, even on advanced, end-stage cancers. But his findings were generally ignored in medical research, and clinical medicine continued to treat breast cancer with little interest in the extraordinary tool of group psychotherapy.

Is Medicine Enough?

Americans are rarely tentative in their reaction to a challenge, and on December 23, 1971, when the late President Richard M. Nixon declared war on cancer, there was great optimism and enthusiasm. With the signing of the National Cancer Act, the National Cancer Institute was created with the charge to "comprehensively and energetically exploit scientific leads to combat the disease,"[3] with full federal funding for research and treatment.

In the treatment of cancer, surgery and radiation had long been in use; during World War II, an accidental explosion of mustard gas in Italy demonstrated that chemicals known as nitrogen mustards might be useful in suppressing some forms of cancer.[4] This seemed to be a promising basis for effective cancer treatment, and a great deal of research was launched to explore the effects of pharmacological treatments.

The National Cancer Institute and the American Cancer Society had been powerful leaders in the prevention and treatment of cancer, and they emphasized the need to find ways to destroy cancer cells and increase the body's resistance to disease. So strong was the faith in our ability to find a cure for cancer that the NCI in 1984 set as its goal to cut cancer deaths in half by the year 2000.[5]

How successful has medicine been in using its current techniques to reduce the occurrence and mortality from cancer? The death rate from cancer *increased* by 7 percent between 1975 and 1990 (figures controlled for population growth and death from other diseases),[6] and since 1971, when the "war" started, there has been an overall improvement in five-year survival of only 4 percent.[7]

These figures represent overall cancer statistics, but each disease shows its own patterns. The incidence of some cancers, such as cancer of the cervix, uterus, stomach, and pancreas, has decreased, while others, such as breast cancer, have shown an increase in incidence and mortality.

These figures should not obscure the real improvements in breast cancer treatment over these years, with breast-conserving techniques developed as an acceptable alternative to mastectomy for many women, new chemical and hormonal treatments like Taxol and Tamoxifen coming into use, and the side effects of chemotherapy and radiation better controlled.

Breast cancer is different from other malignancies. It is easy to assume that general statements about cancer apply here, but often they don't. Breast cancer is less predictable than other types of cancer and appears more often to be influenced by factors outside the body. Each woman's response to treatment is different, with hormonal status an important factor. The disease is subject to long dormant periods, and a majority of women who are diagnosed with primary breast cancer will experience recurrences at some point in their lives.

The current understanding of breast cancer is based on the idea that malignant cells take root, develop, and dominate the body, disrupting its healthy functions. Cancer growth is conceptualized as cells gone wild, ungoverned by the standard regulating forces of the body, a dramatic but not wholly accurate view. This perspective has little explanation for tumor dormancy, for example, in which breast cancers, or their offshoots, stop growing and spreading, as in Marylu's case.

Breast cancers are not all the same, however, and, the rate of growth differs from person to person. One woman's breast cancer may have a course of 10 years, while another has a course of 110 years, giving the appearance in her lifetime of a curable, short-term illness. Put another way, current research can't explain why primary breast cancers don't all recur quickly and why they differ in the pace at which they grow.

Many of the factors that predict breast cancer in the general population are not strictly medical factors and have to do with the way women live their lives. These include a woman's age at the birth of a first child, marriage, menopause and menarche, family history of breast cancer, and social class.

There are new and promising directions in research on the causes of breast cancer as well, including great interest in oncogenes, which seem to promote cancer when they have been damaged, tumor suppressor genes that work to prevent cancer, and cell mutations that lead to cancer. At some time in the future, gene and enzyme testing may help determine which women are likely to have a recurrence of breast cancer.

There are many intriguing findings in the research on breast cancer. Why is it that profoundly blind women are half as likely to have breast cancer as women who are fully sighted?[8] Or that women with larger breasts are more likely to get breast cancer?[9] And critical questions, such as what will prevent cancer and what will put tumors into remission are still largely unanswered.

Given the very limited gains for $25 billion in research funding over the past two decades, it is reasonable to question whether medicine's capacity to improve outcomes in breast cancer is limited. Just as war is too important to be left to the generals, it may be that the war on cancer is too important to be left to medicine.

In an age of cost-conscious health care, research funding that promises more of the same results is likely to be challenged. Mammography screening is currently under attack by some who consider it costly and ineffective in improving outcomes. New treatments, which seem so promising when first announced, often end up having limited utility. Autologous bone marrow transplants, for example, which involve strengthening the post-chemotherapy immune system with infusions of preserved bone marrow, are estimated to cost an average of $115,800 for each year of life saved.[10]

Certainly breast cancer research must continue, with as much funding as possible from both public and private sources. The gains of past years have been real ones, and if research efforts have not achieved a clinical cure, perhaps the reason has more to do with unrealistic expectations of medical therapy than with wasted research financing.

In the United States, health maintenance is usually seen as a doctor's job. Only in the past few years have people seen personal habits as important to health. "Visit your doctor" is still the primary health care advice, and as a consequence people often expect more of medicine than the field can offer. A good illustration of this is the current national health debate, which isn't a controversy about ways to be healthy, but instead an argument about the most acceptable means to reimburse medical caregivers. The underlying premise is that the more money there is available for medical care, the healthier we will all be.

The prevailing view of health care casts the patient as a passive recipient dependent on doctors for a good outcome, a good consumer seeking better treatment from medical personnel, with consequent frustration.

Our environment influences the way that we behave. When you find yourself in some circumstances, for example, an exciting ball game, your behavior may be like that of others, so that you clap, shout, move your arms, stamp your feet, and so forth.

When you find yourself in a medical setting, you are more likely to agree with medical caregivers rather than questioning or arguing, to defer to a doctor or a nurse for decisions, and to avoid taking the initiative, acting independently, or setting a course of your own.

Obtaining good medical treatment may seem to require patients to act in these ways, but when these responses are detrimental, they characterize a psychological affliction called dependent personality disorder, in which a person's emotions and decisions are tightly bound up in the need for others' approval.[11] Women have much better treatment outcomes when their behavior involves taking the initiative, actively exploring health-enhancing opportunities, and speaking their own judgment, behaviors that will be explored more fully in chapters 7 and 8.

So it is wise to be aware of the ways that outside influences shape our behavior. But there is more at issue than how to use medical care effectively. Medical treatment of cancer is only the first step after a diagnosis of breast cancer. It is easy to see surgery, radiation, and chemotherapy as solutions to breast cancer, but in fact they only open opportunities for a restoration of health. Medicine by itself cannot produce a body brimming with health and vitality. Good health is generated from within, not imposed from without.

Getting enough rest, not smoking, getting regular exercise, controlling alcohol consumption, maintaining a healthy weight, and eating a nutritious diet are all important as well to help your body utilize treatment to maximum advantage. If you have breast cancer, you need to use medical help fully, but you must supplement it with your own work, for medicine is not enough. Women have unique strength in this, for women's ways are healing ways.

Using Psychology to Boost Breast Cancer Treatment

Psychology has always been a spooky science; if you tell people at a social gathering that you're a psychologist, you may suddenly find yourself alone at the punch bowl. But the field is changing, and so are popular beliefs about mental health. Most people know that psychology involves more than being either crazy or sane, that all of us could use some help in reducing stress and upset in our lives.

The relation between psychology and health is a growing field of study that now offers ways for patients to use psychological skills, developed over a lifetime, to boost the effect of cancer treatment. Current research reveals some startling findings, like those of David Spiegel, that demonstrate that under the right conditions, psychology can have a dramatic impact on the course of breast cancer. But how this has its effect is complicated; in research it is called a treatment interaction.

Having an alcoholic drink can be a pleasant part of a social event, and driving a car is an easy procedure, but when these two are combined, they produce consequences that are very different from either one alone. Similarly, having chemotherapy produces one outcome and having psychotherapy produces a different outcome, but when these two are combined, the effect is to strengthen the power of both.

The effect, as the mathematicians say, is multiplicative or synergistic, rather than additive, and the result is more powerful than either one alone. What occurred in David Spiegel's research was that psychological forces changed the effect of the medical treatment and led to consequences that neither alone could have caused.

Without doubt, biological factors are most important in predicting how a woman will do with breast cancer, and patients with long disease-free periods and few tumors do the best over the course of their illness. But feelings and thoughts are biochemical events.

We may for convenience' sake refer to body events as either thoughts, emotions, or behaviors, but this is merely a form of speech. Any event involving a live human body is biochemical and affects all other parts, because of the delicate balance among all forces in the system.

This makes it easier to understand why an emotional factor called *joy* in one research study can give a good indication of how a woman will do in breast cancer treatment. What did joy mean, and how do you have joy when you have a serious illness? As described by the researchers, joy seemed to stand for some combination of resilience, stamina, energy, vigor, cheerfulness, and positive mood. Patients who felt hopeless, helpless, worthless, unhappy, and sad tended to live far shorter lives than those who scored higher on the joy variable.[12]

When we think of an emotion like joy, images and feelings come to mind. With every emotion, however, there are chemical and electrical shifts in the body as well, and these affect the climate in which cancer cells exist. Some of these are not conducive to health. The two most potent and damaging psychological states are helplessness/hopelessness and social isolation, since they have chemical and electrical consequences for the body. Psychological states before diagnosis may set the stage for a poor response to treatment, or treatment itself may cause problems. When damaging psychological experiences are intensive during oncological treatment, they overburden an already strained system and force the body to divert its resources to deal with them.

With the upset of troubled emotions comes turmoil in the endocrine and the cardiovascular systems and a change in the body's chemical balances. This puts more demands on the body's resources. The situation is a bit like that of an emergency room suddenly called on to handle the victims of a fire and a plane crash at the same time. When resources are split too many ways, reserves are depleted, and effectiveness in any direction is limited. It's all one body, and our energy needs to be concentrated in the most important pursuit.

The reason that psychological support can boost medical treatment has to do with reducing the demands on the body's resources. Psychological treatment alone is not a viable alternative to medical treatment, but as a strengthener of medical treatment, it is a great empowering agent. It does not offer miracle cures, for there are no real miracles in medical treatment, only the healthy forces of a body hard at work trying to regain its balance.

In the past, psychological treatments have been touted as magical, mystical solutions to critical health problems, and they have had their following, perhaps because miracles touch a strong emotional chord. Psychological fanatics would dismiss the body as a figment of the imagination, and as a result medical treatment that includes a psychological component can seem suspect, soft, or unnecessary.

This view of healing fails to draw on the female wisdom that understood healing long before the advent of modern medicine. The need for emotional sensitivity and support, the power of genuine emotional relating, the sense of belonging in relationships and community are all essential parts of restoring health.

These are not generally dealt with in medical treatment plans, but they have a profound impact on health outcomes. In fact, psychological forces make themselves felt in the body, as you know when you see fear registered in sweaty hands, or anxiety in a stomach ache. Physical forces have an effect on our emotions too, so that when we feel pain of any sort we automatically feel fear at the same time.

Using psychological techniques to bolster treatment is not a cure for breast cancer. Rather, such techniques are an attempt to link the good life with the strongest treatment. In doing so, the wisdom acquired over a lifetime of experience can serve us well if we trust our inner voice.

The research that is described in this book is not the final word on the forces at work in breast cancer, for we have only begun to see the complexity of this powerful disease. Breast cancer is an enormously diverse illness, with eight histologically pure tumor groups and many combinations of these possible in an individual patient. And research is full of errors. It is not clear that the findings regarding cells in a laboratory petri dish are the equivalent of the extraordinarily complex setting of a woman's body. The findings in research depend heavily on what we are able to measure. Before there is unambiguous data, there must be good instruments, and at present there are woefully few.

Although it would be better to be absolutely sure of the promise of new approaches to breast cancer treatment before using them, the need to help patients must prevail. If we use treatment techniques that do no harm to patients, the worst that can happen is that they will not help as much as we hope.

Treatment for breast cancer must begin with all of the best that surgery, oncology, and radiology have to offer. The rest comes from within you. This is good news for women, for the emotional perceptiveness and relational skill that comes intrinsically to women offer great power to enhance medical treatment for breast cancer.

Marylu's extraordinary health is the result of an interaction between her medical treatment and her powerful internal voice. When I began to think about her experience, I wondered if women could learn to combine these two forces.

Chapter Two

The Power inside Us

I thought of Marylu when I got the call from Jane. Jane's daughter and mine had been friends since they met in nursery school at age three. They were remarkably compatible, these two, and they had progressed from mudpies and roller skates to experiments with hairstyles and rock music. They were always in motion, dreaming up adventures and full of ardent, emphatic descriptions of their escapades.

But this time the call was not about children. Jane had gotten the results of a breast biopsy, and the news was not good. Lab analysis revealed primary breast cancer, and a mastectomy was recommended. Her voice on the phone, usually warm and chatty, was strained and tight. She reassured me that she would be fine, that she wasn't worried about the surgery, and that I shouldn't worry either. It was her concern for me that made my throat close and my eyes water. Dear Jane, I thought, a good woman, a mother, a friend. Please, Lord.... I was frightened, and sad. And I would do anything to help.

My thoughts went to Marylu and her experience with a very different form of breast cancer. I remembered how upset she had been but also, how methodical and organized she was in using her clinical skills and knowledge on her own behalf. A good deal of psychological research was already available. Would Jane like me to take a look and see if there was anything helpful?

"Sure," she said, "I'll take any help I can get."

During the fall of 1989, I first heard a news report on the radio that David Spiegel at Stanford had released findings that group psychotherapy had doubled the survival time of women with advanced breast cancers. Jane didn't have this form of the disease, and hers was only primary breast cancer. But that was no small thing, and this was an important person. She was, after all, Emily's mother, and although others might not notice, I knew that she was Emily's whole world.

I had steadily followed the research on psychology and cancer ever since adolescence and had been captivated by Lawrence Le-Shan's riveting reports in the 1960s. Although he couldn't support all of his theories with the extensive research efforts and funding they deserved, his belief that feelings and malignancies were closely connected made fascinating reading.

I started my search for information by calling around town to find out where there were experimental psychotherapy groups for women with breast cancer. I called the American Cancer Society, the National Cancer Institute, the hospitals, and the oncologists to find out who was applying David Spiegel's findings. When I asked whether the Stanford findings were being used in clinical work, most often the response I got was "David who?" Then I tried the professional associations, like the American Psychological Association, and the cancer patients' organizations. As a last resort, I wrote to the drug companies that produce the chemotherapy drugs. I even contacted David Spiegel himself, a gracious and compassionate man, but a realist who acknowledged that it would be a long time before patients or medical people could fully accept his findings.

In most cases, I seemed to be the only one who knew about the psychological treatment news on group psychotherapy and breast cancer. And I was clearly not the most expert voice on the topic. But everyone I asked about it who was in the business of treating patients knew nothing. Or worse, they knew that some of the overblown claims of earlier decades, that psychology could cure cancer, had been disproved, and so they assumed that psychology had nothing further to offer.

Although I could not have known it then, this was to be the beginning of years of searching, done primarily in libraries, but also by mail, telephone, and travel. I had told Jane that I would find out if psychology could help with breast cancer, and I knew from watching Marylu that somehow it could.

What I learned is reported in this book, an interpretation of the research from many laboratories and projects. What it says, in summary, is that psychological forces, internal forces peculiarly feminine in nature, can be used to boost the impact of standard medical treatment for breast cancer.

The ordinary ways that we deal with strong feelings, our mental problem-solving habits, and the way we relate to others around us have a lot to do with what happens after a diagnosis of breast cancer. And all of these patterns are subject to our control and can be changed.

How Thinking Affects Healing

How can thinking destroy warts? Warts (*verruca vulgaris*) are caused by infection of a papilloma virus and often recur after medical treatment. It's hard to believe that how we think can affect these small but irritating growths of tissue. With the wide range of thoughts that go through anybody's head, if one idea were powerful enough to cure warts, we would surely have noticed.

But hypnosis is a form of mental activity distinctly different from ordinary thinking, and it activates other parts of the central nervous system outside the brain. It involves activity at a level deeply embedded in the body, not accessible through ordinary channels of thought. There is good evidence that hypnosis is able to influence physical activities inside the body.

In one study, psychotherapy using hypnotic trance to destroy warts was particularly effective, and three-quarters of the patients using trance treatment had no further recurrences.[1] It is not clear why this form of mental activity can have a physical effect, but it does.

Not only in the treatment of viral infections does hypnotic work have an impact. It can alter the normal course of the body's healing powers. In particular, it can make a difference in burn injuries, which are among the most painful and difficult to treat. This is because the destruction of parts of the skin system makes it hard for other organs to compensate, which handicaps the healing mechanisms of the body. The necessary tasks of draining fluids, fighting infection, and bringing nutrition to wounded tissue all become more difficult.

When patients are admitted to the Alta Bates Hospital Burn Center in Berkeley, California, it is usually because their burns are serious and painful. One group of patients who had hand burns, mostly from electrical flash explosions, was given hypnosis to support medical treatment by changing the blood flow and tissue temperature and by providing pain relief. For purposes of comparison, the hypnotic treatment was applied to only one hand, while the medical treatment was applied to both. After several days of treatment, physicians were easily able to identify the hypnotically treated hand because of the accelerated healing.[2] Using thought processes and the central nervous system had clearly enhanced the body's capacity for healing itself, even with serious tissue damage.

The effect of hypnosis comes from forces within us that are poorly understood but nonetheless powerful. They are there inside, latent until we draw on them and most powerful when they are unfettered and free of too much intellectual processing.

The idea that these internal forces, which we call psychological, influence cancer is an old one, but until recently it seemed more folklore than science. In recent years researchers have begun to explore the range of connections between the mind — or the central nervous system — and the endocrine/hormonal system, and disease processes. Our ways of thinking trap us in a perception of the body as made up of many separate parts, when in actuality they all infiltrate one another. Mind and body are only labels that we use to describe groups of interlocking systems that comprise an integrated circuit.

Curing vs. Controlling Breast Cancer

Breast cancer is a formidable disease, one that afflicts 2.6 million women in the U.S.[3] and claims more than $6 billion in health costs and lost productivity.[4] To suggest that it can be cured just by thinking right is clearly nonsense. But some women, like Marylu, have a particularly effective response to breast cancer, one that involves no experimental drugs, no special treatments, no gurus, and no magic. It makes sense to examine why some women are so skilled at healing and to see what makes these women different.

Cancer is a puzzling and complex disease, with many mysteries. If cancer is diagnosed in one identical twin, why doesn't it occur at the same time in the other twin? Why does chemotherapy work for one patient and not for another? Is there a personality that is prone to breast cancer? Does stress cause breast cancer? Do bad marriages? Bad relationships? Bad children?

This is a powerful disease, and biological factors are critical in predicting outcome. Clinical studies indicate that if a woman is diagnosed with breast cancer, she has an 80 percent chance of a recurrence at some point in her life.[5] For some women, the cancer reappears two years after treatment, but for others it doesn't reappear for forty years. And for some it never recurs.

A great deal about breast cancer is unknown. The extraordinary advances in recombinant DNA technology have led to the production of interleukin-2 and interferon and their use in clinical trials. These can change the body's immune cells to produce more powerful fighters in the body and have led to high expectations but limited gains in helping patients. These treatments have an astonishing success with the occasional patient but no effect with many others. Clearly, there are invisible forces that have the power to radically alter the way the body uses experimental treatments.

Basic research in breast cancer treatment is complicated by enormous variety in the disease forms and the way that cancer cells generally behave. Although we group many cancers under the one name of breast cancer, no two cancers are ever exactly alike, and the range of differences in people makes even the same histological type different from person to person. Sometimes the disease factors are predictable, but other influences in the environment change the course of the disease. This is clearly illustrated by the fact that blacks in the U.S. get cancer only slightly more frequently than whites (8 percent) but have a much higher mortality rate (35 percent).[6] Something appears to be affecting the course of the disease in blacks to make it more lethal and to reduce the good effects of medical treatment.

Some cancers, such as pancreatic cancer, are largely invariant in their course and seem to be unaffected by anything. Other cancers, in particular breast cancer and malignant melanoma, are highly variable and difficult to predict with patients. There are far more unknowns with these two cancers, and the diseases are more affected by nonmedical factors. Although breast cancer and its general characteristics are widely known in this culture, the disease is much more complicated than it seems.

Often when women have breast cancer, there are more cancerous cells present than actually show up on examination, and women may have more than one tumor group as well, with 15 percent of women on primary diagnosis having cancer in the other breast.[7] Some breast cancers are never found at all in a woman's lifetime, as they fail to become clinically noticeable. Autopsy studies have found that 25–30 percent of women have either *in situ* or invasive breast cancer that would have otherwise gone undetected. Given two women, each with the same type of breast tumor, why does one grow and become a problem, while the other grows slowly or not at all? Why does this process of slowing down a tumor's growth happen naturally at various points in many cases?

Only some of the physical factors that affect the rate of breast tumor growth are understood, but slowing down the process may be a more promising objective in cancer research than finding a cure. The goal of curing breast cancer with early detection is always worth working for, but it is only the *first* response to breast cancer. Even though there is a great emphasis in breast cancer treatment on removing all of the primary tumor so that it doesn't spread, it is clear from the research that the time that cells break off and travel to other parts of the body is long before anybody can tell that there is any cancer present.

Cancer cells grow by doubling; the first one produces two, which then produce four (and then eight, sixteen, thirty-two, etc.), and it takes at least thirty of these doublings before there is a mass that can be felt. The breaking off and spreading of tumor cells usually happens before the twentieth doubling, at which time the tumor is probably still undetectable by standard tests like mammograms or self-examinations.

This means that when there is a spread of cancer in the first five years after treatment, it is not the return of the original tumor that has occurred, but rather the emergence of new sites that were seeded before treatment.[8] These continued to grow and develop at their own pace, and finding them means only that more treatment aimed at these sites is needed.

Recurrences are always upsetting because they imply that medical treatment didn't work, but this is a misinterpretation. The body has been able to slow down and hold in check this extra cancer for longer than the original one. It may be that the doubling time for the first tumor and the recurring tumor are different, but nonetheless the immune system has done a reasonable job and has not failed.

Cell-doubling times vary with each form of breast cancer, and also with the original cancer and its new sites. Cancer cells can have vastly different characteristic features, so that one form may have a doubling time of 44 days and another may double only once every five years.[9] Tumors that are affected by hormones (estrogen receptor positive) are slower growing than others, with an average doubling time of 580 days. Estrogen receptor negative tumors in contrast have been shown to have an average doubling time of 203 days.[10]

The doubling time of cancer cells in a tumor affects a woman's health because it indicates how fast tumors grow and the relative power of the disease. The most reassuring tumors are those whose cells double once in a long time.

The results of what occurs in the reproduction of tiny tumor cells shows up in the outlook for a woman with a specific form of the disease. If a woman of 45 with breast cancer had a tumor cell-doubling time of once every five years, then she would have to be 195 before the cancer could be diagnosed. This would not technically be a cure of breast cancer, but the slow growth rate of tumors allows for enormous control in a patient's life.

When we look at how psychology affects breast cancer, we need to focus on what slows down or speeds up the growth of tumor cells, for it is this that determines how long a woman survives and the length of healthy periods or remissions. For some tumors, the growth rate changes during the life of the disease, sometimes speeding up and sometimes slowing down. Sometimes cells left over after mastectomy or lumpectomy may stay in the system, with their future course difficult to foresee. They may pick up speed in doubling, or they may lie dormant or grow very slowly for many years.

Hormones, Nerves, Feelings, and Immune Cells

Often during menstrual cycles, women experience a time when they can feel emotions more strongly and sense the working of various hormones, both physically and emotionally. This offers women a unique opportunity to understand the interplay of the central nervous system, the endocrine system, and the immune system.

Cancer responds to hormones also, and estrogen receptor status is an important influence on tumor doubling time.[11] When the hormonal environment is changing during menopause, the effect can sometimes be seen in tumor growth.

Instead of thinking of breast cancer as a battle that is won or lost, it makes sense to look at malignant cells more like plants growing in soil where growth is affected by many factors. No garden is ever completely cured of weeds, and a wise gardener tries to limit unwanted growth by controlling the surroundings.

This is not the way that breast cancer is typically viewed. The claim that the disease is 85 percent curable if found early has led women to great anxiety about whether they have had frequent enough mammograms, breast self-examinations, and so forth. This early detection approach suggests to some that the only way to deal with breast cancer is to identify and destroy it early, and although this is advisable, it is only one of several responses to breast cancer. In addition to full medical treatment for primary breast cancer as well as recurrences, a woman needs to use psychological treatments to expand the power of medicine. Current research indicates that this work can make a profound difference in the course of the illness.

In fact, many breast cancers continue to recur even after a woman passes the five-year cure milestone. Although women often feel doomed when this happens, there is a great deal that they can do to enhance their health; the recurrence, after all, is not a sign that they are dying but only an indication of one more place they must deal with the disease. About two-thirds of women first diagnosed with breast cancer are likely to remain in remission for ten years or more, while about one-third are likely to have a recurrence before that time.[12] The course of breast cancer over a woman's lifetime is notoriously unpredictable, so it is wise to use all possible help in dealing with the disease.

When women have no further symptoms of breast cancer at the five-year exam, it is tempting to assume that aside from routine checkups their work is over and they can retire as breast cancer patients. But women who have been successfully treated continue to be at risk, and they are fifteen times more likely to die of the disease than other women.

When women go through the trauma of diagnosis and the ordeal of treatment, remaining healthy to the five-year exam can feel like salvation. If a woman sees breast cancer as curable instead of chronic, it can seem that she has had her life returned to her at this point. Recurrences are then shattering, for they seem like complete defeat and often cause greater psychological distress than the first diagnosis.

The problem lies in seeing breast cancer as an acute illness, a one-time event in which a patient wins or loses, instead of considering it as a chronic condition, one that must be controlled and managed over a long period of time. This fundamental misconception of the disease has led to trauma, helplessness, lawsuits, and panic.

It has also led to undue pessimism about a woman's power to enhance her health and has given rise to unrealistic demands on medicine. Many believe that having a good prognosis and enduring the rigors of standard treatment, including sacrificing a breast and undergoing chemotherapy, should insure a return to health. In fact, the disease is more complicated.

This conception of the relationship between women, medicine, and disease underestimates women's resources for dealing with breast cancer and overestimates the power of the illness. Certainly breast cancer is a fearful and dangerous disease and deserves all of the best responses of modern science. But there is a whole arsenal of powerful techniques that is generally omitted from breast cancer treatment that can improve the outlook for women with breast cancer. These techniques draw on skills that women in this culture develop quite early: psychological insight, a striving for interpersonal connection, the ability to commit to relationships, and a high tolerance for interdependence.

The Logic of the Body's Reactions

Have you ever had the experience of hearing two people use the same expressions, like "It was like a pig in a poke," or express the same opinions when you spoke to them separately, so that you wondered if they had a private relationship? Sometimes people having extramarital affairs give themselves away in this manner, incriminating themselves by carelessly revealing common expressions or opinions.

Researchers who study body systems have had the same experience. They have found that the expressions and language used by the immune system are used by the body systems that govern our thoughts and feelings. If these systems communicate directly with one another, it is likely that they have a great impact on each other. The chemical messengers between these systems [neuro-peptides, steroids, catecholamines, and others], speak the same language in the immune organs and in the central nervous system, our thinking and feeling apparatus.

This may seem pretty obvious since you know that your thoughts affect how your body feels and that sensations in your body (like a toothache) affect your thinking and feeling patterns. But this is a new idea in science and until recently could not be supported with hard data. It still encounters general resistance and consequently has a big influence on how we deal with a disease like breast cancer.

Let's look at what happens when Mrs. H. is unwell and goes to her doctor. After a careful examination and a number of tests, he tells her he can find nothing wrong, which should be good news. Instead, she is disheartened, he is uncomfortable, and she is deter-mined to get a better idea of what's going on. He suggests that the cause of her symptoms may be stress and sends her to a psychol-ogist. The psychologist finds a number of sources of emotional difficulty in her life and helps her to deal with them, but she still doesn't feel very well, and so she goes back to her medical doctor. He does more tests and then refers her to someone else, probably another psychologist.

Clearly, all of this back and forth isn't doing anything for Mrs. H.'s health or peace of mind, and it is likely to make her feel inadequate and foolish on top of feeling sick. By dividing her into pieces, it becomes impossible to understand how her various parts affect each other. When caregivers begin to consider what makes her feel sick and what makes her well, they may notice that her blood sugar level goes up when her daughter gets nasty and her blood pressure goes down when she pats her dog.

The separation of the mind from the body shows up most clearly in the separation of the disciplines of psychology and medi-cine. In their training, psychologists and physicians have very little instruction in the business of the other, and so they both operate like the blind men who describe the elephant according to which part they are touching.

The two professions themselves are not organized in a way that allows easy talk, because they have no common language, unlike the patient's body systems that do share common communication. For the healers, the major means of communication is through professional journals, where reports are given of research findings or clinical treatments. But psychology and medicine have few journals whose fields combine or overlap. There are loads of psychology journals, and even more medical journals, but it is rare to find one that reports research from both fields together.

When the two professions do talk, they speak different languages. Psychologists may say that stress causes affective and cognitive interference, which physicians have trouble interpreting. When physicians say that stress affects opiate peptide levels and lymphocyte activity, psychologists are left scratching their heads. Even with computerization, the two fields use different data bases, so they know little about what the other is doing.

The result can be what occurs in one city in upstate New York. In a large professional building on the main street is one of the world's top researchers in stress and anxiety, a man who publishes widely and offers a great deal of psychological help to people who deal with stress. In the building next door are two large groups of physicians, each dealing with the effects of stress on the cardiovascular and endocrine systems. They know nothing about the work of the stress expert next door, and so each profession is limited in the strength of its treatment.

Psychology originally developed as an academic field, and it is only since the Second World War that the field of clinical psychology has become popular. There is a mighty war in the profession itself between clinicians, who feel that they are a lonesome minority, and researchers, who feel that clinical psychologists are prostituting themselves by selling their expertise. This conflict recently reached major proportions and threatened to tear apart the large American Psychological Association when research and academic psychologists threatened to withdraw and form their own professional organization, separate from the practicing clinicians. Not only do the professions make a separation between mind and body, but the mind is also subdivided into separate categories.

So the way that our study of the human being is approached makes it difficult to combine our knowledge and make it work for patients. Psychology and medicine do not communicate well and have not found ways to pool their understandings about feelings and physical responses in the human body. Psychologists themselves often fail to help one another in advancing their wisdom about how the parts of a human being operate together.

But the body knows. In the same human being, the mind and body communicate with each other with extraordinary speed and accuracy. If you doubt this, put yourself in the situation in which my aunt found herself. She was a young Dutch immigrant going for her first job interview in this country. She was very nervous. She had washed her clothes the night before, bathed herself, and fixed her hair just so. As she walked through the waiting room, which was full of applicants, up to the desk of the stern matron doing the interviewing, she could feel things loosening, and all of a sudden her underwear slipped down to her ankles.

Perhaps you can feel how the body hears and registers the thoughts and emotions in this situation. The sweat across the upper back, the damp armpits, the red face, the tingling hands, the lightheadedness, all illustrated, in milliseconds, the thoughts of alarm, humiliation, shock. In medicine and psychology, there may not be a direct communication, but within the body, our feelings and our visceral reactions are always one.

It is most easy to see this connection when there are excessive reactions to powerful situations, as in my aunt's case (she did get the job by the way). Where we are not terribly upset or excited, we may see no external evidence of internal reactions, the shooting chemicals released by this or that memory, the flashes of fire inside us when we are angry, or the surges of sadness and anxiety that may come with anticipation of an experience. And because we can't observe these changes inside us, we may believe that there is nothing happening, that these are only thoughts or feelings, and that they have escaped the body's notice. Or we may make assumptions that this or that event should produce one or another set of feelings and then ignore the genuine reactions that we do have. We dispute our own body's messages, saying, for example, "Why am I so down? I have no reason to be depressed."

The study of stress connects the body with the mind and has caused researchers to look at both. But the same kinds of assumptions that mislead us in looking at our own reactions have also misled researchers. It is easy to assume that certain things should be stressful to people and then to interpret whatever they do as signs of that stress, ignoring the fundamental logic of the body's emotional reactions.

If we want to know what is stressful, we must discard our beliefs and notice what makes us physically tighten up. On the other hand, if we want to know what is relaxing, we have to watch those experiences and thoughts that cause us to loosen up.

It's hard to imagine a more stressful activity than skydiving, or freefall parachuting. At least most people assume that this is stressful. In this hobby, the jumper is in the air unsupported for a minute or more, has a falling speed of between 90 and 200 miles an hour, and a forward speed of up to 60 miles an hour. Not surprisingly, jumpers show the effects of their experience in their physical measures. Heartbeats of up to 230 beats per minute have been recorded, and it has been suggested that some of the cases of accidents with chutes failing to open are actually due to cardiovascular failure.

But there is a small proportion of sky divers who have exactly the opposite reaction, who find falling at high speeds to be highly *relaxing*, so that their body seems to register the experience in a very different way.[13] Their blood pressure and pulse drop to peaceful ranges, and there are all indications of more relaxed functioning.

So although we know that the mind and the body interact continually, we have to look closely at each individual to see how the mind perceives experiences. We can be sure, however, that the body reacts to the mind's interpretations. And the way that our bodies react involves our immune function and our health.

Psychology Is Not Mind Control

Any discussion of the relationship between the mind and the body opens the door to nonscientific explanations of disease. Since cancer is an enigmatic disease, it has frequently been approached from a mystical perspective, with supposedly vast mental powers invoked to cure it.

This puts cancer patients in a difficult position: they can feel pressured to control their thoughts and so cure their disease in service to someone else's magical view of the mind.

The brain has always been seen as transcendental, having potentially strange and magical powers. When people think of the role of the psyche in illness, it is easy to slip into this sort of invalid thinking. The sensationalistic supermarket newspapers support this approach, since every issue seems to have a headline about somebody who cured cancer by mind control.

But mind control has nothing to do with sound psychology; it means thought control, and all of us know how hard it is to control thoughts. Anybody who's ever had to stay awake through a boring lecture knows what a challenge it is to control where our thoughts go. In dealing with cancer, feeling anxious or depressed can seem dangerous to health, even though there has never been any research supporting this belief.

The combination of these beliefs has led to the emergence of breast cancer treatment programs that claim to offer mental cures for cancer as an alternative to good medical care. Often expensive, these programs prey on the fears and hopes of people dealing with serious illness, and their occasional successes are probably more a reflection of the determination of patients to fight for health than any real help from the programs.

More insidious are the well-meaning helpers who see cancer as the unconscious choice of a patient in response to twisted psychological needs. Stemming from early Freudian thinking that everything that happens to a person is caused by unconscious motivation and that nothing occurs randomly, this explanation sees cancer as an expression of a death wish inherent in all living things and most commonly observed in depression.

There are many problems with this kind of fantasy thinking about breast cancer. It assumes a total and magical control over health that in reality eludes human beings. Merely having thoughts has little effect on health, and most adults have learned through many years of battle with ourselves that the things we want are not a matter of magic. They take hard work, constant practice, self-discipline, advanced planning, and lots of wisdom and maturity. As somebody once said, the harder you work, the luckier you get, and so it is with health as well.

The assertion that we can gain mental control over cancer also assumes that we fight a hidden mind that works against us subconsciously and can destroy us, a kind of Mr. Hyde under our good Dr. Jekyll. While it is true that the mind operates on many levels and that we may not like to notice, for example, that we are eating far too many desserts, this is not exactly the plot of a hidden personality working against our own best interests. It is instead the mundane bad habit of ignoring our own behavior and its consequences. Most of us are aware that regular exercise supports health; it is not, however, a death wish that makes us skip it, but rather the more elementary human habits of laziness, passivity, and avoidance.

Insisting that breast cancer patients lack mind control and need to learn it adds another burden to their illness and makes cancer treatment a test of character. If getting cancer is a sign of failing to have a good psyche or the right thoughts, then the cancer patient can be pressured to redeem herself and her health by getting it right. Cancer patients are often spoken of in patronizing tones: they are "heroic" and "courageous" on a great health battlefield where character shows itself. And we are more than condescending in portraying patients as valiant. Rarely do we hear a cancer patient described in human terms, and somewhere there must be one who is a sniveling coward or a fool.

In one sense, pop psychology has come to replace religion as a source of spiritual reassurance. In the early days of this country, ill health was considered a sign of God's displeasure and a strong impetus to atone and reform one's character.

Now cancer patients sometimes see themselves as psychological deviants, people who have given themselves cancer because of a warped and damaged psyche. Penance takes the form of unearthing their pathological process and permitting themselves to be well. It is a compelling idea, since we are all full of shortcomings that can easily begin to feel causal in the face of a randomly occurring disease.

People who get breast cancer, however, are not psychologically deficient, and neither are they in some way more insightful or more admirable than others.

When women try to deal with breast cancer, deifying them only serves to widen the distance between them and others and to make them feel more stigmatized and isolated. There is nothing ennobling about having cancer, and it does not necessarily improve human character. Good and bad people get cancer, and good and bad people get well, the cowardly and the brave, the admirable and the despicable. There is no need for a review and overhaul of one's character and integrity, but there is a need for lots of hard work, for that is what makes good luck. Fortunately, the kinds of things that need doing to maximize medical treatment come easily to women, and although such behavior is often seen in this culture as foolish and feminine, it is in fact life-enhancing.

There are lots of good ways to augment health and work for long remissions in breast cancer. You don't have to have splendid character, courage, and determination, but you do have to do your share in backing up medical treatment.

Keep in mind that in this culture a diagnosis of breast cancer brings with it some degree of psychological upset and includes a loss of self-esteem, guilt, failure, and shame, partly because people can conclude from the media that breast cancer is preventable if we eat right, live right, and get regular check-ups. People have their own beliefs about why breast cancer develops, and personal myths abound as well. Wearing no bra, having injuries to the breast, having many sex partners, or breast feeding children have all been offered as explanations for breast cancer, even though there is no research support for any of these.

We live in a social and political climate that holds people responsible for their health, even when this is not justified. Although there is some connection between breast cancer and diet, alcohol consumption, exposure to industrial chemicals, radiation from sunlight, smoking, pesticides, vehicle exhaust, estrogen exposure, age of menarche, number of children, and so forth, no one has been able to suggest a dependable way to avoid breast cancer.

Because there exist nonmedical ways to enhance health, this does not mean that illness is a sign of neglect or failure. Instead, it offers a source of help from the set of skills we've learned through living, which now can be used to reinforce medical treatment. Sometimes habits and patterns learned accidentally become useful in new circumstances.

A good illustration of this is Marilyn, who grew up in an intolerable situation. The youngest child in a family of five older brothers, she was continually forced to do all the housework and cooking, and she was beaten when she resisted. She was sexually abused by her brothers and her father and even sold to their friends. But she learned to frighten them off by waiting until they were asleep and then taking small nicks of an ear or a finger with a small, very sharp knife that nobody ever saw, because it fit perfectly into a crack in the wall beside her bed.

When she was fourteen, she left home, taking all of the savings of each family member with her, and disappeared without a trace, never to have any contact with her family again. She made her own way in the world and by working hard achieved some success in her own business. When she ran across problems in her business with organized crime, she fought back hard, even though it meant losing a great deal. At thirty-five, when she developed a severe cardiovascular ailment and breast cancer as well, she wasn't upset. After everything else she had dealt with, she knew how to handle trouble.

And she did. She made the changes she needed in her life, and got well, and stayed well. (And Marilyn, if you're out there somewhere reading this, I know that things are going your way.) Who knows why she got cancer? Who knows why she survived such a hard life at all? The early patterns of fighting for herself became a lifelong posture, and she knew how to listen to the internal voice that took care of her, even when she was very young.

Psychology and Medicine

Learning, looked at in one way, is always an indication that we were formerly unlearned, ignorant, and inadequate. Such is the human progression. We can deal with this either by claiming to know everything or by finding ways to get more of what we want from life and borrowing from the experience of others, particularly as it is systematically reported in clinical research. We don't all have to find our own way, like Marylu did, and we can avoid having to reinvent the wheel by using one another's experience.

Good health, like good baking, is the result of a complicated mixture of ingredients and processes that produce what seems like magic when they are combined properly. When my daughter first tried to bake a cake, she followed the instructions carefully; when it said to mix the ingredients *by hand,* she put her hand in the bowl and did just that. When she finally got it right, it seemed like magic and she thought she had a special gift, but she forgot the number of times she had to practice before the result was edible.

Medical care is crucial to treating breast cancer, and no responsible approach can fail to include it. But it is not enough, and there is a great deal more that needs to be done to back up and strengthen medical treatment. Some of it may seem so familiar and ordinary that its power is overlooked.

We are used to looking to science and technology to solve all the problems of modern living, and with health, as well, there is great faith in this direction. Although there may be great debate on how to finance health care, the belief is that improvements in health come from improvement in medical treatment.

In the past, however, the greatest advances in disease control occurred when there were changes in the way people lived. The advent of public sewers and the clearing of swamps made enormous changes in the health of whole populations, even though they were not medical advances.

In the same way, changes in human attitudes and patterns of social support may be the next frontier along which human health will advance. In order to maximize the effectiveness of medical treatment, we may need to revise our cultural attitudes about the way that we use our minds in disease treatment.

When I first went to the American Society of Clinical Hypnosis training program in 1981, I was ready for entertainment. Trained in traditional cognitive psychology, I saw hypnosis as harmless nonsense. My first session involved listening to the surgeons' section discuss the use of hypnosis in place of standard anesthesia during surgery. When I asked a down-to-earth dermatologist from North Dakota if she believed what we were hearing, that verbal directions to a patient could replace the powerful medications that numb the body during surgery, she told me that she routinely removed warts from the hands of long-distance truckers using hypnosis and that she wasn't hearing anything new.

As the information at this conference piled up, I realized that I was at a loss to understand or categorize what was occurring and that traditional psychology had no way to explain these events. That manipulation of thoughts could produce changes in the body's normal pain thresholds as well as in blood circulation and healing was evident, but the reason was not.

I left the conference with the understanding that psychology and medicine had been stymied by developments in research and clinical practice that could not be explained by any of the things currently understood about human beings. Now, many years later, more of the same clinical experiences such as hypnosis have accumulated, and there is still little understanding of why a verbal experience such as hypnosis can change the body's workings.

Confronted with data that makes no sense, like burns healing and warts disappearing with trance induction, medicine and psychology have done what science has always done with unexplainable findings. They have ignored these developments and continued in their old practices with their established beliefs

One view of scientific change is that our cultural beliefs determine what we look at and what we can perceive and understand.[14] What we can't understand, we assume is error, and we ignore it. As more and more information piles up that doesn't make sense and old explanations don't seem to work anymore, a crisis develops.

This is precisely what is happening in both psychology and medicine. When a breast cancer patient with advanced, spreading cancer gets well, through no external intervention or magic, neither medicine nor psychology has an organized way to explain it. As these events accumulate, old beliefs come under fire.

But there is great resistance to questioning established scientific beliefs. We continue to look to medicine for an explanation that we believe must be there somewhere. We eagerly greet news of medical breakthroughs in chemotherapy treatment because we expect that this is the source from which they will come. But the best that medicine has been able to offer, after decades of research, has been a public relations effort that presents a chronic disease as curable and advocates a focus on prevention because of the absence of advances in treatment. The real advances, which cannot currently be explained, are ignored and not made available to patients like Jane.

As the reports of patients like Marylu accumulate and the research continues to show the same trends, we will become aware of a revolution occurring under our feet, of a radically altered view of the way that the human organism nourishes itself and of the internal resources that can be brought to bear in dealing with disease.

Strengthening the Body's Fighting Response

There is obviously more available than medical treatment to help cancer patients, although medical treatment is the foundation of the techniques discussed here. For someone like Jane, a woman with children and a busy life, how can psychological factors be used to enhance the response to standard breast cancer treatments? Evidence clearly shows three psychological factors that affect the course of breast cancer.

The first has been called *social support* and deals with the way that we relate to people around us. Sometimes this involves a sense of belonging and participation with others, and sometimes it refers to the concrete help we receive. Social support in various forms, including marriage, family relationships, friendships, psychotherapeutic relationships, group belonging, and so forth, generally have the effect of lengthening periods of healthy functioning with breast cancer. In the next three chapters, these influences are explored, with an eye toward using them to back up medical treatment.

The second psychological influence of importance is the *ability to deal productively with negative feelings*. Note clearly that this is not the same as the ability to be happy or have happy feelings, but refers to the capacity for *coping* with negative feelings. When negative feelings can be clearly identified and handled productively, so that good results follow, the outlook for breast cancer patients becomes more promising.

When negative feelings are pushed aside and ignored, they appear to influence the way the rest of the body's systems work. Not only does repressed anger make us uncomfortable and fail to energize us to find more serene solutions to problems. It also changes various immune measures and affects the body's response to disease.[15]

The third factor has to do with the *level of helplessness and hopelessness that a person feels* and how these feelings are managed. This is directly related to dealing with negative feelings, since the result of ignoring or burying negative feelings is that we fail to solve problems and get what we need, and end up feeling helpless and hopeless. The despair that follows is predictive of less happy outcomes in dealing with the disease. In chapter 6, these issues are dealt with so that the problems they present can be used to strengthen medical treatment.

But medical treatment itself presents many challenges and can be traumatic and demanding. Psychology offers a rich source of help for dealing with treatment, both in understanding personal reactions and in using psychological techniques to reduce the impact of the treatment experience. If you know, for example, that the time after treatment ends is likely to involve high anxiety, it will be easier. If you learn how to use systematic desensitization, it will be even easier, and all of your system's resources can then be devoted to enhancing health rather than being used up by psychological stress.

In chapters 7 and 8, the emotional impact of breast cancer is explored, along with psychological techniques that can be useful when used in connection with other people.

In the last chapter, we explore ways to strengthen our systems to build resistance to breast cancer and other forms of disease. For if psychology can help medicine and the body to respond to breast cancer, there are many ways that it can be used to maintain good health.

This book contains information and ideas that will make sense to women at an intuitive level. But American females are so much in the habit of hiding their insight and stifling their inner voices that they may be surprised to see their natural inclinations supported by psychological research.

Chapter Three

Immune Cells and Emotions

I should have known that it would be hard to talk to Jane about psychotherapy, but I had forgotten all the things that I knew about her family when I called her.

"I don't need counseling," she said definitely. "I'm doing fine."

"I know you are," I said honestly, "but that's not the reason for using it, not that you're not doing okay. The research shows a clear advantage for women with breast cancer when they get psychotherapy in addition to medical treatment. They stay healthier. They live longer." I let the meaning of it sink in.

"I just can't see the point," she said after a long pause.

It is hard to see the point of sitting around talking about feelings when you're struggling with a frightening illness. It may seem frivolous or sappy or, worst of all, like a sure sign that you can't cope. And most cancer patients refuse psychotherapy, even when it's free. In one study, 69 percent of cancer patients turned down free counseling when it was offered as part of a research program. Interestingly, if patients feel that their participation would help science, they are more willing to become involved.

For Jane, psychotherapy would be a doubly frightening prospect. We had grown up in the same small town, and I well remember her older sister and the events of our childhood. Julie was a pretty girl, but strange, and as a child she was always silent, with large haunting eyes. When we became teenagers, she got stranger, and she began to do things that first amused and then alarmed all of us. One day she took off all her clothes in the main hallway of the school, which embarrassed everybody and horrified Jane. Another time she disappeared for days, and the whole town searched for her. They finally found her under some bushes, bruised and sick and incoherent.

58

As we grew older, there was a series of doctors who tried to help, sometimes coming to the house when the ambulance had to be called. We knew that her life was a horror, but nobody had anything to offer her. And so we all avoided her, except sometimes I would visit her with Jane at the state hospital. Her years there were a nightmare, with Julie screaming whenever visitors would leave, and sometimes when they would arrive too.

So Jane's feelings about mental illness were more painful than most people's, and she needed to stay as far away as she could from head doctors and analysis. Psychological treatment was for mental illness, and it invariably meant defeat and despair.

It wasn't hard to understand why Jane thought that psychotherapy had nothing to do with breast cancer. It *is* hard to see the connection. But the connection keeps turning up in the research studies. Again and again.

How Immune Cells Work

In factories in the bone marrow, thymus, lymph nodes, and abdominal organs, protective cells are grown that keep the body's house in order. Many of these, such as the large macrophages, tackle foreign substances and deal with dead waste material of the body.

A special group of immune cells is manufactured in the thymus gland behind the breast bone; it includes the stalking natural killer cells and their assistants, the helper and suppressor cells.

These cells are not the body's only means of resisting the growth and spread of tumor cells, for they combine with interferon, antibodies, and other forces. But they are a powerful force in the battle against cancer cells, and their workings have been of primary interest in research. Sometimes natural killer cells seem to lose their power. They may ignore or fail to recognize tumor cells, so that they don't attack or respond to threatening cells. When natural killer cells do work, they do so by attacking alien cells, destroying them and then tracking similar cells in surrounding tissues. Other immune cells will clean up after them, but killer cells do the work of guarding the body's house.

Sometimes immune cells do their work too well, attacking transplanted tissue or the body's own tissue in error, as in Grave's disease or Lupus. Their action can cause serious illness without any true disease present, so powerful are they. They depend on antigens on the cell's surface to identify cells as wanted or marked, although sometimes this identification system doesn't operate well, allowing enemy cells to slip by. Natural killer cells are armed with a powerful weapon that involves the ability to *lyse* unwanted cells, that is, to shoot an antibody or amino acid at another cell, causing it to break down.

The strength and number of natural killer cells is important in cancer outcomes, because it predicts how long a person can stay healthy. Unfortunately, at present there are no cheap and routine tests for natural killer cell activity level in patients, so we can't find out what's going on inside us. Other immune cells, such as the macrophages and B-lymphocytes, are all important to health, but for cancer the focus of research has been on natural killer cells and on how they respond to psychological forces. There will in the future be new laboratory instruments that allow us to see and measure various cells more accurately, and some researchers are freezing their cell findings in anticipation of that day, so that they do not lose potentially useful information. For the present, our understanding is rudimentary. Here's what is known.

Immune cells, such as the natural killer cells, work to check the progression and spread of cancer cells, but they have not been shown to control the appearance of malignancies. Considering that mutant cells must appear with some frequency in the body, it may be that these killer cells destroy cancer cells quite early, unless they cannot recognize them as mutant cells.

There is clearly a connection between the spread of cancer and the action of natural killer cells. When natural killer cell activity level is down, it is related to the spread of the cancer to the lymph nodes. Early stage tumors often draw lots of killer cells, but advanced cancers draw few, and the level of cancer development seems to be related to how active the cells are.[1]

We can get a pretty good idea of what affects natural killer cell activity levels. One researcher has suggested that instead of seeing the immune system as an army ready to do battle for our health, we might more accurately see it as a sensory organ, much like our eyes, ears, nose, or skin.[2] He suggests that the immune system senses things directly, without getting information from our thought processes and without reasoning, and then it reacts. Certainly our body's systems are connected, and the brain, glands, and immune cells and organs all communicate through the same chemicals and receptors.

Most research has shown that stress gets in the way of the immune system's working. This seems to occur via the release of chemicals such as adrenaline, noradrenaline, cortisol, prolactin, progesterone, and glucose, which affect the way that immune cells function. It may be that stress hormones neutralize the fighting power of natural killer cells.

It is particularly difficult to measure stress and its effects because of the differences in what people see as stressful. What is upsetting for one person may be amusing to another and catastrophic for a third. Most importantly, what is stressful for us is usually what we can't cope with, so the range of the coping patterns we have learned is also important. The first time we encounter a new situation, such as driving a car, we are likely to feel stressed, but as we develop effective and rewarding ways to deal with the situation, we feel less stress and we may even enjoy a challenge that was once unpleasant. On the other hand, when our patterns of dealing with stress don't work well, then the challenging situation is stressful again and again, with feelings of failure accumulating at each repetition.

Learned Responses

How can a person have a real allergic reaction to a silk rose? The power of the immune system is specific and awesome. Most of us have no idea of what occurs inside our bodies until something outside produces a big enough reaction to be noticed. An anaphylactic shock reaction is one demonstration of the power of internal reactions, whether we see them or not.

My son was seven when we first learned about the awful power of the immune system. He was a sturdy child who never paid much attention to his own discomfort. That's why, when he came in from playing in the backyard and said he didn't feel well, I got concerned, since he rarely gets anxious either. But he was clearly not feeling right, and he was quiet, with his mouth all screwed up tight. I noticed a mosquito bite on his lip, but as I reached to touch it, two more appeared on the other side of his lips, and then three more, so that there was a circle of lumps around his mouth. This all occurred in the seconds it took to reach out and touch his face.

He began to pull at his back. I took off his shirt and saw what seemed like a huge mosquito bite that was at least twelve inches long on his back. As I went to touch it, it disappeared under my hands, and another one appeared further up his back. Not understanding what was happening but aware that lightning-fast changes were occurring in his small body, I grabbed my car keys and put him in the front seat, his small face dazed and frightened. By this time his face was red and he was wheezing while the bumps kept coming and going on his skin. Now I noticed something truly ghastly. His eyes were watering, but the water wasn't coming out. It was swelling the membrane that covers the white part of the eyeball, so that his eyes were covered by water sacks that began to bulge out hideously and hang down over his cheeks.

At this point my heart was racing and I was driving as fast as I could, while trying to speak soothingly to him. I went through red lights and up over sidewalks, the accelerator to the floor, and prayed for a police car to pull me over. But none did.

There were two hospitals next to each other, and when we entered the first, there were drug addicts and knife fight victims on the floor, but no doctor in sight. The nurse told me to wait while she tried to quiet a child with a broken hand, but I knew that we had only moments left now. I stood for just a moment, waiting. And then a voice inside told me to move, to find someone who could help.

With little David limp in my arms, I raced to the hospital next door, down the basement steps in through the back door to the emergency room. The nurse there was a true emergency room nurse. As we came in, she put her arms around a now almost co-matose child and hugged him; in her hand was the small button hypodermic which injects adrenaline.

The change in David over the next five minutes was truly astonishing. The water bags hanging out on his cheeks began to recede, and the membranes pulled back to normal, showing merry blue eyes. The large skin swellings stopped appearing, and his skin became a uniform creamy color. The hives were gone from around his mouth. He sat up and began to breathe normally, and the wheezing stopped. Best of all, he smiled and became interested in the emergency room and made friends with the people there.

His body had suffered this severe reaction and returned to normal in less than thirty minutes. Anaphylaxis is the violent systemic response of a threatened immune system, a response that destroys the body in its overreaction unless halted. Estimates are that 15 percent of people may have this sensitivity, most often to antibiotics, nuts, seafood, and insect stings, and many of them die without ever knowing that they were victims of their own body's defenses.

The power of the anaphylactic response illustrates the body's capacity for defending itself when it perceives a threat. In a person with anaphylactic reactions, when the body first comes into contact with a substance like nuts, it manufactures antibodies called IgE, which remember the nuts forever. At some point, when nuts appear again, the antibodies set off a series of chemical responses, producing histamine and leukotrienes, which attack the skin, blood vessels, lungs, and intestines. The excessive immune response is so strong that it threatens to destroy the whole body along with the invader.

The delicate and complicated structure of the immune system is usually not apparent unless it is shown in outward symptoms. Foreign agents can set off this reaction, but research shows that immune responses, like other body responses, can be trained to appear in response to external signals. The immune system is also affected by emotional influences like trauma.

Stress seems to have a large impact on how all of our immune cells work. In physically healthy people who experience a major stress, such as living through a hurricane or losing a job, some research has shown a drop in the ability of immune cells to multiply and fight off invasive cells.[3]

We have a big dog at our house, with an impossibly long tongue and an extraordinary capacity for drooling. Drooling is an automatic salivary response to food in canines, and this dog taught us a lot about the relationship of learning and body processes. When we first got her, she would drool when she started to eat. Then she started to drool when she saw her food being prepared. Then it was when we took out the bowl. After awhile, she started to drool when she saw the big bag of food come in from the market. After a time, when we looked at her and said, "Are you hungry, poochie?" her mouth would start to drip. And now, since I've gotten in the habit of taking her with me on my late night trips to the ice cream store, she starts to drool when anybody says goodnight.

The kids realized that they could make her drool whenever they wanted to without her ever coming near food. It wasn't that she was very smart; obviously she wasn't or she would have caught on that when they would pretend they were coming in from the market, she wouldn't end up with a bowl of food. But her central nervous system had drawn a different conclusion, and it acted on what it had learned was the truth. When one of the kids would innocently say, "Is that Mom coming home from the store?" out would come that absurdly long tongue, and long strings of saliva would puddle on the floor.

Salivation in a dog begins as an automatic response to food, but then it generalizes to other, nonfood sights and sounds. This process can happen randomly, as when she started to drool when the bowl appeared, or it can be deliberately conditioned.

We tend to think of our body's ability to fight off disease, our immune system, as something hidden and cellular, and it is hard to imagine that immune responses can be trained. But all mammals function with similar contingencies, and drooling is only one example of a physical response that can be shaped. We learn to breathe, feel hungry, get sleepy, yawn, blink, cry, and laugh in response to conditioned cues. The capacity for these responses is inborn, but the link to external cues is learned.

Is the immune system like the salivary glands, and does it learn to respond to external events and cues? The prevailing view has always been that the body's protective response is self-contained, untouched by a person's reaction to his or her surroundings. But in 1975 a laboratory experiment with rats, an experiment that went wrong, changed the course of research on the immune system.

When Robert Ader was trying to condition rats to turn away from sweetened water, he did so by giving them a drug to make them vomit when they tasted the saccharine water. His purpose was to test whether you could destroy a natural attraction to sweetness if you hooked it to an unpleasant experience. This would be like yelling at the dog while she was drooling to get her to stop. If the rats began to turn away from the sugar water, it would prove that you could override a natural response.

Sometimes laboratory research runs into mundane technical problems. Microscopes get dropped, graduate students graduate, the computer breaks down. In this case, the rats in the experimental group were a sickly bunch and kept dying off at an unusually high rate, so it was hard to get the study finished up.

When research goes awry, everyone begins troubleshooting to find the problem. Somebody noticed that the drug used to produce vomiting in the rats when they drank the sugar water also happened to be a chemical that had the power to turn off their immune systems. Even though they had gotten the nausea drug only once, the rats kept responding to the sweet water as though they were still getting the nausea drug at the same time, the drug that also turned off the immune system.

This was just like my dog learning to drool when the grocery bags came in, even though she wasn't getting any food. The living system in both cases reacted to a cue for an event, even though the event itself never occurred. And with the laboratory rats, since their immune systems kept turning off because of the sugar water, they got sick and died.

Can humans turn on their immune systems to the sound of a bell like dogs can drool?

It may be the case, although the research to demonstrate this is fraught with difficulties. The least that can be said is that the immune response is far more affected by external influences than anyone ever believed and that the idea that it operates independently of learning is now impossible to sustain.

In *Beyond Freedom and Dignity*, B. F. Skinner, one of the great figures in psychology in this century, argues that human beings need to pay close attention to the conditions that shape their behavior, those deliberate and accidental contingencies that develop and shape a life.[4] These may range from salivating to the tune of "You deserve a break today," to the relaxation that comes over a fretful child at seeing her mother's face. Skinner argues that human dignity and autonomy can result only from an awareness of the contingencies that control us and that there is no true human freedom if our behavior is all controlled by cues in our surroundings. In the health arena, we need to look carefully at the forces that provoke and suppress our immune response, or they will occur randomly and affect our health outside our control.

Many factors affect the body's protective forces, and some of them can be influenced by our behavior and intellectual patterns. Some of these are accidental pairings, like the dog learning that the car in the garage can mean food in its mouth, and some of them are more complicated linkages. But this opens the possibility that just as the kids learned to make the dog drool whenever they wanted, people may be able to direct their immune system to work harder when they need it.

This sounds far-fetched, but the research exploring these possibilities is already underway. Dr. Janice Kiecolt-Glaser, a psychologist, and her husband, Dr. Ronald Glaser, an immunologist, found that they had more in common than romance when they began to link their two fields of psychology and immunology by means of a series of research projects. One of them involved changing immune responses of students.

Medical school is a trying experience for young people, and it shows in the strained and haggard faces of medical students. During exam periods, things get more tense, and measures of the immune system taken on medical students during these times show a clear drop.

The doctors taught a group of medical students a technique that temporarily reduces tension by slowly and systematically relaxing every muscle in the body. Developed by Herbert Benson at Harvard, the relaxation response is an orderly exercise that takes about twenty minutes and turns down the body's idle speed.[5] This may sound easy, but it takes a great deal of practice and self-control for this to have an effect and show clear benefits. The medical students who learned the relaxation response and practiced it regularly stayed healthier through their exams. Laboratory tests showed that there were measurable physical changes and their immune functions were stronger than students who did not use the relaxation sequence.[6]

All of our current thinking in medicine says that this should not happen, that a mental exercise cannot have any effect on the activity or potency of lymphocytes in the body as they track down and destroy health threats. But this point of view assumes that thoughts have no chemical basis, that they happen somewhere down the street from where our bodies are, and that they have a phantom existence in air molecules or light rays, instead of having their being in chemical configurations inside us. Thoughts are in fact chemical realities, and the idea that they should affect and be affected by other chemicals in the body, like the neuropeptides and amino acids that are the basis of cellular immune response, merely puts them back in the same body that they come from. It all happens within us.

The chemical signals that go with thoughts get linked with the chemical signals that turn on or turn off immune cell action. And so there are predictable health results from certain kinds of human events.

Psychological Forces That Affect Natural Killer Cells

The activity of certain kinds of immune cells has been a focus of breast cancer research, in part because current technology limits the choice of experimental measures. You can study what you can see and measure. Natural killer cell activity levels have been of particular interest, because they are a reliable predictor of axillary (underarm) node status, that is, of whether the local breast cancer has begun to enter the lymphatic system and travel through the body. This is important to know because breast cancers that spread require special treatment.

Since natural killer cells track down tumor cells and lyse them, it makes sense that as their numbers go up, the spread of breast cancer slows. And patients with high natural killer cell activity levels are likely to have fewer lymph nodes with cancer. Identifying the conditions that help or hinder the operation of these immune cells has been a primary goal of research in the psychology of breast cancer, and some influential forces have been identified.

When there is a loss of an important human relationship, it is correlated with a drop in immune response. In marital relationships, regardless of whether partners love each other, the relationship nonetheless structures their lives, and the loss of one person is usually a serious stress for the other. Folk wisdom tells us that illness following widowhood is not unexpected, and the psychological research supports this, showing that a spouse is more prone to serious disease after being widowed.[7]

When men are widowed, their lymphocytes seem to have more trouble proliferating, and these levels fall, reducing their body's defenses.[8] At the same time, a man is likely to experience powerful, disturbing emotions of anger, anxiety, and sadness. The conditioning of these responses, like a dog's drooling, can become accidentally conditioned to irrelevant parts of the surroundings. A man who is widowed in the springtime may have a drop in his immune reaction as part of the emotional trauma, and these feelings and immune reaction drops may become internally connected. In subsequent years, he may have the same chemical and emotional reactions to the signs of spring in what is termed an anniversary reaction. This is the mind's reaction to profound loss and may involve unexplainable moodiness, irritability, and depression during the weeks before the actual date of the past event, as the body anticipates, on a subconscious or cellular level, the remembered pain.

How our body reacts to an event depends a great deal, however, on the way that we interpret it. When there is a loss of spouse due to one's own choice, for example, when a woman makes a conscious decision to separate from her husband, the immune system does not register the event as an injury and does not show the same drop in function.[9] Our beliefs about our control over life events and their benefit or danger to us greatly affect how our bodies register experiences; we shall explore this subject more extensively in chapter 6.

There are many different kinds of events that can affect the delicate balances of hormones, neuropeptides, and amino acids in our systems. Sometimes these events are not personal but rather community traumas. In 1979 a damaged nuclear power plant caused great emotional upset among the residents of Three Mile Island, who feared a meltdown and contamination of their families, homes, and community. A similar community eighty miles away had concern but not the same panic level, since they were not in danger.

When measures were taken of blood pressure, heart rate, and immune function over a six-year period, the Three Mile Island residents showed a drop in immune function in five measures. The ordeal of living in a community under siege by uncontrollable forces apparently affected the residents in a way similar to that of people who incur other types of losses.[10] We can only guess at what associations were made at a cellular level, but like the rats who suffered reduced immune function in response to sweet taste, a change occurred in body processes as the result of exposure to external events.

The connection between external stressful events, psychological reactions, and body processes is a concern because it is difficult to see, and often the results are not felt until long after the events are over. For people who work at jobs where there is frequent exposure to danger or risk, these experiences can result in an increase in personal injury accidents and serious health problems.

Emergency service organizations have become concerned about the relationship between traumatic events and physiological reactions, and many of them have instituted special preventive programs for their workers. Police, firefighters, emergency medical technicians, and disaster workers are now considered to be at risk of disability as a result of strong emotional experiences. The American Red Cross has taken the lead in creating programs to protect their rescue people from the physical consequences of observing trauma, and even the toughest disaster workers have begun to accept their own vulnerabilities.

If all of this is hard to follow, it should be. Contingent links in learned behaviors are extraordinarily complex, and it is difficult to figure out what is connecting to what. Suffice it to say that we need to be aware that our immune system is more like a sensory organ, closing down at the anticipation of a blow and opening out under receptive conditions. For just as surely as the immune responses can constrict under certain circumstances, there are influences that expand our body's defenses and boost their strength. In breast cancer we want to limit, as much as possible, how often the immune system blinks.

The great difficulty with understanding the immune response is that all of it happens outside our awareness, making it seem imaginary. We can't see it in action, but repeated research studies have found certain predictable connections. A woman's level of fatigue and how much social support she feels she has, for example, are good predictors of natural killer cell activity level in breast cancer.[11]

Women who believe that they get lots of help and support from others generally have high natural killer cell activity levels. It may be that the help and support are not actually there and they are reacting to a belief rather than a reality. As in the case of the asthmatics responding to a fake rose, the body can only respond to its perception of things, as filtered through the sensory organs and thought processes. A fake rose can elicit the same response as a real one, whether in romance or in asthma, and the body operates as though its perceptions were the only reality.

It is not only immune responses that get conditioned to external or internal cues. When someone undergoes chemotherapy, irrelevant events can be perceived as part of the experience. This is why years after treatment, hospital smells or certain foods may stir up all of the same sick feelings that they did originally. The body's systems react as if the complete sequence of events, medications included, were happening.

Psychotherapy and Breast Cancer

As we consider the effect of psychological forces on the body, it can seem that the random pairing of personal experiences with physical processes is the main way this happens. But there are other psychological experiences, planned and regulated, that also have an impact on physical functions, the most familiar being psychotherapy.

Across a number of research studies, there is a clear trend of results that indicate that psychotherapy raises the level of immune function. Why should this be? Nothing physical happens. Perhaps somebody talks louder here or there in therapy or cries, but nothing obvious occurs on a physiological level. At least, not to the naked eye. But there is an effect, and it seems to come from the central nervous system's influence on the immune system; it is similar to what happens when the central nervous system makes the eyes fill up with tears. Psychotherapy changes our perceptions of people and events and opens a way to release powerful feelings.

This process of expressing feelings generally improves immune function, whether it happens in speaking or in writing, while suppression gets in the way of the activity of immune cells.[12] Holding back is a natural reaction to stress for many people, and in some situations it may be the best response, because it can allow us to reflect on decisions, evaluate risks, and plan our response. In other situations, holding back out of fear or shame may be a prelude to burying feelings and making ourselves unaware that we have them.

How does expression or suppression affect immune cells? Studies of women with breast cancer who live for a long time show that they are more likely to pay attention to feelings and deal with them directly and continuously. Women with repressive personality styles, on the other hand, may report few emotional upsets or turmoil, but they are more likely to be sicker with breast cancer and not respond as well to medical treatment.[13] A free flow of feelings, particularly negative feelings, seems to go along with a free flow of immune cells.

How do we know if we are repressing? Repression, after all, means an insensitivity to our emotions, and it can be hard to see what's there if we are emotionally blind. Highly repressed women often appear extremely, impossibly well adjusted psychologically. They are likely to think about happy things, to avoid dwelling on the bad, and to show no emotional distress under any circumstances. It can be hard to tell the difference between serenity and a veneer of serenity.

Highly repressed people are poor at dramatic stage acting because they have no personal experience to draw on when they need to demonstrate a wide range of human feelings. When feelings are stifled, there is little color or variation in a person's responses to life experiences. The facade presented is bland, unflinching, and tells little of what goes on inside.

When we habitually repress feelings of anger, fear, or sadness, we limit the ways we have to show them, and after awhile we may forget how they feel. We will certainly be limited in the choice of ways to express feelings, since we won't have had much practice.

A woman with repressive patterns has little interest in emotional distress signals, since these can threaten her sense of balance and competence, and she is therefore likely to ignore them. When asked about her feelings regarding her breast cancer, she is likely to say:

"It's no problem."

"I can handle it."

"There's nothing to talk about."

"I know some women get really upset, but, thankfully, I'm not like that."

"I'm very open about my feelings, and I would talk about it if it upset me."

"You just can't let these things get you down."

There is nothing pathological about these reactions when they appear in response to life's routine upsets, for example, having to pay a fine for an overdue library book. But if a person has just gotten hit by a truck, which is the equivalent of breast cancer diagnosis and treatment, these responses work to seal off all the fruitful turmoil that makes for adjustment. They also cut off the possibility of real contact with other people, because the genuine person and her unique reactions are hidden, and other people are likely to reply in kind, giving shallow, insensitive responses in conversation. What's more, these reactions deny the reality of the body's needs. When there is trauma, our physiological systems need attention whether we choose to notice or not.

When people keep feelings inside or repress them, there are changes in the blood pressure, heart rate, and skin conductance, and these are all summary measures of much broader fluctuations in the body's many systems. In contrast, when people share upsetting information with trusted others, this appears to relieve physiological pressure, and the body reaches a more balanced state.[14] Even the brain reacts: when we talk about superficial topics, the right and left brain generate different wave activity, but when we talk about difficult, emotionally charged subjects, the right- and left-side brain activity are congruent.[15]

Psychologists in training usually worry a great deal about what they should say when they do therapy and what advice they should give. Much more important is how well they listen, for helping people distinctly verbalize their feelings is the great power of psychotherapy.

Increasingly, cancer patients are using psychology to maximize their response to treatment. Today's therapist is no longer the spooky doctor who reads your mind but is instead a skilled technician and caring helper who works with a patient to help her get what she wants and enhance her health.

Why is it particularly important to express emotions in difficult situations? The main reason is that when we are confronted with something exceedingly stressful or overwhelming, we tend to shut down our coping process. In the face of trauma, it is impossible to be reflective, balanced, and wise, because the pressure of potentially overpowering feelings is so strong. And the feelings tend to pile up, clogging all of the body's problem-solving channels.

When Maria was diagnosed with primary breast cancer, she could not bear to think about having cancer, and she told no one. She put it out of her mind, except when she had to go for treatments, and she worked hard to hide her illness. As she recovered from treatment, she consciously avoided thinking about the illness. Three years later, her married daughter was diagnosed with breast cancer, but Maria was paralyzed by her feelings. Although she deeply loved her daughter, she could not bear to confront her daughter's feelings about the disease. Neither could she talk about it with her daughter, who would have been badly hurt at having been excluded from such an important event in her mother's life.

Talking as a Way to Reduce Stress

When we are dealing with serious life problems, most of us tend to think the same thoughts repeatedly, and our thinking reinforces itself. We look for reasons for our predicament, and our thinking can easily become circular, so that we end up blaming ourselves.

We know that when people go through stressful experiences, it helps to talk about it, and we may even notice ourselves repeatedly describing a car accident or an operation as a way to absorb the incident and make sense out of it. Reviewing it many times may serve to normalize an unusual event and to gather social support and friendly reassurance from others as well. In the American Red Cross, this need to talk has been recognized in volunteers who deal with disaster. When there is an earthquake or plane crash, Red Cross workers therefore spend a great deal of time in groups talking about their rescue experiences and reliving them in words until they lose some of their sting.

Even with the advent of fast-paced machines in modern life, like computers, supersonic planes, and fast food services, human psyches still need the same amount of time to assimilate new and traumatic experiences. This means that we may express certain feelings the first time we describe a traumatic event and then react with somewhat different feelings by the fifth retelling.

Our emotions change when we introduce new information, and when we speak about our experiences, our feelings change just as they would if we listened to any new voice speaking on the subject. Our thoughts and our feelings often represent distinctly different perspectives, and they each change when confronted with the another.

When we first hear "cancer," we are likely to hear an alarm bell, or maybe even a death knell, because of all the prior associations we have formed. Some people feel that having cancer is the same as dying. Alarm reactions tend to set off neurological and hormonal signals. When these associations and beliefs are examined in psychotherapy with another person, we are likely to expand our automatic associations and develop other images. In response to the word "cancer," we might picture, for example, a concerned doctor's face, a long period of taking pills, and good news at future testings.

It may be hard for us to be aware that we have strong feelings in response to stressful times, since repression is rarely a balanced decision that we make after careful consideration. Instead, it is the mind's way of protecting us from too much information. In a crisis it may feel like we have no feelings at all, as the mind draws a curtain over our emotions to protect us from overload.

This is why when someone we love dies, we may feel nothing at the funeral or during the first few weeks afterward. After three to six months we may feel much more of the impact of the loss, as our protective systems gradually allow us to confront the trauma. After the decisions have been made and the necessary action taken, our emotions come back, sometimes in force.

When feelings are hard to feel, we may become aware of our psychological state by noticing physical signs like great fatigue, tense irritability, or tearfulness. Biological indicators may show that certain things affect us strongly. After a few sessions with a therapist, most people get a better sense of their genuine feelings. The energy required to repress emotions can then be used productively in places where the body needs it more.

Psychotherapy is a safe way to regularly and routinely release strong feelings and to clear the intellectual deck for the work that has to be done, both in thought and behavior. By saying our thoughts and feelings aloud, we take a more careful look at them, and often we change our thinking. Dealing with emotions openly reduces their power, makes our experience seem more legitimate, and takes away some of the stigma we may feel.

Talking aloud helps us avoid self-blame, and we gain support from a sympathetic listener (ourselves). Most importantly, therapy allows us to move on to more fruitful problem-solving. The beneficial effects on health come from clearing away the burden of stress on a system already dealing with disease. Stress has physiological costs, and psychotherapy allows us to give our energy to an already challenged system.

There is a way that you can demonstrate this to yourself if you are dealing with breast cancer. If you find that you have trouble sleeping because of tension or anxiety, it will help if you clear your intellectual deck. You need to get up and, using either a tape recorder or pencil and paper, record all of your thoughts and feelings continuously. Get down on paper whatever comes to mind, whether it is relevant or unrelated to your day and plans. Dredge up everything you can, and don't try to make sense of it or be fair or present a reasonable appearance. Don't edit or correct, but do try to be as clear as possible.

Do this for several nights, and then look at the effect on your sleep: how quickly you get to sleep, how long you sleep, and how rested you feel. You're likely to have the same results as one researcher who found that the act of releasing emotional tension allowed the body's other processes to work much better.[16] By breaking up the logjam of feelings, we allow the emotional process to become fluid, and our other systems can then reach a new balance as well.

Feelings are not always easy to identify, and things have different meanings for people. A woman who discovers a lump in her breast during a pregnancy will have a different reaction than a woman who discovers a lump while going into action as a fighter pilot. It is these perspectives that are important, and they vary from person to person. A woman who feels her life is threatened may respond with anger to a diagnosis of breast cancer, while a woman who feels incapacitated may react with helplessness and depression. Experience shows that most women respond with a combination of these.

There are additional ways that psychotherapy influences health when you have breast cancer. This disease involves so many new problems and questions that it may seem that you have to remap your life. A therapist can be a caring outsider who helps to choose the best options. With all of the trivial and not so trivial issues of the illness and treatment, it can conserve a woman's energy to schedule a regular time to handle problems and work steadily at solutions, with some coming quickly and others taking more time. This also helps you avoid obsessing over these issues during the week, as there is time set aside for them.

Organized research programs that have provided psychotherapy for women with breast cancer usually show a clear benefit. Mood improves a good deal, there is a reduction in anxiety and depression, and people find workable solutions to practical problems.[17] These therapy programs generally involve a focus on thinking and behavior and rarely explore childhood and early memories as is the case in traditional psychological treatment for disorders.

Julia, an elderly breast cancer patient, used to joke that her therapist was actually her administrative assistant and social secretary. Their goal was the building of a more extensive social network, and their therapy sessions had evolved into planning meetings for the week.

It makes sense that routine psychotherapy would be helpful. In this arrangement, you talk about yourself and think about yourself in a way that is not common to most women, particularly women who have been married or raised families. A good counselor continually draws the focus of discussion back to you, even though you may be used to thinking about others and planning for their needs. What's more, a therapist focuses on current feelings, not your philosophy of life or your rationalizations, but how you feel at the moment.

What does this accomplish? It gives emotions a place to go, instead of settling in physically like an ingrown toenail. Negative emotions turned inward usually result in hopeless and helpless feelings. Saying feelings out loud drains them of their power, even if you already acknowledge that they are there. When their power is gone, they begin to change as you develop a new perspective. To voice aloud routine feelings of hopelessness and helplessness, paradoxically, gives one power.

Women with breast cancer are usually extremely reluctant to participate in psychotherapy or most experiences that deal with emotions. When they do, the results are enlightening. Women are most likely to accept a recommendation for psychological treatment when it is made as part of the medical treatment plan, which requires that oncologists be familiar with psychological treatment methods (this is rare). In general, women who are youthful and of higher socioeconomic class are more likely to follow such a recommendation. People are most likely to participate if they believe it is important for the good of science.[18] This seems to take the stigma out of using psychological treatment and reassures women that they are not dependent on help to cope with breast cancer.

The Faith Courtauld Studies

Steven Greer at the Faith Courtauld Unit of King's Hospital in London has been following a group of woman with breast cancer for a long time.[19] It began when he selected 160 women who were about to have a biopsy for breast cancer, before they knew any results or had undergone any procedures.

Prior to their biopsies, they were given a series of psychological tests. Greer was interested in measures of their emotional state, including depressed feelings, anger at themselves or others, anxiety levels, stress and coping methods, relationships, marriages, and work histories. Luckily, a large number of women were willing to help with his research, thus providing information of great value to others and to the study of cancer.

After the biopsies were done, the women were grouped according to whether they had breast cancer or had negative results. Greer found a clear difference in the two groups in several of the psychological measures, most importantly, in the way that they handled anger. He found that the women who turned out to have breast cancer generally expressed anger less often than the other group, and when they did, it was often in the form of sudden explosions. His interpretation of this was that those women had a habitual way of coping with stress or threat by suppressing emotions as long as possible until they came out in outbursts of temper. This is a finding supported by other research.[20]

After studying their coping styles for a longer period, he was able to identify five patterns that characterized women's behavioral responses to dealing with breast cancer:

1. *Fighting spirit:* When a woman utilizing this pattern is diagnosed with breast cancer, she understands and accepts what is being said, and she is optimistic and generally active on her own behalf. She is characteristically determined to do as well as she can

with the disease and works at enhancing her health. Sometimes she may be seen as aggressive, ornery, and difficult, but her behavior is not negative and has a level of vitality in pursuit of her own best interests. As Marylu put it, it's not fighting against something, but fighting for something.

2. *Denial:* A woman dealing with breast cancer may refuse to recognize the seriousness of the situation, and carry on with her life in the same ways as before, as much as possible ignoring the change that a breast cancer diagnosis brings. Sometimes this may be fruitful, but in this style there is considerable energy diverted to maintaining a schedule and keeping up appearances rather than mobilizing for life.

3. *Stoic acceptance:* When a woman with this pattern is diagnosed with breast cancer, she shows little emotion throughout the process. She may not register any thoughts or feelings at all, which can be confusing to those around her. There is a high level of acceptance here, too high, which can be a form of fatalism. For some women, a diagnosis of breast cancer, with the possibility of death, can be less frightening than other things happening in her life and may initially seem like a relief.

4. *Helplessness/hopelessness:* When a woman is dealing with breast cancer, she may feel continuously overwhelmed by knowledge of the disease and descend into an enduring passive state. There is a preoccupation with horror and death, and her thoughts and feelings increasingly disable her. There is little anger or hostility and sometimes no reaction at all to others and instead an enormous emotional involvement with herself. To outward appearances, a woman may appear serene and relaxed, but inside she may feel panicked and defeated.

5. *Anxious preoccupation:* In dealing with breast cancer a woman's behavior can show obsessive thought processes in which a great deal of thought and attention is given to checking and making sure of things. There is repetitive thinking, compulsive rituals and checking, and in general an attempt to use up feeling in stereotyped, useless behavior.

These styles of dealing with stress and trauma develop early in life and appear in response to any trauma long before breast cancer becomes an issue. They may be learned from parents or developed in response to unrealistic expectations in childhood, or they may simply be responses that have produced good results in

the past. In challenging situations, we usually try one response after another until we find a successful one, which is then repeated
in future situations that are similar.

Most people use all five of Greer's coping responses from time
to time, but Greer was concerned with how a woman's characteristic coping style affected her recovery.[21] In looking at the
women in their group, the researchers on the Greer team were
able to gauge the relation between adjustment styles and breast
cancer. After fifteen years of observing women in the study, there
were clear differences in how women fared with breast cancer
according to their predominant coping style. Women who handled stress with either a fighting spirit or denial were more than
twice as likely to be alive and well fifteen years after diagnosis, as women using stoic acceptance, helplessness/hopelessness, or
anxious preoccupation.

Fighting spirit and denial are different from the other three
styles (stoic acceptance, helplessness/hopelessness, and anxious
preoccupation) in that they involve energy and a forward direction. They offer a determined response, and although they may
not make the best use of a woman's resources, they do show a
determination to prevail, a diving in, rather than an avoiding or
withdrawing. With either of these two ways of coping, a woman
moves forward into the challenge of breast cancer with energy and
fortitude.

There may be practical reasons that certain coping styles produce better results. Women with a fighting spirit characteristically
bring a good deal more energy and vitality to their efforts, and so
their goals become more reachable. They are also far more likely
to draw on their relationships for help, using emotions to connect with others. Aside from the impact of these stages on immune
function, active coping patterns of dealing with the disruption and
inconvenience of disease are far more productive.

Stoicism, helplessness, and anxious preoccupation all have a
strong element of passivity and immobilization, and it is likely that
these styles close off promising sources of help and approaches
that can enhance health. It is probable that they are detrimental
to optimal physical responses, and they also limit creativity and
energy available for dealing with the routine problems resulting
from breast cancer treatment.

Adjuvant Psychological Therapy

Can these characteristic coping styles be changed? If a woman wanted to increase her chances of dealing well with her illness, could psychology offer any ways to help? Or are these fixed coping patterns, perhaps genetically determined and as unchangeable as height or skin color?

Steven Greer has set out to find out. He has created a psychotherapeutic program that helps with the stress of breast cancer and its treatment and strives to develop health-enhancing circumstances in a woman's life, along with fighting spirit. Called *adjuvant psychological therapy*, or APT, it works to change feelings by revising thinking and beliefs.[22]

It is not the same thing as the traditional psychological treatment aimed at women who can't cope. In fact, teaching fighting spirit to women who have breast cancer requires a certain level of psychological health, for women with severe psychopathology have little energy for this sort of work. These are in fact two quite different endeavors, and they cannot be successfully combined.

It is also different from regular medical treatment and needs separate arrangement to be effective. APT requires a suitable treatment setting and it cannot, for example, be offered at bedside in the hospital when there are others present, for then confidentiality is destroyed. It cannot be interrupted by medical caregivers doing routine rounds and must have all the safeguards of office psychotherapeutic treatment. It is also important that the therapist and medical caregivers coordinate treatment so that caregivers understand the independent effects of medical care and psychological upset.

Greer looks at ways to use thinking ability to strengthen the body's response to medical treatment and to clear away obstacles to maximize fighting response. Recognizing that medical treatment forces passivity on patients, he works in APT to develop a more energetic stance. In short-term treatment (six or more sessions), often involving family members, a therapist helps the patient to examine and change her habitual reactions to crises. This usually involves exploring her internal monologue, which is often negative, and challenging her through reality testing.

APT also uses anticipation of stressful events, rehearsing them and planning ways of coping with them that are most effective.

In addition, an ongoing activity is the planning of events that are maximally pleasant and confidence-building. Sometimes skills are taught, such as relaxation training, and often communication is improved between family members. The purpose of the treatment is to build on a person's strengths and overcome feelings of helplessness and hopelessness.

How this might work is illustrated by the experience of Ann. At fifty-three, Ann was diagnosed with breast cancer and underwent lumpectomy, radiation, and chemotherapy. When APT was suggested to her, she was reluctant to use it, since she often spoke with her priest and, she said, she did not want to dwell on her difficulties.

In eight sessions at which her husband was also present, Ann found that in the face of most life stresses, her response was generally to pray and then wait to see what God offered. She believed that trouble was God's way of trying to teach her something and that it meant that she needed to change something about herself. When she felt challenged, it automatically indicated that something was wrong with her. She felt that if she were a good person, there would be no crises in her life.

This led to the two stress habits of eating and watching television, which often went together and usually made things harder for her. When she was engaged in these activities, she felt more relaxed and less confused, but she was concerned about the effects of inactivity and overeating on her health and mood.

As she began treatment, she felt confused and upset because she could not identify why she had gotten sick and what she was supposed to learn from it. She decided that it must mean that she should learn to bear pain silently and to keep her faith. Her husband assumed that she refused to talk to him because she couldn't rely on him, since he had lost his job several years before. When he had to take a lower-paying job, he felt less useful as a husband and provider.

Both partners were surprised to learn that whenever Ann dealt with her tension by turning on the television, her husband found himself automatically thinking, "I'm no good to her." As they both examined this openly, he became aware of her need for him, and they both came up with some specific ways that he could be helpful in the current circumstances, for example, accompanying her on her doctor visits and asking questions. Coincidentally, he looked at his thought patterns and found ways that he needed to change his hopeless/helpless feelings about losing his job and to take action in his occupational area.

In APT, neither Ann nor her husband changed their personalities, although they did learn more about the habits they had developed for solving problems and were able to make them more fruitful. Both were healthy people psychologically, and treatment helped them to streamline their problem-solving, thus preserving their energies for better uses.

A somewhat different case is that of Annabelle, who at thirty-eight was diagnosed with breast cancer. She had lived with her boyfriend for three years. Visibly upset and angry at her diagnosis, she was ready to fight with everyone, from the doctor who gave her the diagnosis and the nurses who provided treatment to her boyfriend. One day when she felt particularly irritable, she slapped her doctor when he told her to calm down.

In APT she examined her thought patterns and noticed that although she had lots of fighting spirit and was used to conflict, she often drained off energy wastefully by fighting futile battles. These were often driven by hysterical thinking that developed from unvoiced fears blown out of proportion. Her mental monologue included the following refrains:

"If I have to have another chemotherapy treatment, it will be awful, horrible, unbearable!"

"I can't stand any more chemotherapy!"

"The last chemotherapy ruined my life!"

"If I have to have more, I can't stand it!"

As Annabelle listened to her own excessive thoughts, she became increasingly emotionally upset. When her boyfriend tried to calm her down by speaking rationally to her, she felt that he was dismissing her fears and ignoring her worries, and so she usually exploded at him.

In APT Annabelle used relaxation therapy, which she practiced several times each day, and she learned to think more serenely about challenges. In doing so, she was able to temporarily put aside her strong feelings in order to plan action that would help her. She found, for example, that she was able to arrange a systematic desensitization program that greatly reduced the side effects of chemotherapy. Of particular importance was that she and her partner got into recreational routines that took them out two nights a week, allowing them to enjoy their favorite activities and each other.

In this case, what looked like fighting spirit was actually anxious preoccupation with frightening thoughts and personal inadequacy. These led to excessive, emotionally draining confrontations that exhausted Annabelle and alienated her from others. In therapy she learned to calm her insides and draw on outside supports to make better use of her energy.

Can APT affect coping styles? Can it develop fighting spirit? Will breast cancer patients improve their outlook by working on their thinking habits through this technique? The answers to these questions must come from research that will take years, perhaps decades, to complete.

There are a host of studies that suggest that various kinds of psychotherapy for breast cancer patients improve the quality of life, reduce depression and anxiety, and improve relationships. In addition, research findings indicate that psychotherapy boosts the effects of medical treatment and results in a brighter prognosis for patients. These studies also indicate that behavior patterns that increase emotional repression make for a gloomier outlook with breast cancer.[23]

The Health Effects of Behavior

Recently medicine has begun to apply the tight research design requirements that have long been characteristic of psychology. Research design and statistical analysis are a basic part of psychology, which has long relied on these to deal with the often murky field of human behavior and individual differences. This realm of techniques seeks to answer the question, how do you know that research results mean a real difference and are not accidental, the result of random variation in human beings?

Psychological research has held itself to a much higher standard than other fields in evaluating results, and many of its findings, although indicating that treatment techniques were powerful and effective, had to be discarded because they did not meet the strict requirements imposed on the methodology. Such is the case with the Heidelberg Prospective Intervention Study. The study has many flaws in its design, but its results are strong ones, and the flaws do not necessarily negate the information gained. Like any research advance, it needs to be replicated, but its results are in line with the trend of research in this area, although the magnitude of its effects may be exaggerated.

One of the smaller projects in this study dealt with the effects of combining chemotherapy with twenty to thirty sessions of individual psychotherapy for breast cancer patients.[24] Sessions included problem-solving, looking at beliefs and expectations, relaxation training, and positive thinking. Women with breast cancer explored their reactions to their disease and their ways of dealing with the events.

The treatment offered is called "creative novation therapy." It is based on the belief that personality differences determine health, and that these can be changed. Also called "autonomy training," this treatment emphasizes helping people to evaluate whether their usual ways of thinking and acting get them what they want from life. Behavior that helps us in the short run may not offer any long-term benefits.

The researchers believe that many neurotic problems result from an emotional dependence on others, which prevents people from making decisions in their best interests. When there is too much attention to others' demands and too little attention to one's own care, psychological needs are unmet, and symptoms like hopelessness/helplessness appear, leading to unsatisfying relationships and unhealthy life choices.

This is well illustrated by the case of Edith, a woman who had been married for many years and treasured her home life. She had been diagnosed with breast cancer after her oldest child graduated from high school, and she had been successfully treated for several recurrences. Her husband carried on a separate life, which kept him away from the house for most evenings and weekends. As the children grew up and left, he spent less and less time at home and also contributed little financial help to the household, forcing Edith to maintain their home. Eventually he moved to the west coast, where he could take up car racing, which he enjoyed.

Edith was left with the choice of continuing a lonely, frustrating marriage or divorcing him and risking further loneliness and financial strain. The aim of treatment here was to help her look realistically at her alternatives, to deal forthrightly with her dependence on her husband, and to help her to find ways to live more happily.

After a great deal of active thought and exploration of options, she decided to divorce her husband and hired a lawyer to contact him. Interestingly, he immediately changed his behavior and returned home, apparently in a state of high anxiety. This led to a dilemma for Edith. Her choice was to postpone the divorce proceedings for one year and keep track of his choices. But she had changed a good deal. As she put it, "I learned that I was stronger, smarter, and more valuable to me than I thought and that he just wasn't the only choice in life."

In the Heidelberg studies, it was predicted that psychotherapy aimed at improving patients' life satisfaction by changing habitual responses would have an impact on health. In one part of the study, breast cancer patients receiving standard medical treatment were followed.

The patients, women with metastatic breast cancer who were treated with chemotherapy as well as cognitive/behavioral psychotherapy, showed a substantial increase in survival time, while women who used only chemotherapy increased their survival time very little. The effect of psychotherapy alone was not very powerful and neither was the effect of chemotherapy alone, but together they seemed to have a significant effect.

An additional finding of the study was that psychotherapy affected patient lymphocyte levels during treatment. Using cortisol to represent a complicated system of chemical interactions involving peptides and hormones, the researchers suggested that acute stress in humans increases cortisol levels, leads to feelings of hopelessness and helplessness, and produces a drop in immune responses. If this is so, then psychotherapy that deals effectively with acute stress and resulting feelings should raise the lymphocyte levels.

Whatever the mediating process, lymphocyte levels do generally drop during breast cancer treatment, and this can be an obstacle to continued chemotherapy. Usually, the strength and frequency of treatment is determined by a woman's immune tolerance.

The researchers found that women who had only chemotherapy showed a steady decrease in lymphocytes, while the women who had chemotherapy and psychotherapy showed a decrease at first, but then a steady *increase* in lymphocytes.[25] Apparently, the psychological treatment worked to strengthen the immune response and offset the effects of the chemotherapy.

So although a great deal of our current understanding about immune cells is based on the chemical and biological interactions between them and other body cells, the issue of how they respond to psychological forces is a new frontier. It is an exciting frontier, with several trends clear in the accumulated research results.

The immune system is closely tied in with the central nervous system and the endocrine system, with many interlocking pathways and shared messengers. Of great current interest are the natural killer cells, which seem to be particularly responsive to emotional states.

If your immune system is strong and healthy, you may have no need for ways to enhance or bolster its functioning, although research suggests that you may want to write about traumatic events to clear away some of the ill effects of normal trauma. But if your system is under attack, you need to limit the extra demands on your system that come from stress and draw on others for help. Psychotherapy can help you clear the way to be most effective in using medical treatment to deal with breast cancer and in drawing on relationships in a way that maximizes outcomes. Certain kinds of psychotherapy seem to be more effective than others.

Chapter Four

Women's Conversations and Cancer Cells

Dear Abby:
This letter is an answer to the one from the girl who said her boyfriend didn't like her friends and he said she spent too much time with them and she had to make her choice.
Tell her to remember that boys come and go but your friends are for life.

Love,

Kristin in Mobile

Female friendships in girls and women form a large part of a female's social network, and this is increasingly true as women get older. Women share their deepest feelings and most powerful experiences with close friends, and often it is these people who help them get through life's crises and problems.

There are two ways, among others, that women are different from men. They talk a great deal more with each other than men do, and they live an average of eight years longer. Could these two facts be related? It wouldn't seem so, but women's talking apparently affects health, and cancer cells in particular.

David Spiegel at Stanford knew the value of women's conversations in comforting and soothing women who were dealing with the emotional turmoil of breast cancer. Over many years, he and his colleagues often ran groups in which women shared feelings and helped each other deal with advanced cancer and its effects, and the beneficial results were well known in psychology. Women who spent a year in their support groups in conjunction with their medical treatment had more positive moods, felt stronger and more optimistic, and felt better physically. In contrast, women who received routine oncological care had a good deal of negative moods, fear, and discomfort.

The additional finding that the women who were in psychotherapy groups lived on the average twice as long as women who were not raised the question of how women's conversations could have such a powerful impact on health.

What goes on in group psychotherapy? The subject of much study, group process is a complicated and intense emotional experience.[1] In the Spiegel groups, two forms of behavior were emphasized and developed: emotional expression and interpersonal support, both of which occurred through interpersonal communication.

In weekly conversations lasting ninety minutes, small groups of women shared their experiences and their feelings and listened to each other with concern and encouragement. These ways of relating are characteristic of the way that women typically converse when they seek to connect with one another, but the group psychotherapy structure helped this occur more rapidly and intensely. Why did this affect the course of advanced breast cancer?

It may be that when women talked about their illness, they realized the importance of medical care, and so they followed their doctor's directions more closely. Or perhaps they took better care of themselves, got more sleep, or ate more nutritiously. Maybe by being more insistent, they persuaded their doctors to give them more or better treatment. But a growing number of research studies suggests that there may have been a more powerful force at work.

It is likely that the immune function of the women in the support group was strengthened so that it was able to checkmate cancer cells for a longer time. Research shows that stress and the hormones it produces interfere with the immune system, and so reducing stress might take the burden off the immune system and help it function more efficiently.

There was another effect that showed up in David Spiegel's groups that suggests a protective force at work. The more often women attended the groups, the greater the impact of treatment, and the longer they lived on average. Attendance and survival time were related to each other.[2]

It is easy to overlook the significance of this finding in cancer research, where most studies involve the development of new drugs for chemotherapy treatment. But results of this magnitude, involving a doubling of patient survival time, have been extremely rare in cancer research. What's more, the Stanford findings are particularly impressive because advanced cancers don't generally respond to treatment, so to get any change at all is a real achievement.

On a human level, for women dealing with a rare and difficult disease, here was treatment meant to be supportive that was incidentally life-extending, and with no side effects or inconvenience.

The group treatment was not uniformly successful and did not affect all women in the same way. When women used group psychotherapy for advanced breast cancer in combination with medical treatment, the average group survival time was twice what is normally expected for women with this form of breast cancer. But within this treatment group, there was a good deal of variation. Some of the women didn't physically benefit much from the treatment, although all reported emotional gains. But some of the women lived much longer than the group average.

Metastatic breast cancer is very different from primary breast cancer, and this research may not seem relevant if you have primary breast cancer. But if there are treatments that make such a difference with this relatively intractable form of the disease, it is worth investigating whether the same treatments can affect milder forms of breast cancer, perhaps in preventing recurrence.

Spiegel's research should not have been such a surprise, but our beliefs about illness are such that it was a stunning result. Earlier work, much of it problematical from a research design perspective, had suggested the same trends. The Simontons, a husband-and-wife team, he an oncologist and she a psychologist, had worked with patients with advanced cancers of many types and found that with psychotherapy their patients survived twice as long as the average.[3]

But there were many criticisms of the Simontons' work based on faulty research design. How could anyone know, for example, whether the patients who came for treatment were just like all other cancer patients? Perhaps they were healthier to begin with, and so they would have done well with or without the Simontons' treatment.

It is important not to throw out the baby with the bath water, here, however, for the research clearly points in the direction of an effect. And the job of science is to continually refine results so that cause/effect relationships become clearer.

Fortunately, David Spiegel's work continues. With help from the National Cancer Institute and the Nathan S. Cummings Foundation and in conjunction with the University of Rochester, there will be a much larger research study at twelve centers around the country to study the effect of support groups on women with breast cancer. Only this time it will be with women who have early, easily treated cancers with a very positive prognosis. The final results on this technique should become clear by about the year 2015, and it seems likely that the findings will change the outlook for women with breast cancer.

Spiegel's original work was with women with metastatic breast cancer, advanced cancer in which the biological process dominates and where psychological factors were assumed to have a minimal influence on the course of the disease. Is there any evidence that early cancers can be affected by teaching people to be expressive and supportive, that is, to talk the way women do?

Fawzy Fawzy at UCLA

A man with an improbable name got some improbable results at UCLA. Fawzy I. Fawzy, research physician, and his medical team looked at what happens if you work with healthy cancer patients, people who have a good prognosis and have every reason to believe that they will recover from their illness and do well.

Malignant melanoma is the kind of skin cancer that we all worry about when we think about getting too much sun. It is a dangerous, invasive growth that appears most frequently on the back or lower body regions, and, like breast cancer, it is highly unpredictable. While most cancers follow a relatively predictable course, malignant melanoma and breast cancer are the two that have shown the most variation in outcome. But both of them benefit from early treatment and have a favorable prognosis.

For his research Fawzy recruited melanoma patients who had gotten the standard medical treatment for their illness, which usually consists of surgery to remove the tumor and the area around it. In half of the patients, however, there was an additional treatment, which involved meeting in small groups for ninety minutes weekly for six weeks.[4]

In the melanoma treatment groups, there were a wide range of conversations. Health education was offered to help patients plan activities that would fit with their treatment program, and illness-related problems were explored. Changes in appearance, dealing with the medical system, and coping with the stress of their experience were all discussed. Patients were also taught relaxation skills as a form of stress management.

There was a heavy emphasis in these groups on solving practical problems, with help from the group in thinking up solutions and trying them out. Sometimes these were common problems, such as how to pass the time in the waiting room, and sometimes the issues were more personal, for example, how to deal with loneliness and isolation. The focus in these groups was on emotional expression and reciprocal help, common elements in women's conversations. Exploring feelings, helping each other, and offering reassurance and support were objectives as well.

Men don't usually join groups to talk about psychological problems, although women frequently discuss problems with friends. The UCLA program was a way for people, men and women, to discuss feelings openly, support each other, and look for solutions to common problems. Patients were asked to participate "for the good of science," and so nobody had to admit to experiencing any emotional turmoil regarding their malignant skin cancer. These conversations may have felt like "women's talk" to some, but they had a powerful impact.

Patients in the psychological groups learned to enjoy life more. They learned to solve problems faster and better and to concentrate on things they enjoyed. They developed the habit of arranging activities that were uplifting and energizing and of getting rid of obstacles. Patients in the control group, who had no access to this type of help, in contrast, were more inclined to use avoidance and social withdrawal (including drugs or alcohol) to deal with the stress of the cancer experience.

But the results involved more than just the patients' quality of life. Fawzy Fawzy's results were predictable from David Spiegel's findings with women who had advanced breast cancers.

After six months, Fawzy's patients had better psychological coping skills, and this continued and increased over the next six months. After six years, patients who had this brief psychological treatment had much longer periods of health and only one-third the number of deaths as those in the control group.[5]

The reason that the group treatment patients lived longer and healthier can be found in changes in their immune function. At six months, group treatment patients had better immune function and changes in the natural killer lymphoid cell system. There were increases in the percent of large granular lymphocytes and natural killer cells along with increases in the cytotoxic activity of these cells.

These differences in immune response were accompanied by changes in patients' moods, so that as their depression and anxiety decreased, their immune response increased. Where patients became more assertive as well, there were parallel increases in immune function.[6]

This way of talking and communicating, a way that is personal, emotional, and reciprocal, has a stronger impact than just helping people to feel good. It is a natural way for women to talk to each other, unless they are blocked by social convention or circumstances, and it is the basis for forming relationships with people.

The Heidelberg Prospective Intervention Study

David Spiegel and Fawzy Fawzy looked at how late and early cancers respond to changed patterns of relating and communicating. A large study in Germany tried to create these types of supportive/expressive relationships to see if this would *prevent* the development of cancer.

All research findings are open to challenge, and the mission of good researchers is to be careful in their own research conclusions and critical about everybody else's. Such is the way that science proceeds. This is an essentially conservative approach and insures that nobody gets too enthusiastic and draws unfounded conclusions.

This is worth considering in looking at the findings of the Heidelberg Prospective Intervention Project, mentioned above, one of the most massive studies of health in recent years. The conclusions drawn from this study are highly suggestive rather than conclusive, but they are still important, as they indicate a trend that appears in other research as well.

The group therapy work in this study comprised one part of a large and complex research effort. Hans Eysenck, one of the great figures of modern psychology, and Ronald Grossarth-Maticek, his partner, sought to predict diseases on the basis of personalities. From a very large pool, they chose people who were highly stressed and vulnerable to disease. Then they formed matched pairs in which each member was of the same sex, age, and personality type, and had the same smoking history. Since these people were all at high risk for contracting disease, the effects of their group treatment would be most likely to show up here. From each pair of stressed people, they randomly chose one person to go to the group treatment sessions while the other would serve as a control, that is, a comparison without treatment.

Psychological treatment groups met between six and fifteen times, and each session lasted several hours. There were between twenty and twenty-five people in each group, and their discussion concentrated on the problems patients had identified for themselves and how they needed to change to find more happiness and serenity in life. The Heidelberg groups operated in ways similar to those of David Spiegel and Fawzy Fawzy, but their members didn't have any illnesses.

Seven years later, the researchers looked at the health of all the participants to see if there was any effect from having been part of a psychological group treatment. Although there have been serious criticisms of the design of the research project, there was a clear benefit to participation in therapy groups. In general, people stayed healthier longer, and if they got cancer, they tended to live longer.[7] What's it like to be in a group like this? One woman described it like this:

> "At first, I was worried. You know, I'm older and I thought maybe people would think I was an old bag. But then I figured, what the hay, I'll try anything. They were nice people. We talked a lot and I didn't feel so isolated. My friends would never ask me about the cancer, you see. I was sorry when the group ended, but one gal still calls me."

When people join cancer support groups, it is usually not because they have no one else to talk to or because they are psychologically troubled. Most members have a good friend and family support system, but they may have more difficulty with the medical network. In general, people who join cancer groups are of higher socioeconomic status, younger, female, and with more social resources than other patients.[8]

The research studies suggest that sitting around and talking, talking the way that women typically talk, has an impact, a very large impact, on health. If this is so, why don't these good results happen when people get together to go bowling or when people share a hospital ward? To some extent they do, a subject we examine in the next chapter. But let's look at what makes group psychotherapy different from support groups and groups of people who get together to be supportive.

Women's Conversations, Deep and Superficial

In her groundbreaking research with women and adolescent girls, Carol Gilligan and her colleagues theorized that women struggle with the conflict between wanting to live in genuine relationship with others and the need to express emotions clearly.[9]

The drive to connect with others, to share emotionally, is fundamental to a woman's psychological health and offers her strength and structure in understanding who she is. Without the chance to connect honestly with others, women experience a crisis in which they feel cut off and unable to have faith in themselves.

Women's ways of communicating are geared to these needs and are different from the social conventions of the larger society. Although women don't always need to relate in expressive/supportive dialogue, they must have ample opportunity to do so, most especially when they experience great emotional turbulence, as with breast cancer. Sometimes women form informal support groups to share their experiences and express their feelings; they have varying levels of satisfaction and success.

In support groups that arise spontaneously, there can be many forces operating, some positive and some less helpful. Each person has her own needs and her own idea about the directions a group should take. It is to be hoped that everybody has good manners, although that is not always the case. A larger problem may be the operation of what Richard Renneker calls PNS, or pathological niceness syndrome.[10]

PNS involves reflexive niceness, niceness that comes out before we realize it, when we say things that are reassuring, flattering, pleasant, and optimistic but do not necessarily express how we really feel. These communication patterns reflect the expectations for women in our culture, that they will fit a "nice girl" image, that is, that they will be pleasant and comforting to others.

The motivation for excessively pleasant behavior in women is a wish to make things relaxed, to encourage others to be pleasant, and to build a sense of group feeling. It is a habit pattern based on the assumption that getting along with others requires making them comfortable rather than being emotionally expressive.

At times, many of us overdo being pleasant, saying things that are not completely sincere, trying to create pleasant illusions and smoothing the conversational traffic flow. Sometimes this is truly the best approach to a social exchange, but, like dressing up in your Sunday best, it can become a serious interference to living a normal life if used constantly. At times of severe stress, habitual niceness can make us feel trapped inside our own feelings.

Exclusive reliance on this way of relating can make a woman feel that she is disappearing as a distinguishable human being. When these patterns emerge in groups, it is difficult to redirect people without trained leadership.

Lay support group experience is distinctly different from the psychotherapy groups described earlier in this chapter. When people strive to be nice instead of being real in a leaderless, loose group, the beneficial emotional effect is considerably less than that of structured group psychotherapy. A participant can even begin to feel that negative feelings are wrong and a betrayal of the group. Some support group members have reported being asked to leave because of their negative attitudes.

Lay support groups have made a great contribution to patient health and welfare, as they have sometimes been able to forge a bond of emotional trust and mutual support that has given members a way to relate and connect. Some groups arising from the mutual need of people suffering a common experience, although having little structure or format, can make a good contribution to patients' moods. What are the effects on health of participating in such support groups?

The research literature on cancer support groups is difficult to interpret because of the great variation in what constitutes a support group. They can be any size and may meet once a month or less often. They may offer information or guidance, and often they operate with spontaneous leadership. Some of them, such as Y-ME (a breast cancer survivor organization), Reach to Recovery (a peer counseling support organization), and CAN ACT (the Cancer Patients Action Alliance), offer very different types of help to cancer patients, and each of them serves a separate and significant purpose.

In addition, there are many types of illness support groups that have a religious or political orientation or affiliation or are part of a hospital treatment program. Sometimes groups form spontaneously within a neighborhood or community organization.

In contrast, there is much less variation in the structure and rules of traditional psychotherapy groups. Meetings are weekly or more often, involve no more than ten members, and require long-term commitments. They operate with a clear consensus on keeping confidences, attendance, and conversational focus, and their purpose is to share feelings and offer support. The available research on these types of groups shows a clear effect on cancer patients' survival time.

With informal lay support groups, the results are not the same. One study of lay support groups, for example, evaluated the effect of Bernie Siegel's Exceptional Cancer Patient groups in New Haven and found that those groups had no measurable effect on survival time.[11] Participants received weekly cancer support and family therapy, individual counseling, and positive imagery to take control of their illness. The key element most likely to affect health outcomes would be the opportunity for cancer patients in these groups to communicate and make connections. However, it is not clear from the study how these groups operated or whether they were support groups or true psychotherapy groups.

There was, moreover, a special aspect of this treatment not present in the Spiegel, Fawzy, and Eysenck groups. The assumption was made in the exceptional cancer patients group that patients choose to get cancer to serve psychological needs and that they can then control it themselves by using mental images and optimistic thinking. This premise was incorporated into the group work and may have undermined the group's effectiveness.

This was different from the groups of Spiegel, Fawzy, and Eysenck, which concentrated on controlling living rather than disease and on planning life to have the most satisfaction. There was little interest in these groups in what caused patients' illnesses, or in trying to help people to mentally control the disease. Instead, the emphasis was on limiting its impact and expanding the other areas of living, for example, pleasure in relationships.

A group is a powerful organism, with more strength than the sum of its parts. The power of a mob or an army illustrates that groups can be something other than what individuals plan them to be. Groups of individuals who are vulnerable both physiologically and psychologically need trained guidance to help them achieve their full potential and reach their goals. Often individual habits and patterns interfere with a group's progress, but a skilled leader can get everyone pulling together for the common good.

In a group it is easy to slip into distractions, particularly when conversation provokes procrastination or avoidance, and a leader can help keep everyone on track. Sometimes people need help in speaking up or expressing themselves clearly or in learning to listen. A good leader can help to set workable ground rules that enable everyone to relax and focus on the task at hand.

"We had a support group awhile ago, but it didn't work so well. One girl wanted to talk a lot about Jesus and there just wasn't any way to get around her. I finally quit."

Everybody needs help in a group conversation, sometimes just help in getting a word in or maybe help in breaking up a long silence. Dominant personalities may need to challenge leaders, but a trained person allows everybody else to be responsible for themselves. It is wiser to place the job in the hands of someone who can see the group from the outside and take a larger view of what all need to accomplish. Although women often spontaneously connect with one another, the experience of dealing with breast cancer makes this a more complicated process.

Group Psychotherapy: Concentrated Connecting

It was January 6, 1994, and New York City was suffering one of the coldest winters on record. Usually this season in the city is moderate, but this year it felt like the Arctic. When I was a child, we used to go to Coney Island down by the ocean on the hottest summer nights to ride the roller coaster and eat hot dogs. But everybody knew that by January nobody would be there at all because the stiff winds off the ocean and the roaring breakers piling in set your teeth chattering. That was why on this January day the sight in front of me was so unbelievable: middle-aged men, paunchy, jowly, in boxer short swim suits, obviously not physical fitness freaks, raced about in the Atlantic waves. Members of the Arctic Ice Bears Club of Coney Island, they jumped into the water, soaking themselves over and over, and, oblivious to the wind chill of minus eleven degrees, shared hoots and smiles. The contagion of good feeling, bravado, and skin resistance seemed to strengthen all of these fellows and allow them to do together what would have been unbearable for an individual alone.

Groups give special power to individuals, opening the potential to do things that they could not otherwise do or that would be vastly more difficult. Sometimes groups even change the physical experience of an event and our reaction to it. All cultures recognize this power, and the most important rituals always involve invoking community power to enhance the individual.

Sometimes groups overpower the individual, and they may block either good judgment or irrational fear. When my Girl Scouts needed to taste soy milk and goat milk for a merit badge, I knew that if the older girls tried it, the rest would be readier to take the risk. On the down side, the power of a mob to build and intensify individual feelings can be lethal.

Management of large numbers of people usually relies on small units to effect outcomes. During World War II, small combat groups were the source of individual strength, and psychiatric breakdowns were seen as the result of problems in the unit that interfered with a soldier's sense of belonging and support from his buddies.[12] Group support provides not only emotional strength, but it affects what goes on inside the body. Psychological research has shown that when people anticipate pain, companionship can reduce the stress of the experience.[13]

At their best, groups can strengthen and focus the power of individuals. Western cultures, with their premium on individualism and independence, have often disdained groups and reliance on them, even though, as in all cultures, the group, whether it is business, sports, social, family, or other, is still the basis of our society.

This disdain for group attachments is more of a male than a female characteristic, as men in this society voice great concern for independence and self-reliance. Instead of group identification, men often depend on a female partner to give them a sense of belonging and support.

In contrast, women are usually more comfortable with dependence on others. Rather than sacrificing a sense of self, group membership seems to enhance individual identity by connecting with others.

Why do groups work? The experiments at Stanford, UCLA, and Heidelberg offer good evidence that women's ways are powerful in enhancing medical treatment of some forms of cancer. Why?

There are certainly practical benefits from being part of a group. Sharing common problems, getting ideas for new solutions, and overcoming the challenges of cancer treatment are real gains. Women who can express feelings and give and receive support become more efficient patients, using better health practices, pursuing more powerful medical treatments, and getting information from other women.

Connecting with others offers a new set of standards in dealing with the cancer experience, so that a woman can mentally refer to the opinions of other women and try out ideas against their reactions. This may be particularly important for women, since they respond to stress with an increase in behavioral inhibition, become tighter and more constricted,[14] and relationships can help them to relax, plan, and take promising risks.

Any group develops its own rules about which subjects are acceptable for discussion, so that you know what you can say and what you can't. It may be okay, for example, to tell jokes at the PTA, but not at the church meeting. In group psychotherapy, the rules for conversations are clear. They are meant to develop insight, share understandings, offer support and compassion, and build individual stamina. Everyone must gain if the group is to be a success.

Sometimes sharing with others can help us revise personal rules that no longer apply. When Gail explained to her psychotherapy group that she was relieved rather than unhappy when her husband died of a heart attack — and she explained that he had been an alcoholic for many years, verbally abusive to her, and cold and unresponsive to her children — it helped to say it all in a public forum. She was able to revise the rule she had learned from her family, church, and neighborhood that it is a woman's responsibility to make a marriage work at all costs. It was easier for her to see her situation more realistically and accept her emotional response to it when she considered it with a group of supportive intimates.

Sometimes the feelings that go with the experience of breast cancer are tangential to the illness, but stirred up by it. When Beatrice got breast cancer at sixty, her major concern was not the disease itself, but a sense that she had wasted her life in an impulsive marriage to a man who was a true stinker. She felt that she had not had enough courage to leave the marriage and instead had passed up all that was important to her. In sharing her experience and feelings with others, she came to forgive herself for her choices and began to live in the present, making plans for the life she wanted and enjoyed.

Sharing feelings with others helps to put things in perspective, to "de-catastrophize," in the words of Albert Ellis,[15] so that what may seem very large in our private thoughts is diminished when examined with friends.

Perhaps the most powerful effect of interpersonal connections is the opportunity to join with other human beings in a way that helps us to feel more like ourselves. This seems to go far deeper than the thoughts that stimulating conversations stir up, although we are apt to become more optimistic and self-confident when we have contact with others.

In conversations where we clearly express our feelings, we are most ourselves, and confidence and self-esteem rise as a result. This is not an isolated retreat from others or a narcissistic display. It is a full connecting, with all parts of ourselves at risk. Connection with others in which we are genuinely ourselves with all our vulnerabilities has consequences that go far beyond our emotional comfort.

In an intensive care unit, a comatose patient is totally unresponsive — except that she shows a slowing of pulse when her hand is held. The body has many levels of reasoning and perception that bypass the brain, and our response to other people goes far deeper than our thoughts about them. Whether we are the person being touched or the person reaching for others, the connecting affects us.

Perhaps this is characteristic of all mammals, for it occurs in other species as well. When Ivan Pavlov first studied the effect of presenting meat to a dog at the sound of a bell to see if he could produce salivation by the sound of the bell alone, his own presence interfered. His dogs began to salivate when they saw *him* rather than the bell or the meat, and their pulse and blood pressure changed as well. He had to build an isolation chamber that cut off all their contact with him.[16]

We respond to other people in many forms and on several levels. In some casual contacts, for example, the neighborhood group, the format may be merely catching up on news and reestablishing contact and might take the form of:

"How are you feeling? You've got the best doctor in the world. He really helped my brother-in-law. You're really lucky that they caught it early."

Often our conversations follow established patterns, and it is intrusive or disruptive to change them. Women with breast cancer may feel trapped in some social situations if there is no comfortable way to emotionally connect with others. People want to make a difference and have a positive impact, and where this is not possible, everyone is frustrated.

With breast cancer, the need to connect is strong, but the opportunities are few. The comforter cannot be direct and effective, and the sick person cannot be comforted, and neither feel much in touch with the other, for no feelings have been communicated. But in new situations, in a group like Spiegel's, for example, there is the potential for a new pattern, with relating on a very deep level.

"Are you lonesome?"

"Do you get scared at night?"

"Do you ever get mad?"

These are not questions that are asked routinely, not even in the intimacy of our households. Families are a powerful group form, one that has many purposes, including providing companionship, establishing a homestead, and rearing children.

There is, in short, a lot of business to be done in a family, and there are typically set hierarchical relationships, including that between older and younger members. Emotional exchanges may not be a comfortable process in the home.

To transform a family so that people express feelings freely can upset previous arrangements, and this may be more difficult than helpful to a woman with breast cancer. In the family group, a woman is often the central caregiver and emotional organizer, like the hub of a wheel that others look to for help and support. In this role she and the family both benefit, and it can be disruptive to try to change these patterns when illness strikes.

When Karen asked her family to discuss their feelings about her breast cancer, she tape-recorded their replies (mostly questions) to her query regarding how everybody felt about her illness. They said:

"Are we done yet?"

"Why do we have to keep bringing this up?"

"Can I go?"

"I have to go to the bathroom."

"Mom's fine."

"I thought Mom was fine."

"This is boring."

"Mom, are you really okay?"

Legitimizing the Woman

To be diagnosed as having breast cancer is a powerful experience, one that leaves a life forever changed. The human psyche needs help in absorbing powerful experiences and in rearranging life assumptions. Our most significant human events such as birth, death, and marriage, are all commemorated by complex social rituals. They give meaning to the event, and help us to understand our feelings, for example, when we cry at a wedding because we are aware of the loss of a child and the beginning of a new life stage for the family.

Rituals also allow us to set aside a period of time and emotional energy for adjustment so that we experience our feelings and then, after a period, move on. After the graduation, we get back to the normal business of life, but with some new expectations.

The most important role of rituals is to bring us into contact with others who share our experience, support our feelings, and ease our transition. Ceremonies like baptisms and funerals point out that no matter how humble, we have a place in the culture when we pass through. When changes occur, rituals give us a way to connect with others emotionally and to be ourselves, while we draw on others' support through the transition. Sometimes these expressions can seem stereotyped and superficial, but they are nonetheless a means of connection; they allow us to experience and express genuine feelings that may not be acceptable at other times.

Our emotional transition is made more difficult when a major life event cannot be marked by a ritual observance of some sort, as for example, when a person is missing and presumed dead but there is no funeral, or when a child elopes. It may be difficult to deal with the complex and intense feelings that such change stirs, for there is no established format for connecting with others.

When a child was murdered in upstate New York, the frozen ground and heavy snows made it impossible to recover the body for many months. It was not until there could be a funeral that the family and the community could begin to heal. Social rituals are a powerful form of psychological support.[17]

There aren't many social rituals in which a woman is the central figure, and women rarely have major changes in their lives eased by ceremonies that center on them. Rituals involving men — in marriage or widowhood, for example — offer women a role of significance, but it is a derivative significance. The changes a woman experiences, for example, on retirement from parenthood at the last child's graduation, have no testimonials, and so women make these transitions alone.

Even though breast cancer represents a major change in a woman's life, it is usually a private change. Often the illness is kept secret from everyone except close friends and family. The experience is a very private one, and appearances are kept up so that nothing on the surface seems changed. As a society, we admire a woman's ability to carry on, and it is flattering to hear said:

"She's amazing. You would never even know that she had been sick. She just took care of it and told everybody that she was fine and went to work and kept the house clean. She never complains about it, and she says she doesn't like to talk about it because it upsets her family."

If a woman whose daughter had just eloped responded in the same manner, we would not be openly admiring of such a stoic response. With breast cancer, the society expects women to "handle it," and to do so privately as a reflection of character. This denies a woman the opportunity of public support, both for her health and for the feelings she experiences through the crisis. As one woman put it, "When you cry at your husband's funeral, people comfort you, but when you cry with breast cancer, you cry alone."

The experience of group psychotherapy can serve the purpose of a ceremonial or ritual observance of an important life event and can help a woman adjust. A psychotherapy group can be a "circle of lament"[18] where women of wisdom and sensitivity join to share deep feelings and acknowledge the profound significance of an event in one woman's life. In so doing, the group helps a woman develop a new understanding of herself and her life and to protect her sense of personal value and worth in a time of change.

Group psychotherapy usually involves some degree of structure, for example, in the sharing of news at the beginning of each session. In David Spiegel's groups, the sessions always ended with a hypnosis exercise, shared by the women as they focused on caring for themselves, which can be as a powerful benediction for the group experience. These experiences happened week after week for the participants and marked off an important adjustment period in their lives.

By belonging to the group the women resolved the dilemma of having to choose between being themselves and connecting with others. In psychotherapy they could be genuine and emotive while deepening their relationships.

Cancer as a Communication Block

Back when my grandmother was young, nobody ever said "cancer" out loud. If my mother had to refer to it, she would say that somebody had "CA." The newspapers still observe this so-cial taboo, describing death from cancer as "after a long illness," which everybody knows means cancer.

When Caroline was diagnosed with breast cancer, she had just broken off a difficult relationship with a second husband, one who had been involved with other women. The pain of ending the mar-riage got mixed up with her dread of cancer, and she came to feel that the cancer had made her unlovable. She told only her mother that she was ill, forbidding her to tell anyone else. Caroline con-tinued to work at her job, making various medical excuses and acting happy and chipper at work.

Now, eighteen years later, she deals with the experience as though she had committed a shameful sin. She is afraid to share with people that she had breast surgery and reconstruction, which seems more shameful now that it has been hidden, and the longer she keeps her secret, the more fearful she becomes of disclosure. This has become an obsessional problem for her, so that she mentally ruminates over it rather than enjoying her days.

The psychological term for this reaction is "stigma," and it oc-curs with many other chronic illnesses, but especially with cancer. When people first perceive themselves in the "sick" category as opposed to the "well" category, they may react with self-prejudice, blaming and alienating themselves and expecting the larger society to do so as well. This may be why in one study cardiac patients had more adjustment problems after leaving the hospital than they did before, even though they were substantially healthier when they left.[19]

The sense of being outside the group, beyond the pale, is an experience that many people face at one point or another and it may have little to do with the way people actually treat us. In a health-conscious society, it becomes a personal failure to be sick, so that developing diabetes or high blood pressure can lower your good feelings about yourself. As one patient told me:

"People talked differently around me than they used to and changed the subject when I came into the room. Nobody mentioned sickness, death, hospitals, operations, cancer, doc-tors, or medicine anymore, and it seemed really strange. It was strangest when I was with people who knew I had can-cer but others, newcomers, didn't. When a subject like Paul

Tsongas [a presidential candidate who openly discussed his lymphoma] would come up, there would be a silence, and then one of my friends would introduce some bright new topic, like what the library board is doing this year. It even made for awkward pauses when breasts were mentioned, like once when someone talked about mothers nursing babies in public, and the conversation really slowed down."

It gets hard to separate what is real change and what is change inside yourself after a breast cancer diagnosis. It may seem that nobody is very open now, because there are several different perspectives: patient, doctor, relative, friend. As with any change in relationships, casual words can take on new significance, and old phrases may seem to mean something different now. Decisions about how to act are not so obvious, for example, in a casual conversation, should a woman mention that she has cancer?

How do women cope with this new social problem? Some women like Caroline try to avoid it entirely by keeping the information to themselves. Other women tell only close friends and then relate differently to those who know and those who don't, so that the sharing becomes a bond and the withholding becomes a wall.

Some women take a different tact. Another patient shares her story:

"I assumed the role of the neighborhood cancer expert and decided to instruct all of these women about breast cancer. Every time I heard somebody say something that was in error or that grated on my nerves, I would explain to them how that feels to a woman who has had breast cancer. There were lots of times when I just cried because I could see that they just didn't understand, like when my best friend said that she was sick of "tits and ass" girls in commercials. I just got crying and I couldn't stop, and then I felt horrible for making her feel so bad."

A woman begins to see her relationship to others as different, since she still belongs to the old groups, but her new experiences and learnings now set her apart. If her attitudes to cancer were fearful or critical before she was diagnosed, she is likely to have strong prejudices against herself.

A woman may not be sure whether she wants to be treated the same as other women, or differently. Women who have lumpectomies sometimes have more psychological stress than women with mastectomies, perhaps because their experience alienates them from others who do not recognize the drastic change in their lives, making it more difficult to connect. When others reassure her that she still belongs, that she is the same as ever, and they feel the same toward her, this may produce confused feelings.

"You hate them. All those women who look fine and act like they pity you. How dare they feel sorry for me!"

For many women, the need for contact and connection overrides everything else and may seem to require self-reliance and self-denial. A woman who is used to being the fixer, peacemaker, and team player may try to normalize the situation for others by acting happy and hiding her feelings.

This often sets off a similar reaction in friends and relatives, who want to avoid upsetting a woman dealing with breast cancer. Others may act as though everything is fine with them and with her, and the pretense spreads, locking everybody into a consensual silence. It is easy to confuse this consensual silence with insensitivity or indifference, for they can feel the same to a woman who is ill and frightened. What's more important, everybody starts to feel that their reactions are the wrong ones and that they have to hide their real feelings.

It is this well-intentioned conspiracy of silence that is particularly troublesome, for it isolates women with their feelings and disrupts the relationships between them. Without these connections, it is hard for a woman to feel valid and whole. Most importantly, a woman's connections have a major impact on health.

Occasionally a woman may find that others are preoccupied with her illness and attribute most of her behaviors and comments to it, rather than to the ordinary fluctuations of her personality and mood. Other people may intrude on her emotionally by asking questions or prying into feelings that are normally private. In the worst situations, a woman with breast cancer may become the object of anyone's theories about what causes cancer and what she should have done to prevent it or should do to get over it.

Perhaps the most common reaction to the social awkwardness of breast cancer is to normalize the situation too quickly, so that a week after a mastectomy a woman is acting and behaving as though nothing had happened. To see the breast cancer as "cured" after treatment is a way of reestablishing membership in the mainstream.

But a woman is apt to feel more herself with those who have a sophisticated understanding of sickness and health. To feel a genuine sense of belonging has to involve feeling accepted for oneself, with all of the vagaries and contradictions inherent in human nature. But to be truly accepting requires a certain degree of wisdom, and this is possible only with experience.

Women's Communication

Women use conversations to connect with one another and create an emotional framework for themselves, according to Deborah Tannen, author of *You Just Don't Understand*. Men and women talk differently because they have different goals in speaking. Her work on "genderlects" proposes that men use conversation to gain power and control over others and that they preserve their independence and status by lecturing, monologuing, advising, talking down to others, and monopolizing the conversation.[20]

Women, in contrast, use conversation to develop rapport and draw closer to others, through confirming and validating each other's observations, supporting each other, and finding common ground on which they can agree. This allows them to form intimate, supportive relationships and to develop a sense of community. It also explains why communication problems are considered a primary problem in male/female relationships.

If Deborah Tannen is accurate in her observation, what happens to a woman's communication when she has breast cancer? In general, women are less likely to attempt conversation with men who are not intimates,[21] and with a husband, lover, or close male friend the conversational format can make it difficult for her to share.

If she tries to discuss her illness with a man, he is likely to give her advice and want her to take it. There may be pressure to resolve the transitional problems of dealing with breast cancer, even though these will not be responsive to fast, decisive action. He may indicate that there is too much conversation about the subject or even that a woman is wallowing in her feelings about it, or he may begin to compete with her for the crisis spotlight. Worse still, he may change the subject and seem to dismiss the whole issue and her feelings. The problem is not so much that he can't understand the ideas involved, but that he can't use language in a way that supports the woman's needs.

In relationships with women, the situation may feel more familiar because other women's speech follows the same format, but there is such a difference in information levels that the exchanges initially may be difficult. If one woman has experienced breast cancer and the other has not, the conversational exchange will be unbalanced.

Often women need to find new ways to relate, for a diagnosis of breast cancer can seem to disrupt the established patterns. Everyone takes a step back emotionally, and then the choice must be made between whether to deepen or limit the relationship.

It may seem safer to resort to male forms of communication and concentrate on maintaining position or establishing self-reliance and strength. It may even seem that this gives a sense of being acceptable or belonging.

You may feel that this is what is wanted by those who care about you, for if you withdraw from relating, others may do the same. With some people, speaking directly about your feelings or experiences may be upsetting, while others may brush off your reactions.

You may sense that others want you to be like them, to see things their way, feel as they want you to, and that relationships with them depend on your doing so. This is a difficult problem, and people who encourage us to be ourselves are rare; when they do, most often it is because they are comfortable being themselves.

It may be that before breast cancer you were able to operate in superficial relationships without much uneasiness. Breast cancer causes such strong feelings, however, that it doesn't work very well to try to hide them, and there is strong motivation to change these old habits. A psychotherapy group can be a place where women can use their language to connect with others to take the pressure off older, temporarily strained relationships.

This sort of group uses problems to build a sense of belonging and identity that enlarges a woman's former social net and adds a powerful sense of support and refuge when the adjustment becomes confusing or overwhelming. Most importantly, it allows her to use all of her connecting skills to make a positive contribution to the lives of others and to gain as a result.

A woman's distress gets full respect in a psychotherapy group because it is a part of her. It is met without judgment and used to deepen connections. The medical research indicates that this kind of experience, this form of talking, when it is practiced by men or women, alters what happens to immune cells in the body. It will require decades of research to confirm, detail, and tease out the contingencies between communication and cancer, but it is clear that women's communication benefits health dramatically. Conversation that makes emotional connections is bad for cancer cells.

Self-Disclosure

"I'm not angry," he snarled, his face getting redder by the *moment. "I don't know why you'd think I even care what you say."*

Most of us get unnerved at the idea of sharing private thoughts and feelings, but to a large degree our facial expression, body postures, tone of voice, and so forth reveal us far more than our words. When people think about joining therapy groups, they often worry about being put on the spot to say what they think or feel, but this is rarely the case in a group with trained leadership. Conversation that involves sharing woes, agreeing with each other's complaints, expressing reactions to the person sitting next to you, accepting feelings that you may not want to hear about, giving reassurance, and trusting others can feel very risky.

In most television shows, when somebody talks about feelings, it all ends happily at the end of the half hour, and it turns out that the feelings expressed really show a person's integrity and strength of character. But most of us are not so emotionally attractive when we reveal feelings. Sometimes we're petty, mean, dishonest, insensitive, stupid, or irresponsible, and our feelings, fleeting though they are, can make us look pretty bad in our own eyes. This explains why we generally try to hide what we feel and why it seems dangerous to share our feelings.

Breast cancer stirs up such strong feelings that it is hard to keep them to ourselves, and it is a burden on the body's operating systems to add this demand to the illness and treatment. It's like asking a woman with breast cancer to work lots of extra hours at her job, and it just doesn't seem fair.

Releasing feelings strengthens the body. When, for example, a woman is widowed, she will have fewer health problems in the year after the loss if she talks about her husband's death and expresses her feelings often.[22]

When feelings are strong, keeping them to yourself causes the mind to obsess on them or to use a lot of energy to avoid obsessing on them. The natural process of emotional expression gets blocked, and the result is the same as when a baby is prevented from crying: the feelings are intensified, and a whole separate problem develops.

Keeping secrets, particularly about strong emotional experiences, doesn't seem to be a safe practice. In one study of heart attack victims and sexual activity, it was found that 80 percent of sudden death heart attacks during sexual relations occurred when the liaison was secret and illicit.[23]

Sharing one's secrets, for women, is a way of developing deeper and more trusting relationships with other women. In most friendships, women begin with small secrets, and then test the bond with increasingly sensitive confidences. The worst betrayal of a friendship is in disclosing the other's secrets.

In a psychotherapy group, the ground rules are set at the beginning, so that self-disclosure and sharing one's secrets becomes a safe but not obligatory thing to do. Listening to others share their feelings also fosters the connection and deepens the sense of belonging.

Can this help explain why group psychotherapy boosts cancer treatment? In a study at Southern Methodist University, James Pennebaker and his associates found that having traumatic experiences in childhood was a good predictor of health problems in adulthood, but only under certain conditions.[24] If the upsetting experiences were discussed with others and feelings expressed, there were no health differences from those who had a serene childhood. The conclusion to be drawn here is that keeping secrets puts a strain on health, but that sharing feelings supports the body's defenses.

Some events are more likely to be disclosed than others. If a child is hit by a car, for example, it is likely that family and friends will discuss the episode at length, with everyone sharing feelings, opinions, and personal observations. People will remember how they heard the news, what they first thought, other similar experiences or stories they have heard, and so forth. The situation is quite different however when the experience is exceptionally painful or shameful.

If a traumatic event is a parent's suicide or the abuse of a child, there will probably be little discussion, and it may be kept completely secret. Unexpressed childhood trauma, that is, upsetting experiences and feelings that are kept secret, are a good predictor of adult health problems.

Assertiveness in Setting a Life Course

Keeping feelings secret makes it impossible to speak for yourself, for assertiveness requires a belief that you are entitled to preferences, idiosyncrasies, frivolities, ignorance, and so forth, and that you cannot justify every emotional reaction or personal preference as being reasonable.

When we hide our feelings we reinforce the belief that they are illegitimate, and we are forced to invent reasons or justifications for our position. If we are in conflict with somebody who does assert feelings, it can seem impossible to argue for our own point of view. Our feelings combined with our logic are the most powerful argument we have for what we need, and being assertive is nothing more than showing who we are.

In speaking, women usually gauge others' reactions before talking and sometimes remain silent themselves in anticipation of disagreement. Sometimes they anticipate erroneously and so fail to risk speaking up and exposing their feelings, even though they would have gotten a supportive response.

It is easier to speak for yourself in a group where there are ground rules and where there is a traffic director. In many aspects of a woman's life, doing what others need is a habitual response, and it can seem strange or irresponsible to focus on oneself. Solving others' problems, putting others first, and keeping the peace are all ways that women traditionally acquire respect. But in a psychotherapy group, the focus is different, and although there is a great deal of help for one another, the group succeeds only to the extent that each person is most truly herself.

Assertiveness used well is a powerful gift to others. It frees everyone from mixed messages or control through manipulation and allows all to be direct and emotionally expressive. It can clear the way for communication and may be a sign to others that you are strong enough to hear their feelings.

It also allows you to have your own shortcomings, to be a person without apology in a world of fallible humans. When the need to be perfect or brilliant or morally right disappears, then human beings can begin to help each other rather than competing or judging each other. Most importantly, it tests out the assumption that the only way to avoid being alone and deserted is to be pleasing to others.

Assertiveness turns up in many places in the research literature on breast cancer, and it is generally associated with better outcomes. It seems to be the key element in Greer's "fighting spirit," and the anger variable in Fawzy's research. Assertiveness here is not aggressive or combative behavior aimed at defeating others. Instead it is a means of speaking clearly and finding ways to get what you need while taking others into account.

There are ways that psychotherapy groups help us practice this. Others let us know if our way of speaking is confusing or obscures the importance of our message. In our group in Albany, members coached each other for better ways to talk to a doctor about medical tests, to insist that a husband watch the children, and so forth.

"Alice, stop apologizing when you ask for more information."

"Joan, you talk so much that I can't figure out which is the important part."

"Why don't you just say no?"

"Zena, you can't yell at him if you want him to take you seriously."

A more basic need is to help members figure out when assertiveness is necessary, which is usually much more often than women use it. A group is able to help by pointing out the constant thinking about a problem that indicates a need to take action. It can help its members see the complaining and resentment, the avoidance or withdrawal from people who behave in an upsetting way, and the scheming to get through to someone that usually indicate a need to speak more plainly.

Assertiveness is a way for a woman to find the proper mix between her feelings and others' needs and preserve her connections with people. "I don't want to come on to the nurse like a Sherman tank. After all, I have to see her every week," said one member.

People often think that joining groups means they are needy and unable to cope, a public admission of personal failure. They often fail to notice that joining a group is a way of *offering* strength and help to others, no matter how limited we may feel.

Participating in a group psychotherapy experience, you make an enormous contribution by offering your support, your wisdom, and whatever unique talents and perspectives you bring. In a major study discussed in chapter 5, women who were active givers, who initiated relationships with other women, and took risks to be helpful to other women had better outcomes with breast cancer.[25]

Compassionate and helpful behavior benefits the doer in many ways. It is an active rather than a passive state, it raises one's self-esteem, and it creates a sense of competence and accomplishment. Most importantly, it increases the connection and sense of social support all around.

Why Breast Cancer Patients Avoid Groups

After a traumatic experience, such as a car accident, loss of a job, or a diagnosis of cancer, self-esteem drops, faith in the future falters, and risk-taking diminishes. To join a psychotherapy group can feel like proof of your inadequacy in the face of a serious illness. In this culture, there is a great value placed on independence, individualism, freedom, and going it alone. From the time of our frontier days, Americans have always respected the concept of the individual man against fate. Joining a group seems to lose the person in service to the mass. If loneliness is the price of such freedom, it can feel like a dignified and courageous stance.

But this is primarily a male value, one that does not jive with the ways that American women have traditionally dealt with stress. Women are the ones who write the letters, call his mother, keep track of the children, follow the doings in the neighborhood, run the welcome wagon, take dinner to the old folks, and generally keep communities together.

Women do not approach relationships as commitments to be avoided or as traps set by needy people who will threaten their independence. Heroic women don't value riding off into the sunset alone but instead stay to talk and relate to others and make the community work. As women have gained more power in the society, they have been inclined to leave behind their unique sources of strength and to substitute male values of freedom from connection as a better alternative.

Although males value self-reliance, their great enthusiasm for self-sufficiency is truly viable only while there is a nurturing female in the picture. When a man's relationship with a woman comes to an end, his health risk soars; divorce for a man is only slightly less risky than taking up smoking.[26]

The cultural emphasis on preserving independence usually surfaces in a breast cancer psychotherapy group. In one group, which included a lawyer, a nurse, an elderly retired teacher, two women who were at home, a waitress, and a secretary, the beginning of the first meeting was very quiet until somebody began to describe how it feels to lie on that examining table (knowing nods), how nice it would be if they would warm up their instruments (murmurs), and how none of the experience feels real at all (yes, say several women).

It becomes clear that women's ways of connecting support the need to be individual and that women are strong enough in themselves to be able to risk being clear with their feelings and experiences. They help one another without losing anything from themselves.

Most women don't know this until they join a group. When they learn that their natural inclinations have enormous potential for boosting health and that, for once, what feels good is also good for you, the group starts to come together solidly. When a group sees the power that it generates and its capacity for enriching each person's life, it takes on a life of its own and may continue well after the agreed-upon termination date.

Perhaps this is as it should be. David Spiegel's groups for women with breast cancer met for only a year. It may be that such groups should run indefinitely. But the relative merits of long-running vs. short-term groups will have to be established by research that will take decades to complete. It may be that groups offer a chance to exert some control over events in one's life that is not possible individually. And research has established that the ability to exert such control over a life stressor enhances immune function.[27]

It is wise to be conservative in experimenting with new cancer treatments and to avoid risking one's health on untried and foolish regimens. There are many alternative cancer treatments available, and although some of them undoubtedly have value, far more often they are exploitative, expensive, and dangerous.

Group psychotherapy is not a replacement for routine onco-logical treatment. On the contrary, it can only be effective *in conjunction with* regular medical care. At this time, however, there is enough research evidence on its beneficial effect to in-clude it in regular cancer treatment. There are no side effects, little expense, and little discomfort as well.

For some women group psychotherapy will have no medical benefit. For many, it will help in coping with the psychological impact of the disease and affect its outcome. With more exten-sive research, technique and practice will be refined to produce stronger and more effective treatment for women with breast cancer and to help develop life-sustaining connections.

Emotional connection seems to be the crucial element in the benefits of group psychotherapy, and there are many ways that women routinely establish emotional connections even before the onset of disease and emotional crises. The next chapter explores the powerful impact of routine life experiences that take place outside formal psychotherapy: women's relationships — with their spouses, their children, their friends, and even with pets.

Chapter Five

Relationships and Breast Cancer

Lucille called me for help when she was seventy-two. It was puzzling that at her age she had developed panic attacks. But that is what they were, and physical illness had been ruled out as the cause of her rapid pulse, shortness of breath, sweating, and racing thoughts.

It was difficult to see the source of her problems at first. As a matter of fact, many good things had happened in her life over the previous year. For almost a decade, she had lived with an old friend in a run-down apartment complex with many other retired folks; she worked mornings at the corner store to make ends meet. She was also an active community volunteer and had just been awarded a fifty-year service pin from the Red Cross.

She had always been protective of her only son, a tinkerer and a bumbler, who seemed destined to a life of mediocrity. But then, this year, he had sold one of his computer inventions to a large company, a small gadget that made programs work better, and to everybody's amazement he had become an overnight millionaire.

With touching enthusiasm, he went to work to improve his mother's life. He had an architect build her a spacious home up on a hill, and he replaced all of her worn-out furniture. A new car, clothes, servants, and a state-of-the-art computer were all put in place before she arrived. By her third month in the house, the panic attacks had started. As Lucille and I sorted it out, the reason for the anxiety became more apparent.

Her son was a loving and generous man, but he had unwittingly destroyed the psychological shell that his mother had constructed over many years, one that protected her from emotional duress. The friends who cared, the familiar faces, the routine encounters

117

with casual acquaintances, the co-workers on the job, all had been left behind in her new good fortune.

Without her shell, she felt, as she described it, "like a naked woman in the middle of a cold, busy street." Her surroundings and her neighborhood had supported and sustained her, and when these were gone she felt profound isolation and terror.

It makes sense to think of the feelings stirred up by your surroundings as your emotional climate. Once you live in a certain meteorological climate, you stop noticing the overall effect unless there are sudden changes. When I moved to Florida from upstate New York, I was amazed that people didn't have to buy new clothing for each season or go through the ritual of putting-on-the-snowpants with little ones or avoid the potholes in the road. It wasn't just that their air was warmer. Their whole way of life was different from up north.

When I moved back north, I noticed the good sentimental feeling that comes from raking autumn leaves, the first snowfall, and the spring thaw that comes after so long. They are all part of climate and affect us at a subconscious level, often without our noticing.

Our emotional climate is far more difficult to measure and understand than the meteorological climate, because our reactions to it are subtle and complex. Sometimes a single powerful event may strike a strong contrast in our daily life, for example, a lonesome New Year's Eve or a well-attended funeral. Neither of these is a good indicator of year-round emotional climate, any more than a 65-degree day in January is a good index of New York weather.

Emotional climate means the sense of interrelation with other people, of feeling like part of a human setting. Psychological research that has explored the effect of emotional climate on disease vulnerability and survival has shown that the more relationships that a woman has, the healthier she is likely to be.[1]

Fortunately, emotional climate, unlike meteorological climate, is under human control, and this chapter examines the ways that we can build our context to support our health. With breast cancer this is particularly important. Social support has a limited effect on most cancers, but with breast cancer it is an important source of strength and is related to the probability of recurrence.[2]

The Need to Belong

The yearning to be part of the human community is as much a physical need as an emotional one. We may block our feelings, but our body systems continue to respond to the emotional climate. This can make us vulnerable physically with no emotional awareness on our part. In one study on a cardiac intensive care unit, heart attack patients were five times as likely to have fatal fibrillation when unfamiliar staff did rounds as when the helpers were familiar.[3] Although we enjoy the idea that we are self-sufficient, our bodies react independently of our thought processes, and they work better when we are emotionally connected to others.

In modern Western civilization, independence and self-reliance are considered signs of high character even though they are not conducive to health. Intuitively, we know that contact with other people is sustaining; in the judicial system, solitary confinement is considered severe punishment. In the concentration camps of the Third Reich, the effect of severing human connections was seen in *musselmann*, a syndrome in which the loss of one's relationships and inability to generate new ones led to death.

The effect of social support may be more profound for women than for men. It is women who seek connection and use their emotional expressiveness to form relationships, while men generally relate to a sole female partner. Social support has been defined in many ways and includes a wide range of relationships, but relating always involves emotional interchange. All social support involves the communication of caring, even if only at the visceral level of hand holding. Failure in this realm may have particularly important consequences for women.

Sometimes the best way to see the impact of something is by looking at the hole it leaves, like the craters left by meteors. What happens when the emotional climate is cold and there are gaps instead of connection with other people?

In Alameda County, California, researchers looked at the emotional climate that individuals live in and followed people over a period of years to determine if there was any correlation between social connections and health.[4] The researchers made sure that their observations weren't biased by the residents' health habits, such as smoking, alcohol usage, diet, sleeping habits, physical activity, or daily health practices.

In this study, the researchers measured social support by looking at the number of relationships people had and how often they got together. They looked at marriage, visits with relatives, time spent with friends, church attendance, and group membership, and tracked thousands of Alameda residents over a decade.

Their findings demonstrated a powerful association between context and body function. Those people with the fewest number of connections were twice as likely to die as those with the most connections. Apparently, living in a setting with lots of contact with others does something positive for one's health.

In other words, if you wanted to know who was most likely to be alive in ten years in Alameda County, one good way to tell would be to count a person's relationships. People with lots of social contact lived longer and lived better as well. This was true whether people smoked, drank, ate nutritionally, exercised, or took good care of their health, although clearly some of these practices would add to one's good health.

The results in this massive study were not the same for men as for women, however. Being married didn't much change a woman's health risk, although for men it was clearly much safer to be married. For women, friends and contact with friends was extremely important. Women between sixty and sixty-nine who had few friends were three times more likely to die than women who had many friends. In the same age group, there was an advantage to being married, but not much.

For men, the main health benefit seemed to come from being married (presumably to a woman). Unmarried men were twice as likely to die as married men, and although friendships contributed to longevity, there was not the same strong effect as with women. The overall message is plain, that women's health requires a nurturing social climate and that friends have a powerful impact.

This effect became even more pronounced in women dealing with a health problem. Disabled women or those with chronic conditions were greatly affected by the extent of social contact. They had one-quarter the risk of death if they had a large social network, even if friends were not intimately familiar with the health problems. Emotional climate has its strongest and most obvious impact when women are unwell.

Women who didn't operate with strong social support were more likely to get cancer in the Alameda County study. Once they got cancer, their chances of doing well with the disease were increased by belonging to formal organizations. Interpersonal connection seems to have its greatest impact when women are needy.[5]

There are big differences in how social support affects health in men and in women and even bigger differences if they are struggling with a health problem. Men seem to depend heavily upon their wives for relationship needs, and marriage has a great impact on a man's health risk. This is less true for women, who are only slightly better off if married. For women, social support in the form of friendships and connections between women is of primary importance in how long and how well they live. If a woman struggles with a chronic health problem like breast cancer, the need for lots of friends and connections increases.

The Impact of Women's Connections on Health

Why should women's friendships have an impact on health? It may be pleasant to enjoy time with friends, but why would this affect what happens inside the body? Relationships offer a great deal to people, particularly if they are ill. This may be in the form of concrete help that comes from contact with others, for example, regarding transportation, housekeeping, meals, or even finances, and help with all of these can reduce the stress in our lives.

Sometimes others help by giving us information about medical care or types of treatments or minor things such as a good video to watch when we're blue. When there are major decisions to be made, a caring person can serve as a sounding board, a sympathetic listener, or even a devil's advocate.

Talking things over with others gives a sense of control, or at least insight, and often helps us to feel better about ourselves. It feels good when another is interested in our welfare and makes us feel connected to the rest of the human race. It may not make us happy and it may not solve a problem, but it changes our sense of self-worth and optimism to share with others.

Sometimes relationships help us to maintain good health habits, although others can encourage bad habits as well. When people try to quit smoking, for example, their ability to avoid cigarettes over the first two months is related to the sense that there is someone there to talk over problems with and that they are not alone.[6] It's not particular relationships that make a difference, however, but instead the general process of living in a social context.

There are complex biochemical effects on our bodies that result from contact with others; these involve the suppression of neuroendocrine and hemodynamic responses and the enhancement of immune responses.

Perhaps you recall that immune function declined for the people living near the Three Mile Island nuclear plant after the threatened meltdown, and this demonstrated how emotional events can affect immune reaction. The impact of traumatic community events on people can be changed by relationships. A more recent study found that when people believed that others were concerned about them, the stress reaction was reduced.[7]

Our body's defenses react to the emotional climate the way that our eyes react to light and darkness. They become more active and healthier in a context of social support. Without a supportive emotional context, defenses begin to decline, and alienation appears to suppress immune function. In medical students[8] and in psychiatric patients[9] loneliness was a good indicator that natural killer cell activity levels were down.

Loneliness is a uniquely individual experience, and we may feel lonely even when we are surrounded by caring people. This is less likely if we share feelings with others, for then we are far more likely to feel a sense of connection and belonging. By taking risks in exposing our feelings, we also free others to do the same, which creates a climate of emotional openness and acceptance.

These types of relationships have a strong effect on our bodies. At the University of Nebraska School of Medicine, a study of elderly people found that among those who confided more, sharing feelings and secrets, there was stronger immune function.[10]

What is social support? It involves so many different forms of relating that the research findings have been confused by the many ways of conceptualizing it. We all know what social support feels like. It's a feeling of being liked, belonging, getting help when you need it. It involves the sense that people care what happens to you and that it matters if you don't show up when they expect you. It often means knowing that there are sensitive folks who will listen to you, people you can count on and who can also count on you, because true social support is always reciprocal.

We also know what is not supportive, even when others intend it to be: giving unrequested advice, minimizing your worries or upsets, being aggressively cheerful, intrusive, or manipulative. These behaviors are not supportive, although they may be the best that people can offer. Sometimes what researchers think is socially supportive is not. When undergraduate students visited elderly people, it had little effect on their immune function, although contact with elderly friends did.[11]

There are many social relationships that have not been systematically studied for their effect on the immune system, but a social support network usually involves a variety of connections. Some relationships are close with lots of confidences shared. Other relationships are superficial, and many involve only companionship without any shared secrets. Another type of relating involves mutual cooperation in some common project where the focus is on the work. All of these have a place in a social network that generates a warm emotional climate.

The effects of social support are particularly powerful for women with breast cancer. In a landmark study, Sandra Levy at the University of Pittsburgh found that women with breast cancer are physically affected by their social context.[12] When breast cancer patients believed that they had a great deal of interpersonal support in their surroundings, they stayed healthier longer. The level of perceived social support was found to predict the level of natural killer cell activity. Levy has suggested that social support seems to be effective in controlling the spread of micrometastases in early breast cancer. But according to David Spiegel's findings, it seems that social support is also extremely powerful in advanced cases of breast cancer as well.

Health doesn't require that we surround ourselves with admirers and helpers. Far more instrumental is the construction of relationships, even less than perfect ones, where our feelings can be expressed freely and where we can listen to others. In this society there is a proclivity for leaving relationships when they become disappointing and for defending one's dignity by refusing to tolerate others' bad manners and maladjustments. Far more beneficial is the habit of astutely noticing and cheerfully dismissing others' imperfections while continuing to strengthen the social fabric of one's life.

In a culture where there is a great deal of movement and where people rarely stay in the same relationships for very long, it is not likely that there will be a surplus of these relationships. But it is essential for people to get a human response from the environment, to get some kind of recognition that we are alive and that we are real.

Contact with others is essential for life and sanity in all mammals. When Dr. Harry Harlow did his famous experiments with monkeys, he found that he could provide for every physical need possible and still not offer enough for survival.[13] Without connection to other living creatures, even unloving contact, his monkeys spiraled downward through crying, fighting, depression, and death. The overwhelming isolation was clearly lethal.

Even with supportive relationships, an extended social network is necessary to buffer the effects of unforeseeable life events. When Dr. George Engel at the Rochester University Medical School studied sudden death in adults, mostly from cardiovascular causes and not including suicide, he found that for 59 percent of the people, there had been a major loss of a loved one just prior to the lethal event.[14] Those who care for those at risk recognize this. In intensive care units, human contact can lower the levels of serum cholesterol or raise it, depending on whether contact is reassuring or stressful. Life presents many problems, and when they are too disruptive and occur too close together, they can overwhelm a normally healthy system.

When Holmes and Rahe studied the relation between life events and risk for disease, they found that people's chances of getting seriously sick increased with the number of life losses coming together.[15] Life is full of problems and traumas happen, but there is good evidence that a supportive emotional context softens the physiological impact. In one study, having a close friend reduced the impact of a traumatic event and prevented the development of more serious psychological problems.[16]

Living with People

There are many types of household living arrangements, with only some of them fitting the image of the nuclear family, with a father/breadwinner, mother/primary parent, and two or three children. The great majority of living arrangements involve combinations of people, sometimes biologically related, in which there are emotional ties and interdependence and which we refer to here as families. Three-quarters of American families will be involved with someone with cancer, and often when a woman gets breast cancer, someone else in the immediate or extended family will have already had cancer. This will influence everyone's reactions.

Enduring family patterns don't change much when one person is diagnosed with cancer, but the initial disruption and stress will affect daily habits. In the first three months after diagnosis, a woman needs a good deal of help with transportation, shopping, housekeeping, and meal preparation. The family's flexibility will be tested, as new arrangements are required to meet new needs. If family members are used to expressing care for one another, then conflicts will be solved relatively easily, because expressing emotions compassionately usually opens the way to solution.

As family members try to sort out how to get the work done now that one member is temporarily out of order, they are likely to use their usual approaches to problems. As one girl said about her family, "Our problem-solving techniques? That's easy: When in trouble, when in doubt, run in circles, scream and shout." And that is very much what her family did when her mother got breast cancer. People argued about who would do the cooking, the oldest daughter screamed that everyone was picking on her, and everybody seemed to be very busy and overworked, even though little actually got done around the house. But their approach did solve one of the major problems of dealing with breast cancer: there was little time to notice or talk about feelings, and nobody had to admit to being frightened, angry, guilty, or overwhelmed.

Cancer stirs powerful feelings in anyone; sometimes people are afraid of the disease, afraid of catching it or of being in contact with someone who has it. It can be particularly difficult to express these feelings when a mother is seen as vulnerable and weakened. There may even be fears that if family members have negative feelings, that could make the illness worse. ("If I get mad at Mom, she'll die," one boy said.)

Often families get into a pattern of being decisively cheerful, so that no matter what anybody feels, it will be overridden by positive comments, reassurance, and smiles. For a woman trying to deal with treatment choices, change in life view, altered social relationships and functioning, physical changes, sadness, uncertainty, a flood of new information, mortality issues, financial requirements, occupational concerns, and disruptions of daily living, forced cheerfulness can feel like trivialization or rejection. With all of the new circumstances of breast cancer, there is a need to talk often and at length with many people.

If a woman's attempts to express feelings and upsets are met with an unresponsive reaction, either lack of interest or reflexive optimism, she may emotionally withdraw and close herself off from others, or she may overstate her feelings, arguing for their legitimacy. Family emotions and physical reactions tend to rise and fall together, and a woman may try to calm everyone down by cooling herself off too quickly, before she has a chance to establish what she needs.

Patterns develop in families to reduce stress and solve problems. They may be useful or counterproductive, but they are all likely to be in evidence during this period. The best indicator of a woman's emotional adjustment is the frequency of talking often and freely.[17] If others cannot share conversations about a woman's situation, they may resort to avoiding her, staying emotionally out of range. Sometimes, though, people are just busy, and another's illness is not the focal point of their lives.

Even though women are usually emotionally sensitive to their families, it can be unwise for a woman to put family comfort ahead of medical and emotional needs. In one study of end-stage renal disease, families that placed a high value on family harmony also had higher patient mortality. It may be that patients were too concerned with cooperation and serenity, which led them to neglect real problem-solving aimed at longer survival.[18] If a woman has to choose between her family's tranquillity and her own health, this is the time to choose health.

Often the family is headed by a woman, and if this is so, it is likely that finances will be a particular problem. Half of woman-headed households with children fall below the poverty line, and two-thirds of poor adults are women.[19] This is no doubt the result of the higher divorce rate, lower job pay for women, the expense of childcare and the requirements of parenting. Illness can be an additional financial burden.

Although families and marriages are conducive to better health in men, the findings for women are more complex. Some research has shown that relationships with family and relatives are not as important for women's health and survival as are relationships with friends and acquaintances at work.[20] This may be because during an illness a woman is not able to operate as emotional care-taker and homemaker, so she gains little good feeling about herself when she fails this primary function.

Since others around her at home are not in the habit of caring for a woman, they will do a poor job of it and not help the situation much when a crisis like breast cancer suddenly arises. The fantasy that often sustains us through the stresses of family life, that when the chips are down others will reciprocate, may be destroyed during breast cancer treatment. The lack of an adequate response by others and the disappointment it incurs may present a serious problem because it challenges a woman's premise about reciprocity in relationships.

Living Alone

If you are living alone, you are not alone in your circumstances. Of the 8.8 million elderly people who lived alone in the United States in 1987, 80 percent were women Many of those who live alone are poor, including 1.1 million elderly widows, with as many near poor, that is, widows with incomes below $156 per week.[21] If you live by yourself, your relationship to your home is likely to feel different after treatment. You may find it harder initially to take care of your household and yourself, and you may frequently feel tired and discouraged. But a home is like a shell that we need to crawl into at times, and it needn't be in perfect order to serve the purpose.

It is wise to avoid making sudden residential changes during breast cancer treatment if you can, since your home is a refuge and this is not the time to disrupt it. While you are recovering, it is advisable to plan your day so that people can visit or help you, keeping a schedule that makes your health needs the first priority. Just as hospitals have visiting hours so that patients can rest and staff can get work done, similarly your days at home must be arranged to use your energy well and to enhance healing.

You may feel, as about a third of breast cancer patients do, that people are avoiding you,[22] and it is worth exploring this. It may be that friends are socially awkward and don't know what to say or what not to say. Instead of hoping that such friends will develop social grace, it will be more productive if you ask for specific help, for example, cooking a lunch or helping with laundry. Other friends may be phobic about illness, medicines, hospitals, and shots and may even pass out on contact with these. If this is the case, or you suspect it to be, you might encourage telephone calls and letters until you feel you are back to normal.

Don't expect everyone to respond with balance and insight to your illness, for people rarely develop such traits in a crisis. The only way we really learn to handle cancer is by having it, and if your friends and relatives haven't had this experience, they will not be able to offer much. You may even begin to feel like a skilled therapist to your relations.

When you return to normal, it is important to draw on a social network and to build and enhance it. Research suggests that family and relatives are not particularly beneficial to women dealing with illness, and that they may even be burdensome. When, for example, a woman with breast cancer has a spouse who is ill, she is likely to have twice as many problems with recovery as a woman with a healthy spouse.[23]

Involvement outside the home in activities that bring you into routine contact with others will be particularly helpful. In one study, work outside the home, whether volunteer or paid, was the strongest predictor of good health for women of all ages. Compared with unemployed women, working women had fewer days of illness, spent less time in bed, had less chronic illness, and felt better.[24]

Marriages and Partnerships

How does marriage affect the experience of breast cancer? Marriage can mean happiness or misery, and the same marriage may be both at different times, or at the same time. This may explain why the research findings on marriage and women's health are so mixed. Some research shows that people are healthier if they are married, but other research shows no significant relationship between marital status and outcomes with breast cancer.[25]

In one major research project, being single, divorced, or widowed was more predictive of survival with breast cancer than being married.[26] Other studies have shown marital status for women with breast cancer to be a risk factor rather than a protective factor with respect to survival.[27] But the effects of marriage for a specific woman depend very heavily on the nature of the relationship between husband and wife.

Although few studies show strong health benefits to women from marriage, it is difficult to interpret the findings. Researchers often assume that marriage is the same thing as social support, but this is a simplistic view of a complex relationship. The high divorce rate indicates that marriage is often unsupportive, particularly since most divorces are initiated by women. Marriage may include a great deal of contact with other people, and so lead to but not offer social support. In general, marriage offers the potential for support when a woman is ill. But a great deal depends on the quality of a husband's reaction to the diagnosis of breast cancer.[28]

Married women who feel that they get little support at home, can't communicate, and are dissatisfied with their relationship generally have a poorer prognosis than other women.[29] Women in poor marriages have increased depression as well as diminished lymphocyte responsiveness. In one study, these women had elevated antibody titers to Epstein-Barr virus, which is evidence that the cellular component of the immune system is not controlling viral infection.[30]

A good marriage is primarily a good friendship, in which two people care for and comfort each other and share their feelings and thoughts without apprehension. Although the research on breast cancer shows an advantage in having friendships, there are many marriages that are also strong friendships, and so the data on the effects of friends on health would also apply here.

Are marriages supportive for women? Marital status was always considered one of the best predictors of health, until researchers began to look separately at men's and women's health. Although the death of one's spouse is usually stressful, it has a far less devastating effect on women than on men.[31] Divorce has much less impact on women's heart attack risk than on men's.[32] Marriage itself may hold different consequences for men and women. It results in a 63 percent reduction in mental illness rates for men and a 28 percent reduction for women,[33] and marriage reduces hospital admission rates for men but not for women.[34]

When a woman has breast cancer, support and help become crucial, and the gaps in her emotional life are most apt to be evident. In studies of American marriages, researchers have found that in married couples aged fifty and older, wives generally give more social support to their husbands than they receive, and they generally receive more criticism than they give.[35]

In a major study of sickness and health in marriages, two married researchers looked at supportive spouse behaviors. They found that right after a diagnosis of breast cancer, husbands were more supportive than usual. However, as time went on, they reverted to the previously described pattern in which the wife offers most of the emotional support and the husband offers most of the negative expressions. But a good deal depended on the wife's symptoms. When there were external indications of illness, there was more support and less criticism.[36]

Although a wife's role usually includes taking care of both people's emotional needs, this is not necessarily a dissatisfying experience:

> "He nags me and he does it a lot, and so sometimes I throw something at him and then he quits it. If he didn't do it, then I'd know he stopped noticing and maybe he's really getting old. It's the same kind of thing as when he holds my hand in bed at night. It's too tight, but anyway he's there."

Is it wise to divorce if a marriage is destructive? In marriages described as chronically abrasive, there are generally poorer health ratings.[37] Continued stress diverts the body's energy to calming the system and away from maintaining cardiovascular, endocrine, and immune balances. Although research generally has shown that separation and divorce are worse for health than widowhood,[38] there are currently no comparisons of good and bad marriages, so it is not clear how bad marriages affect women's health. This is important, for the crisis of breast cancer can move a woman to settle a troubled marriage, one way or another. Although a bad marriage is not conducive to health, divorce also has its costs, and sometimes repair and overhaul are the wiser choices.

The immune system reacts to loss, and separation or divorce may bring grief if there is an end to good times, shared friendship and sex, future plans, financial security, shared parenting, and family connection. When this is the case, the immune system functions less well, and there is a drop in immune response.[39] When a treasured marriage ends in widowhood, a woman will be supported in her grief, but not necessarily if she is divorced. Divorce can mean a loss of a spouse and a loss of one's social context too.

For some marriages, separation or divorce may not be seen as a loss at all, and may offer the opportunity for a happier life. When a spouse decides to leave a marriage because it is unsatisfying or damaging, there is less of an effect on the immune system than when the spouse is left.[40]

How husbands react: A woman's emotional connection to those around her shows up in the way her moods fluctuate during a marriage. She is likely to feel upset, for example, as a result of her husband's behavior and the general state of the relationship if it is not good. For a man, things are different. A husband's moods are more affected by how well he and his wife are able to find solutions to family and household problems.

A woman's need to connect and relate to others makes her particularly sensitive to her husband's responses. "You're too sensitive," he may complain, and she may feel that he is insensitive, but they approach the relationship from different perspectives and needs.[41]

This means that the best way to predict a wife's distress with breast cancer is to look at her husband's reactions, although the reverse is not true. In most research, however, husbands report as many adjustment problems as wives with breast cancer.[42]

There are immediate practical problems with breast cancer, especially in daily chores. In most households, a male spouse will have to take on a good deal more traditionally female work, and there may be child care responsibilities or care of an older adult relative as well. Husbands often show increased stress in physical symptoms during a wife's illness. A man may suffer nervousness, fatigue, sleep disturbance, eating problems, or difficulties in concentration.[43] A wife who must abruptly give up all of her usual chores is likely to have some emotional reactions as well, further complicating the problem. Particularly if partners have taken great pride in their respective roles, this will be a troubled time.

Men and mastectomy: People react differently to new circumstances, and it is important to differentiate a man's reaction to mastectomy and his reaction to his wife. These two may become confused so that one seems the same as the other. Mastectomy is a powerful experience for a couple, but a man's feelings may be expressed indirectly and by proxy. Interestingly, some men develop either very positive or very negative reactions to the surgeon, and may be quite vehement.

A husband's adjustment to changed circumstances after breast cancer surgery depends on two things. The first is the degree of a man's involvement in treatment planning; men who remain outside this process and offer no help at this stage may have greater difficulty in the time following treatment. When a woman is hospitalized for treatment, the extent of a husband's contact with her, how often he visits and calls, is also a good indicator of how easily he will be able to become integrated into the new circumstances.[44]

A woman's medical history affects how a husband adjusts, with men apparently having fewer adjustment problems when a woman has chemotherapy even though this is highly stressful for the woman and her family.[45] In part this may be because the months of chemotherapy generally allow for more expression, exchange of feelings, and a gradual transition to the new experience. In mastectomy or lumpectomy, things happen very quickly, and it may feel as though everything should normalize in a matter of weeks.

Sometimes men remain on the fringe of treatment because of excessive sensitivity to a woman's perceived experience or a sense of inadequacy. A woman may need companionship and sympathy through treatment, but a man may offer advice and self-discipline instead. It may be helpful to specify the help needed and offer reassurance that it is adequate when it is.

Sexual relating will require a different level of intimacy and sensitivity and on the whole will reflect the couple's flexibility at adapting to new life circumstances. When men remain outside the initial parts of treatment, this may be more difficult.

Marital communication: If a man is affected by his wife's illness, how does this affect communication? Is it different from how they share when they both are healthy? According to Deborah Tannen, men use talking to establish dominance and women use it to make connections.

With breast cancer a typical spousal conversation involves a wife talking about her distress and a husband speaking optimistically, which is generally followed by the wife expressing greater distress.[46] This type of exchange is reported by 31 percent of married breast cancer patients.[47] In several research studies, male conversational styles have been identified as a source of communication problems in marriage.[48] This may partially explain why women want more time away from their spouses than husbands do.[49] When a woman talks about breast cancer, she may be assuming that her husband can understand what she is saying, but the exchange is complicated by their sharply different perspectives.[50]

Breast cancer is predominantly a female disease of female organs, and the unique place of breasts in femininity makes it difficult for males to comprehend. Breasts have importance in several areas for women, including nurturing, childbearing, attractiveness, and sexual contact. The content of communications about breasts is apt to be highly charged.

Husbands have a different viewpoint and set of concerns in communication than wives do. In traditional male roles, a man may see his job as protecting his wife from upset, and limiting conversation may seem to be a way to do this. Husbands may feel that they have been truly helpful in doing so. They may also be superstitious and feel that talking about cancer is dangerous and that they should steer their wives to safer topics.

Some of this may be a way for a worried husband to soothe his own fears. Since he cannot look to his wife for the emotional support she usually provides, he may calm himself by avoiding the topic. He may also want his wife to be "strong" as he is being strong by not wallowing in feelings. The stress may even be greater at points for a husband than for a wife, for women generally have several relationships in which to share feelings, but men rarely do.[51]

These difficulties often lead to communication problems that may extend to other areas of the marriage as well, for example, sexual relating. If husband and wife see breast cancer as an unusual and unique experience that calls for self-denial and emotional avoidance, this may spread to other areas of the marriage. If, on the other hand, they become more daring, honest, and creative, they may use these coping strategies instead, resulting in a happier marriage than before the breast cancer.

Women are usually the emotional hub of families, transmitting and interpreting feelings and building an integrated group. When women are expressive of feelings, particularly energizing feelings like anger, they are likely to have better outcomes with breast cancer.[52] In order for this to be possible, it is important that the anger lead to fruitful conversation and good problem-solving.

Human dialogue involves listening and talking, both of which affect the cardiovascular and other systems. Interestingly, being unable to speak involves the same problems as being unable to listen. For some, conversation is a contest or an imposition; for others, it is a way of offering and gaining support.

The experience of breast cancer is a powerful one for husband and wife. It offers the chance to give up old, unsatisfying ways of relating and to experiment with new approaches. For many couples, the demands of the situation free up energy and creativity and can create a deeper and closer marriage.

Children

No matter how old they are, a woman's relationship with her children always touches on the same issues of dependency and self-reliance. Breast cancer complicates these issues by making a mother suddenly needy. A diagnosis of breast cancer is usually followed by immediate treatment, often involving surgery, radiation, or chemotherapy, and requires rapid, profound decisions, with little time available to anticipate and care for the needs of offspring.

It is easy to forget that children at any age are likely to revert to their childish ways in tense times. With young children, we may see them as adults with temporary childish habits of irresponsibility, insensitivity, and general childishness. It's nicer to think that underneath it all they're like the wise and compassionate children of the television sitcoms. But children in real life rarely behave so well and never behave better than the adults who teach them.

Children are childish, not only when little, but also when grown, and they are likely to be most childish around their parents. They are tolerable as long as we are not dependent on them, but with breast cancer everything changes. Routines are disrupted, frustrations are common, adults are tense and preoccupied, small things get neglected, and an air of confusion and urgency dominates.

The organizing influence in the home, the mother, is suddenly incapacitated and needy. She who knew everyone's schedules and requirements now cannot be disturbed, and everyone else must make do. The home may seem to lurch from deadline to deadline with its center of gravity gone.

Women in American culture are the emotional anchors and the practical caregivers, and rarely is there an emergency backup system if they are disabled. The younger the children in a household, the more elaborate the caregiving, but even women with grown children and grandchildren provide care of some sort to family members. How do children react? Differently at different ages.

Preschool children: Little children have such a limited understanding of the world that they may feel guilty and scared at the turmoil of a household following a diagnosis of breast cancer in a mother or grandmother. A normally easygoing child may become clingy or oppositional and be especially vulnerable to the emotional moods of a mother who is his familiar companion. Reasoning is very limited in the early years, and a little one may confuse radiation treatment with radioactive fallout, or believe that if cancer is a family illness, then he has it, and draw all sorts of frightening conclusions about what is happening. The most likely thought of a child is that somehow, some way, he caused her to get sick.

Separation of mother and child during treatment and the emotional distance that may come from fatigue due to surgery or chemotherapy can feel like a loss to a mother or child. When baby-sitters are used, the child may feel neglected or angry at the disruptions and changes and insist on small rituals to regain balance. Husbands, boyfriends, relatives, and friends may all be helpful to a mother with breast cancer, but small children may see them as an intrusion, and loyalty to Mom may require defiance.

If a child has routine contact with baby-sitters and dayoare workers, this may be a powerful source of support for a child and mother. The caring and continuity of adults will help a youngster retain a sense of trust in the world as a predictable place.

When people are away from one another for awhile, they appear to smell different, and a small child may reject a mother come home, claiming that she "smells bad." When the intimacy that was disrupted is restored by a mother's small ministrations and attention, the smell seems to disappear. Provocative behavior can sometimes be a way of insuring that a mother is still operating like an involved mother.

It helps with small children to try to retain daily routines and explain if your behavior is different than usual, giving simple, brief explanations for the illness. It also helps to support a child's self-esteem, listen for the child's feelings without trying to change them.

Mom has breast cancer. That's a sickness that women get sometimes. She's upset and not feeling so good now, but she'll feel better after awhile. She'll still be your mother and things will be mostly the same for you. And you still have to eat your dinner before you can have dessert."

School-aged children: Between five and eleven, children learn the thrill of developing competence and being expert in a few areas. Breast cancer challenges this newfound sense of mastery, because everybody is likely to feel confused and a bit inadequate at first.

Children are also very concrete in their thinking and will have specific concerns about breast cancer:

"Will Mom die?"

"Can I catch it?"

"Have I got it?"

"What will they cut off?"

"Will it leave a big hole?"

"Will she go away until I'm older?"

"Can I watch more TV while she's in the hospital?"

Often children feel ignorant and useless when their mother is ill and ashamed at all the help they need. Sometimes others reinforce this: "How can you bother your mother when she's sick?" But most kids, who want to be good at things, now notice how much they need their mothers. Children of this age normally need a great deal of help in daily life, and often the family is centered on their needs and schedules. Breast cancer changes all this.

When a mother is ill, there is less interest in the children's day and problems. Perhaps there is no one to help with homework, settle fights with siblings or drive the children to school. They may have to give up favorite activities temporarily, like riding their bikes after school, or walking the dog. And this can stir some very uncomfortable feelings, just when nobody seems interested in how they feel.

Parents may be absent, preoccupied, tense, or uninterested, and since kids don't usually verbalize feelings easily, they frequently bury them. Emotions change continuously at this age, and a sunny child in the morning may be a stormy one by afternoon. Children may miss Mom terribly and then be angry when they are inconvenienced by a visit to the hospital.

On top of it all, they may feel like babies for having strong and confusing feelings and having to ask for things from tired parents. They may even be afraid that if they don't stop bothering their mother, she'll get sicker and die ("Step on a crack, break your mother's back ... "). So children may strive to be unrealistically good to try to please their gods.

Children may be angry that nobody pays as much attention to them anymore or cares about their day or looks at them, and they may see their fall from prominence as a failure on their part, leaving them to sad thoughts about themselves. They may also feel socially embarrassed at the attention given by strangers to the family, the intrusive questions of others, and their knowing looks. Children may feign indifference and brush off kindness to deal with these tensions.

It will help to give children brief and accurate information about the illness, and be clear about causation, accepting their fears if they appear. It will also help to attend to children's business even if it seems trivial and teach them ways to feel competent and important.

Teenagers: Parents of teenagers routinely offer a great deal of guidance, and an incapacitated mother may be unable to do so. The perception of sudden freedom may feel like liberation or desertion to a young teen, but a sudden shift to self-reliance will not make a young adolescent mature suddenly. If there are many shame-inducing mistakes, adolescents may blame their parents for their lack of guidance.

Other adult helpers, like grandmothers, can be seen as intrusions and as causing demotion of a teen to a child status, and there may be problems of unrealistic expectations or limited experience with a new adult in the house. Most importantly, a new person in the family changes the special bargains and deals that parents and teens have with each other; for example, a girl understands that Mom may scold about the messy room, but will always clean it. Discipline is based on understanding and bonds between two people and cannot be unilaterally imposed by a new person in the household.

Teen girls may be put in the position of taking over cooking, cleaning, and child care, and this can be felt as an obstacle to a girl's social life and an infringement on her independence. She may have too much time with Dad, not enough time as a daughter, and too little time with friends.

Power positions in the family will also change, with Grandma or Dad or the boyfriend taking over Mom's jobs, and relations among brothers and sisters also readjusting. When a mother returns to her earlier role, there will be another disruption as the newly formed patterns change once again.

For a teen girl, personal attractiveness may be a concern when a mother has breast cancer, and a girl may feel that she doesn't look as nice since her mother got sick, a reflection more of self-esteem than changed appearance. A mother's new appearance, which may be fatigued, balding, drawn, overweight, or aged, may reinforce a sense of social stigma that teens feel about their families, no matter how normal looking they are. It's also hard to talk about a disease that involves unmentionable body parts. What's more, it's hard to feel okay complaining and whining about your parents, which is the currency of teen conversation, if your mother seems to be in dire straits.

One study found that adolescent daughters whose mothers had breast cancer didn't have more problems with behavior, but they had more anxiety about their health, and it tended to show up in physical symptoms.[53] It helped to talk openly in the family, but in general female relatives of a breast cancer patient have more anxiety than male relatives.[54]

For teenage boys, the issues are different in relating to a mother who has breast cancer. As with all offspring, the primary impact will be felt in the relative disruption of a boy's life. New responsibilities like housekeeping or baby-sitting, and inconvenience like lack of chauffeuring will have the first impact.

Emotional responses will come later, when the boy faces the fears stirred by a threatening illness and the change in his mother's strength. The accumulation of inconveniences and disruptions will be wearying for everyone, and the young will likely be most lacking in patience.

Throughout his mother's illness, sixteen-year-old John had been a perfect son to his divorced mother, caring for the younger boys, cooking, driving, and showing genuine concern for his mother. John was always a shy boy, but his mother's illness brought out all of the best in him. When she was well again, however, he resisted, and then openly fought her attempts to take back control of the family. The younger children, confused, divided between son and mother, and the household became very tense. Family counseling over several months helped John to return to a teen focus, in which, not surprisingly, he felt far less adequate.

It will help to sympathize with the disruptions in a teen's life. Bring adult helpers into the family with clear and discussed expectations and emphasize good manners. Kindness and firmness are still the best guidelines for adolescent discipline.

Young adults: Early adulthood is a time when youth see themselves as separate from the family and self-reliant. This is a time for establishing one's own residence, living patterns, and routines, finding a job to support oneself, choosing a partner, and maintaining a social circle. It goes most smoothly when young people have developed skill in organizing their behavior and relating to others.

A mother's illness complicates this transition out of dependency, since it changes the way that the family is arranged. If Mom was primarily a homemaker, it may be difficult for her to continue in this role. If she worked to support the family, her job is now tenuous. Because a woman with breast cancer is incapacitated for long periods, the demands on everyone around her are greater.

Some young adults who find it difficult to try their wings may use a mother's illness to rationalize their fear of separation. The emotional anguish, the increased need for care, and the disruption of family activities may seem like sufficient reason to postpone going to college, to refuse the new job offer, or to cancel plans to move to one's own apartment.

Always a difficult process, leaving home may stir up fears of abandonment and guilt if a parent is ill. Young adults who use a parent's illness to remain within the family will receive a great deal of approval from other family members who view this as a sacrifice for the needy parent.

At times, such a sacrifice may be a good choice, but not if the help is not useful. If it serves to disguise a youngster's fear of moving on, it becomes problematical. A woman with breast cancer is most helped by her children's healthy growth and development and by their genuine concern for her, separate from their own needs.

Young people who have trouble making a separate home may become more dependent if they have no employment or educational pursuits. Living at home without a clear life direction may revive earlier adolescent patterns, such as late sleeping, endless television watching, erratic mealtimes, and poor personal hygiene. When these difficulties appear in a household, they can serve the purpose of draining off the family's anger and anxiety at the upset and disruption of the mother's disease, and this may be why repressive personalities fall so easily to fighting.

Fear of loss is a strong current in young adulthood, as young adventurers like to keep the shoreline in sight when out making their mark. A dependable home and family make adult initiatives seem less risky and provide a haven if retreat is necessary. A mother's cancer diagnosis raises strong fears of loss, and these combined with the anxieties of early adulthood about leaving home may cause youngsters to fail to try their wings.

For young adults who are able to develop self-sufficiency in their work, residence, and relationships, shameful feelings that may result from deserting an ill parent can take a different form. A mother's need for help may be felt as a threat to newly established independence, a ploy perhaps to imprison an eager bird. The difficulties of medical tests, surgery, physical therapy, radiation, and chemotherapy and a woman's need for help may stir up guilt in a young person who feels emancipated and wants to remain so. To return to the family orbit in a crisis may feel like a defeat.

Many young adults, as a group not typically attentive to parents, will have even less contact during breast cancer treatment. After the initial crisis and surgery, the phone calls may come at increasingly lengthy intervals, the visits home may include friends who act as buffers, the conversations may seem superficial and forced. Caring may be there, but a young person may nonetheless avoid an ill mother.

The avoidance may also take the form of forced cheerfulness that blocks out the emotional distress surrounding the illness. The young person wants to help and so tries to be pleasant and upbeat, not mentioning the course failed in school or getting docked at work for lateness. A mother doesn't want to burden her children with her misery and fears, and so she tells funny stories about the nurses in oncology. While at critical points these may be very useful ways to behave, as enduring patterns they isolate everyone by stifling emotional expression.

It will help to encourage young adults to continue on with the transition to independence and to make limited but practical requests for help. Explain the problem of forced cheerfulness, and give young people guidelines for how to help. But above all expect young adult behavior. The ability to relate to others compassionately and still retain a strong sense of oneself requires a depth of character and richness of personality that takes many years to develop.

Friends

Friendships affect our bodies far more than is apparent and can change basic body rhythms. When two people talk to each other, and it's more than just polite conversation, their heart rates tend to speed up and slow down at the same time.[55] Interestingly enough, how long we live is predictable by how involved we are with other people.

There are practical ways that friends make our lives easier, particularly when we are ill. They may give concrete help with housework, meal preparation, or transportation. A friend may be a companion or helper at medical appointments and treatments, making the process easier and more efficient. Most importantly, friends can offer sympathy, compassion, encouragement, and support.

Sometimes with the drastic life changes of breast cancer, there are changes in friendships as well. Old friendships may fade, particularly if they cannot adapt to the situation. New friendships may form from medical experiences or grow out of superficial relationships.

Friendships can offer more to a woman with breast cancer than family relationships. They often have more flexibility, so that a woman can deepen or distance the relationship as the need arises. If there are a large number of friends, there are even more alternatives from which to choose specific forms of help and support. In general, breast cancer patients report more satisfaction with friendships than with family relationships.[56]

Women usually form relationships in the workplace that may not be particularly intimate but nonetheless form a part of a social support system. Whether a woman works as a volunteer or for pay, she is likely to be in contact with other women in what Nancy Waxler-Morrison calls the "colleague network."[57]

Work friendship circles are most common in the middle and lower levels of employment status, so that female bank presidents would have less access to them, but all of the clerk typists and key punch operators would automatically be included. Generally, these groupings involve women who work together, have lunch together, and help each other with weddings, baby showers, birthdays, funerals, and other important personal events.

When a woman has breast cancer, this network can offer concrete help, information, an outlet for feelings, and a sense of belonging. A woman in this structure has control over incoming help and can use it as she needs it without feeling overwhelmed. But most importantly, such a network also gives a woman a strong sense of belonging and of being reintegrated into the social framework. At a later time, she will become the helper to someone else who is facing illness, death, divorce, or breakdown, and she will leave her own crisis behind.

Work friendship circles generally function wherever women operate together in a workforce and where there are limited job opportunities. They are less common in higher income positions or where women are an integrated part of the work force.

In general, women's friendships become more difficult to maintain with changes in the culture. As women have become employed in increasing numbers, there has been less time for friendships. Job pressures, changes, and residential moves have further disrupted relationships.

As women have achieved positions of higher status, they have become more vulnerable to social isolation on the job. The requirements of high prestige jobs can appear to include adopting the male habits of emotional self-reliance, restricted emotional expression, and limited connection with others.

Women generally see relationships with women as a way to make emotional connection,[58] and a feminine approach to friendships is very different than a male's. In conversation, women search for common ground, nodding their heads in unison when they find similarities or intersections, no matter how remote ("Your uncle went to the same hotel that my cousin worked in last summer!"). They also find ways to gradually increase the intimacy of the feelings shared in a conversation, all the while testing to determine whether the other is receptive and trustworthy.

When women talk about breast cancer, it is easier if others have had the experience, but since the anatomy is familiar to all, as is fear of the illness, there is often enough of a basis for a bond.

American culture at the end of the millennium seems to put little value on friendships, and often they are derogated as a "female thing": "you and your girlfriends," with activities seen as frivolous, insignificant, and involving a great deal of superfluous conversation. Friendships, however, make a large contribution to health, particularly for women with breast cancer.

What if you don't have many friends? I recall being a new dormitory director at a state college, freshly arrived one month earlier, struggling to learn the ropes and feeling desperately lonely and sorry for myself. I went to visit Mrs. Graham, a widow of seventy, also a dorm director, and poured my heart out to her: how lonesome it was to live by myself, how unwanted I felt, how much a stranger, and how hopeless it all seemed. She listened with a vast sympathy and then asked gently, those old blue eyes twinkling, "And what have you done for anyone else since you got here?"

Building a network of friendships requires changing life patterns and expending energy to form new connections, not waiting for somebody to call. It requires entering into patterns of sharing activities, lunch or weeding or walking, with somebody. It takes remembering others' celebrations and bad times. It requires keeping others informed of important events, taking emotional risks, and showing deep feelings, concerns, and beliefs. It means the ability to listen to others' private thoughts and feelings, to care about them, and to express your own feelings clearly and with conviction.

It is not a set of skills routinely taught in this culture. Far more often are women taught to be assertive and self-analytical. But the skills of friendship pay off in pleasure and in health benefits.

Pets

Sometimes the research on health and psychology seems like
something out of the twilight zone. It's hard to believe that a dog,
a mangy looking, sad-eyed beast like the one lying up against my
leg, can make a difference in what goes on inside our bodies. But
there are good reasons why dogs have been man's (and woman's)
best friend from time immemorial, when a lizard or bird would
probably have been a more convenient pet.

Watch what happens when you bring along a big soft-looking,
dog-smiling, tail-wagging mongrel to visit folks who aren't usually very responsive. Old folks in nursing homes, angry teen girls,
tough cops — they all tend to smile, reach down, and pat a
friendly, hairy head, almost without thinking.

There is a strong relationship between dogs and cardiovascular
functioning. At the University of Maryland Hospital's coronary
care unit, patients who had been admitted for heart attack or
angina pectoris were followed up after they left the hospital. Neither of these cardiovascular disorders has a promising future, so
there was a specific interest in mortality in this study.[59]

When the researchers divided the patients into groups based on
who had a friendly pet at home, they found that the probability
of dying was more than four times greater if there was no pet.
Apparently, pet care has a positive influence on the cardiovascular
system. This is supported by other research also, which shows that
when an adult pats a friendly dog, there is a healthy calming of
blood pressure. Children as well show this effect, and the presence
of a friendly dog in a room lowers children's blood pressure.[60] I've
noticed in families that the addition of a friendly dog can often
improve everybody's disposition, and that people who love their
pets are usually easy to get along with.

This may have to do with the way that people talk with their
pets, which is much more like the way that women talk to women
than the way that men talk to men. Here are the things that people
said this week when they spoke to my dog:

"Here poochie."

"There's a good dog. Are you a nice old thing?"

"Good dog. Good dog."

"You want to lick my hand? Good dog."

"You want to play?"

"Come here, boy."

"That's the girl."

When they talk to a dog, people usually try to connect, to get the dog to respond. They comment on the dog's feelings, get the dog to do something for them, or stroke the dog. Generally they establish a bond. When women talk to other women, they have a similar approach, although not usually in a condescending manner. Men, in conversation with each other and sometimes in conversation with their pets, seem more oriented to compete or control rather than forge a bond.

Talking to a pet has an effect on a number of body systems and changes the blood flow in a way that suggests a state of relaxation. The heart rate slows while the blood flow increases to the brain and decreases in the surface regions like the fingers.[61] People usually like to talk to their dogs and other pets as well and feel good while doing it.

Having a friendly dog is part of a larger social support network, and there are times when only a dog will tolerate, accept, and still love you. Humans respond to that sort of unconditional love, and it makes it easier to offer it to others and build connections. It's all about being alive.

Chapter Six

Acting Alive: Thoughts and Feelings

I was trying to get across to Jane what it means to be lively.

"Think of Bette Midler," I said, picturing how she was always full of expression.

"As opposed to Queen Elizabeth?" she said.

The one is full of emotion and charged with feeling. The other is steady, unflappable, unchanging. It's hard to believe that all the same emotional currents run through both their insides.

Everybody is alive. Everybody has a heartbeat and moves around, but some people are more alive than others. It has little to do with whether they're healthy or sick and a lot to do with habits.

When you think of a lively person, what are the images that come to mind? I think first of Mary Victor Bruce. Born in an age when women were expected to be subdued, she horrified her family first by getting her pilot's license and then by getting arrested in New York City for flying around the Empire State Building. It was said that she flew in such tight circles that the typists inside could see the color of her eyes. "Going slow," said Mary, "always makes me tired." Later she would break the world record for the longest solo flight and create an air ferry service across the English Channel. She never wore overalls or slacks, preferring a blouse and skirt and pearls, and she refused to be called a "women's libber." At eighty-one she made a spectacular comeback as a pilot, flying a loop-the-loop in a two-seater plane. "What a lark," she said, leaving the field. She lived to be ninety-four.

Liveliness means movement, gestures, facial expressions. Vitality invariably includes emotional expression, action, and the articulation of genuine feelings. Trauma, however, can sometimes close off vitality and emotional expression. Breast cancer can have this effect on women, so that they become inactive and emotionally unreachable. Vitality can also be dampened by the belief that other people will withdraw from relationships if genuine emotions are expressed.

Acting alive can be risky. When strong emotions are felt and expressed, feelings of love, hate, anger, delight, anxiety, and sadness, people react. Rarely do they respond in ways we would choose, and so the possibility of conflict increases. But there's not much security in withholding feelings either.

The alternative to emotional expression is a static inner life, one that quickly becomes obsessive and depressing. The human body and psyche are built for action, and when either must stay still for periods, the result is a loss of functional capacity, that is, they simply don't work as well. When patients have to stay in bed for many days, they may need rehabilitative support for all organ systems to reach full functioning again. Similarly with emotions, without exercise and expression, the system begins to lose its elasticity, putting an additional strain on the body's resources. The body and the psyche become a prison that traps us, and the result is hopelessness and helplessness.

There are powerful forces that discourage us from expressing feelings. When we repress difficult emotions, our bodies manufacture opiates that shield us from the discomfort, but they slow down the immune system as well.[1] Steven Greer's research finds that women who can communicate negative feelings, like anger and hostility, survive longer.

Often what stops us is our expectations of ourselves. We may feel that we need to behave responsibly, to preserve relationships, and especially not to disappoint others. We may gain esteem from being the mistress of our own feelings and believe that controlling them shows good character. It may also seem that stoicism is a self-sacrifice that enhances medical treatment or that protects our family's welfare.

Breast cancer patients are inclined to avoid feelings, but research shows that it leads patients to *more* distress rather than helping them feel better. Trying to avoid dealing with inner turmoil can intensify the focus on it and multiply the daily periods of anxious preoccupation.[2]

How we think has a big impact on how we act and on whether we plan action and make choices that enhance our health. It is easy to assume that personal habits are automatic, caused by fate or some wind-up mechanism set in motion when we were born. We may overlook the powers of reasoning and judgment that have enabled us to get through lots of challenges and problems in our lives.

Everything in breast cancer diagnosis and treatment seems to conspire to pressure women to sit still and be quiet. Medical routines, upset friends, physical discomfort, all of these push a woman to retract emotionally, to become passive and hope for the best, or to avoid all thought. But women historically have done best when they are active and emotive.

What best supports our body's strength and health? Depression and passivity lower immunity[3] and interfere with the good upkeep and maintenance of cells in the immune system, thus disabling some of the body's best protective forces.[4] Taking action, in the form of behaviors or discussion, supports good immune function.[5]

Over the past decade, the media have been filled with reports about how people cured their cancer by thinking positively and keeping the right thoughts in mind. There are lots of suggestions for how people can practice doing this, for example, by imagining the immune system eating up cancer cells.

If you have attempted this, you may have found it discouraging to try to concentrate on positive thoughts when there is so much difficulty in your life. You may even have felt like a failure if you were not able to do what others seem to do.

But positive thoughts have little to do with good health. Giving vent to all strong feelings, however — positive as well as negative ones — clears the way for effective decision-making, and helps us feel better too.

Fear of Thoughts and Feelings

Where did our ideas about positive thinking come from? In the 1970s, the treatment of cancer began to move out of the purely physiological realm, and interest developed in the relation between what goes on in our minds and what goes on in our bodies. Unfortunately, enthusiasm for this connection developed far past the research support for these ideas. Some cancer treatment programs were created purely on the basis of wishful thinking or outright chicanery.

At one "hospital" in Tijuana, Mexico, cancer patients were required to bring a friend or relative who would check in with them and share a room so that they could share "soul explorations." In these exercises, sometimes going on for hours, patients had to remain completely quiet, examine their feelings for misdeeds and failures of faith, and await purification. They would have many days of diagnostic tests before seeing the doctor, although sometimes the doctor never got there at all. Before check-in, patients were required to transfer power of attorney over all assets to the hospital director.

At the same time, there was growing interest in this country in mystical Eastern approaches to religion and health, leading to the development of cancer treatments that were based on non-Western philosophies.

As the dust settled, several popular beliefs became enshrined. The first was that it was possible to cure cancer by having the right mental images and state of mind and that these could be achieved by practice. Some saw this as an addition to medical treatment and some saw it as a replacement, but it was believed that what you think determines your cancer prognosis. And there were lots of popular stories to prove this, moving tales of lives saved by positive thinking, people who were rigidly cheerful and dogmatically optimistic. Clearly, something was happening to affect health in these exceptional cancer patients, but it was not so simple as positive thinking.

The second belief was that people gave themselves cancer because they were depressed, thought little of themselves, or were punishing themselves for a bad childhood. What's more, if they didn't get rid of their bad thinking patterns, it was warned, they would make their cancer spread and they would die, probably because they subconsciously wanted to.

This belief came out of the research that had found that cancer and other serious illnesses are more likely to occur after a major loss, such as a spouse or a loved one dying, and that such occurrence is even more likely if there were profound early losses in childhood.

There are connections between immune function and loss, but the interaction is a complicated one. Margaret Kemeny has found, for example, that HIV-positive men are more likely to develop disease symptoms if they lose a loved one, but this is only if previously they had a fatalistic attitude.[6]

Self-blame in sick people seems intuitively wrong to compassionate listeners, and one of the most painful experiences for a competent, caring professional is to hear a woman dealing with the misery of breast cancer ask, "Why did I need to give myself this disease?" For a psychologist it is particularly disheartening to see the power of psychology used against people instead of in the service of healing. It is not surprising that the application of psychological principles and techniques to boost cancer treatment fell into disrepute after this period.

The consequences of this kind of cancer-as-self-punishment approach were unfortunate, for they made patients judge themselves on the correctness of their thinking and set up cancer as a test of character instead of a miserable affliction. Some patients felt that they had to renovate their personalities in order to recover from their disease.

A whole series of programs developed to help patients achieve the "right" frame of mind. They included various mental exercises that would supposedly rid patients of the wish to do themselves damage. For some patients, the attempt to rigidly control thoughts and feelings led to obsessive-compulsive disorders in which great anxiety and anguish were generated by the drive to have only certain thoughts and to banish others.

A second, more insidious result was to make cancer patients withdraw emotionally and hide their feelings in fear of revealing a flawed character. Even when they didn't believe they had caused their disease, people dealing with cancer were likely to withhold their feelings in fear of being told that they should think positively or look at the bright side.

The tendency to adopt a facade of cheerfulness and courage around others was thus greatly reinforced. This would also protect the patient from suggestions and advice, as well as the offering of books and anecdotes about how cancer is cured with the correct state of mind. To show negative feelings made one seem out of control or weak and might upset others as well. The approach to dealing with cancer changed from trying to be self-analytical to trying to be strong.

The masquerade that patients often adopted was reassuring to them as well as to friends and family; the appearance of strength, energy, and optimism often convinced everybody that all was well. The patient could feel strong at taking care of those emotionally dependent on her and believe that she was fighting cancer by controlling herself and not giving in to her feelings, a sure sign of good character. Others could feel that their friend or family member with cancer was coping well. Unfortunately, all this effort sometimes depleted a woman's energy reserves, deprived her of the chance to relieve her feelings, and separated her from those whom she needed.

When I first saw Jan and Tom, they seemed like the ideal middle-aged couple, trim, athletic and carefully dressed. But Jan complained of constant obsessive thoughts about her breast cancer of two years ago. Her husband, Tom, reassured me that she was fine and that there were no further signs of problems. As part of a routine evaluation, I asked them to leave a tape recorder going when they had dinner together. Their casual conversation revealed a pattern of two frightened people trying to dam up the powerful forces of vitality:

Tom: *"Are you upset about something?"*

Jan: [*long silence*]

Tom: *"Don't you feel well?"*

Jan: *"I'm okay"*

Tom: *"What is it?"*

Jan: *"You'll just get upset."*

Tom: *"Don't start that again."*

Jan: *"I can't help it."*

Tom: *"You have to be strong."*

Jan: *"But I can't stop thinking about it."*

Tom: *"You have to. Do you want to get sicker?"*

Jan: [*crying*]

The tape illustrated how the reactions of others can cause us to alter the way that we deal with our emotions. When Jan experienced the normal worries that occur following breast cancer treatment, she tried to keep them to herself, although they showed in her silence and abbreviated speech.

Subject to his own anxieties, Tom tried to solve their common problem by blocking off emotional expression. Like Jan, he was afraid of a recurrence of breast cancer, but he was also afraid of his wife's feelings.

After a good deal of work, Tom learned new ways to deal with feelings, both his own frightened feelings and Jan's. When he sensed his wife's anxiety, he learned the habit of saying, "Good, I'm glad you have some feelings and you're talking about them. This is life." As he relaxed, Jan began to feel more energetic and vital, which he found reassuring. They both noticed that the more open they became about their feelings, the more transient their feelings became. Fear, anxiety, sadness, once put into words, petered out and gave way to fresh perspectives. Only when feelings were dammed up did they remain static.

The most serious consequence of using energy to avoid our emotions is that as women we lose a sense of ourselves. Women know themselves by speaking about feelings and hearing others' responses. In connection with other people, women emerge from within themselves and speak with their unique voice. When a woman is emotionally silent, it can begin to feel like everything inside her is empty and dead. In giving voice to feelings, we stir our own vitality and are more alive in relating to others.

Perhaps most importantly, spending all of our energy trying to suppress feelings and hide them from others can produce a sense of loss of yourself, as though the real person has died. When you're fighting cancer, it's not good to feel that a part of you is dying, as David Spiegel often points out.

Restoring Your Feeling Parts

It helps to see emotional reactivity as a health habit and expressing feelings as a way to feel and act more alive. Bad thoughts don't cause cancer, and good thoughts don't cure it, but expressing them all clears the way for the body to be at maximum strength.

A healthy human organism is built to process lots of things. We take in food and deposit waste, we breathe in air and expel carbon dioxide and water vapor, we register events and we emote. All of these processes need to take their natural route, and if we inter-fere with any of them, we block up the whole system and strain it. When you're dealing with cancer, you want the whole system to be working as smoothly as possible so that it can work in tandem with treatment.

When any of the natural body processes is blocked, treatments for cancer are less effective. So getting your emotions taken care of is just one more form of housekeeping and personal hygiene.

Our culture has a lot of silly beliefs about feelings. One major premise is that if you ignore emotions such as anger or anxiety, then they'll go away, an approach about as successful as ignoring the IRS. This is a masquerade we do for ourselves, like children pretending that they don't have to use the bathroom, with the re-sult that everybody else notices what we believe doesn't show. In the end, the only person that we really fool is ourselves.

If you have breast cancer, you may feel inclined to keep your feelings to yourself and to try to pretend to others that everything is fine. This may help your self-respect and give you a greater sense of control temporarily. You may also feel that you put up a good front for others and that you don't upset them, so you can feel like a good friend or family member.

You may even find that you tell yourself that breast cancer is really no problem, that if you don't think about it and don't talk about it, it won't bother you. The result is that people around you will admire your courage and dignity, but you will lose touch with your real feelings and your inner core. You are also far more likely to have strong physical symptoms of all kinds, with sudden emo-tional reactions that ambush you, like when you start crying at television commercials. Telling yourself that feelings are wrong or dangerous is the foundation for enduring depression and anxiety, but these self-messages can become so abbreviated and automatic that you fail to notice them.

What's more, some research has shown that patients who are very calm and say they had little need for adjustment to cancer had poorer outcomes than those who were upset.[7]

It will help if you begin to look at thoughts and feelings differ-ently. Let's define dangerous thoughts as those that make you feel frightened, sad, angry, or frustrated. They are the ones that are upsetting to think about, that make you feel stirred up.

Instead of seeing these as threatening or poisonous, let's imagine that they are a kind of Drano for your system, an acidic cleanser that will wash out all of the stuff that blocks you up. Any time that these thoughts cross your mind, you can think, "Ah, a good time to wash out the pipes and get things moving in there!"

The stronger these thoughts are, the more useful they will be, because if they are very weak, you will be able to put them aside and that won't help much. Remember when you were a kid and you didn't like to take a bath, and maybe one day you got to smelling so bad that you had to take a shower? The same process works with dangerous thoughts.

Troublesome thoughts give us an outline of the work that needs to be done inside ourselves and save us from sealing off our insides under a cover of false serenity. Cancer becomes more frightening and lonesome when we ignore feelings and when we fail to grow in the ways that any traumatic experience offers.

Helen had been preoccupied with the conviction that she was going to die after she was diagnosed with a recurrence of breast cancer. She canceled plans for a long-awaited trip because she felt that she was too upset to enjoy it. She forced herself to try to think optimistically, but this only stirred more thoughts about dying.

She became increasingly quiet around her friends, which they took to mean that she wasn't feeling well, and they began to act as though her condition was worsening. This in turn raised her anxiety level even further. As she became more obsessed, she made plans for her own death. She examined her insurance, worked on redrafting her will, and even went to a funeral parlor to prearrange her funeral.

At the time there was a funeral in progress, and she stopped to watch the grieving of family and friends. It struck her that there was a very clear difference between living people and dead people, and she knew which she was. Although she was obviously alive, she had been practicing being dead and mourning herself.

When the funeral director tactfully asked how much planning time for the funeral would be available, she remembered her doctor's optimism that she would be alive for her seventieth birthday the year after next, and she told the director that she wasn't yet ready to make plans. Feeling foolish but full of vitality, she went home, put away her will, and got out her travel brochures.

Change your view of yourself: Begin to picture yourself as someone who can endure a wide range of thoughts and feelings without being wrecked. You may feel emotionally fragile after going through the shock of cancer diagnosis and treatment, but you've survived this far, haven't you? Begin to tell yourself that you are sturdy, enduring, and steady, and that thoughts and feelings don't have the same power as events.

Albert Ellis teaches patients to get over their flying phobia by having them think about crashing in a plane and being blown to smithereens. After awhile, they get used to their thoughts and stop reacting to them; they also stop being afraid of crashes.[8] They begin to see themselves as unable to control everything that happens in the world and as more tolerant of the misfortunes and upsets that occur randomly in this life.

Keep a record of your thoughts: Begin a list or journal that identifies all your thoughts, but in particular the ones that cause you anxiety, sadness, or anger, and keep track over a period of time. Remind yourself of the good effect on the immune system that Dr. Pennebaker's students experienced after writing down strong feelings daily, and give yourself the same opportunity. Begin to notice patterns in the times that the thoughts occur, for example, at bedtime, on waking, when you go for treatment, and also notice when they are not there.

Let the anguish go. Breast cancer is no fun, and it causes most women to feel very bad. If you put these negative feelings into words, you diminish their impact, but if you hold them inside, it intensifies these feelings and makes it all the harder.

One woman did this by creating signs and banners and hanging them all over her apartment:

I HATE BREAST CANCER

THIS STINKS!

Say your thoughts out loud and listen to yourself: As we speak aloud, our own ears are listening, and our brain evaluates what it hears. This is a fundamentally different process from thinking thoughts inside our heads, where something else happens. Silly as it may feel, take a walk or a shower when you have strong feelings and put into spoken words what you feel. Let your mind work on what it hears, edit it, and reformulate it as a way to introduce change into the system.

When you hear yourself saying, for example, "This is awful!

I'm so tired I can't do anything!" your ears will absorb the words, and then your brain will go to work. That same brain that has gotten you through all of the challenges of your life will be listening to those words and reformulating them, saying things like:

"Well, I'm talking, so it's not really true that I can't do anything."

"I can't do all the things I used to and that's too bad."

"It is too bad, but it's not that bad."

"I am really tired, but I can do some things."

"I have been really tired before in my life, and I've gotten through it."

"I wonder if there's anything I can do about being so tired?"

This process doesn't happen when thoughts stay as thoughts, but it does happen when they are put into words spoken aloud. It works best when thoughts are spoken to a caring listener. A thinking mind challenges most of what it hears, and by voicing your feelings, you give your intellect a chance to do its work.

In looking at your upsetting thoughts, the purpose is not to wallow in misery or fear. Rather it is to let the normal process of your reasoning ability do its work and not to impede it with some silly ideas about your integrity being vested in remaining calm and composed.

Keeping mental anguish, despair, or fear inside yourself rarely does you any good, and it can make you feel as though you're not really living life if you can't be yourself. You begin to doubt whether any of your normal and natural reactions to things are right, and it may even seem that your reactions could do you harm.

Does this mean that we have no control over cancer when it happens to us? That our thoughts have nothing to do with how the disease goes? Should we just turn ourselves over to the medical folks and do what they say?

We have a great deal of control over what happens to us, and we can do much to optimize our chances for health with breast cancer. But we must begin with a healthy respect for body and mind. Instead of treating our body as a failure and our mind as a threat, we need to see them as valiantly fighting for their own preservation and entitled to our respect and support for their own healthy response to an unhealthy assailant.

Sadness or Depression?

When we suffer a serious illness that frightens us, disrupts our lives, upsets our relatives, depletes our finances, and causes pain and suffering, a healthy reaction is real sadness. Who could be happy in the face of such circumstances? Sadness is the psyche's way of reorganizing, regrouping, and integrating new information to make a better projection of what to do in the future.

Over a period of time, sadness teaches that life has changed and that thinking and perspective must also change, often for the better. Sadness doesn't go away fast, and you can't speed up the process, but you can do a great deal to ease it along.

When we were children and we developed chicken pox, Mom probably figured on two weeks home from school, oatmeal baths, and distractions to keep us happy until we healed. The same orientation is helpful with sadness. If you respect the organism's healthy response and give it time to do its work, then your sadness will lessen.

There are always remedies and comforts for sadness. The ancient ways of soothing, pleasing, and distracting allow a tired and tense body to find relief from worry and strain. Good friends and creative loved ones can be most helpful when asked to help with comforting, which is a part of healing.

In an experimental laboratory, when rats are shocked in one box, they learn to jump to another box to avoid the shock. But when they cannot avoid the shock no matter what they do, they cower helplessly in their cage. Later on, when there is the opportunity to escape, they are unable to take it, because they have been conditioned to respond in a helpless manner. When the same animals are subjected to implanted tumors, the animals that have learned to be helpless have far less strength at resisting them than other animals who have learned to deal successfully with shock.[9] When we are conditioned to be helpless, our body's defenses don't work as well.

Depression is a different business from sadness, even though it can feel a good deal like sadness, and it has sadness as one component. But depression is more insidious, a kind of rot in our faith in the cosmos that is pervasive and drains us of all energy and power. It lasts and lasts and affects our decisions as well as our activity level.

There are many times in the course of a lifetime when sadness is the dominant feeling, usually when there is loss or disappointment. Sadness is a reaction to a loss, a reflection of the change in one's life because of an altered state of affairs.

Depression, however, is an altered view of *oneself*, so that a self who used to be capable and powerful, able to reach for those things that make life full and rich, is now perceived as helpless, with all its efforts futile. Sometimes this perception of yourself is the reflection of a lifetime of frustration and disappointment, in which all the major things you wanted have been unreachable. Under these circumstances, people learn that they have little impact on what happens in life and that their efforts and plans make no difference.

According to researcher Martin Seligman, depression is learned helplessness, that is, passivity or withdrawal that we develop after having been in many circumstances where our efforts had no impact on events.[10] Many events in our lives can lead to helplessness. Perhaps a parent drank and seemed beyond the influence of your efforts to please, or you may have had real frustration at learning in school, where academic success never happened no matter how hard you worked. Or it may have come from a marriage where being a good wife didn't seem to have any impact on your husband's behavior.

Seligman would say that these kinds of experiences teach you helplessness as a conditioned response, so that when you come upon a challenging situation, you don't think up good ideas or get working to gather information, but rather you become passive and retreat, as though it didn't make any difference what you did.

Helplessness and Health

We all retreat a little when we are either sad or depressed, but why is this important in breast cancer? Look at what happens in a nursing home when patients are either active or passive in terms of their health. When researchers Langer and Rodin changed the perceived helplessness of nursing home patients, they noticed some interesting results. They told half of the building's elderly residents that they had the power to change their days to make them more fulfilling and comfortable. They could do this by rearranging the room decorations, by choosing entertainment, and by selecting other fulfilling and rewarding activities.[11]

The other half of the building residents got the same nice things, but through no effort of their own — they were just given to them, along with a little speech about how much they would enjoy them. When the researchers looked at everybody a year and a half later, they found that the group that had power over the things around them were happier, more active, and more alert, and, most surprisingly, they had only half the mortality rate of the other group. It seemed as though the helplessness of the other group to provide for themselves and to make good things occur in some way affected their ability to survive.

Why should helplessness make a difference in health when it is an idea, a feeling, not a state of the internal organs? There are some obvious reasons: If you feel powerful, feeling as though what you do makes a difference, then you'll probably do more, like taking your medicine carefully, taking good care of your general health, getting exercise and good nutrition. Helplessness in contrast disengages the mind, causing us to shrink from challenge and draining the spirit of its vitality.

You may also more aggressively look for the best treatments and solutions to problems to try to maximize the success of your treatment. There is substantial evidence that while helplessness reduces the power of the immune system, acting powerfully increases immune functioning.

Helplessness as a habitual response to challenge doesn't work very well for people, and it works very poorly for breast cancer patients. When Sandra Levy looked at breast cancer recurrence, she found that it was related to a number of indicators of helplessness, which seemed to predict the length of disease-free periods. So strong were the findings that Levy and Seligman are combining forces to use a twelve-session therapeutic intervention to change hopeless/helpless problem responses in cancer patients.[12]

But wait, this begins to sound like you have to think right or the cancer will spread, doesn't it? That if you let gloomy images into your head then you'll kill yourself? Not at all, because acting alive allows for *all* feelings and even encourages them as grist for the mill. Far from being scared of upsetting thoughts, it warmly welcomes all aspects of your personality and cognitive creativity. Bad thoughts, scary thoughts, sad thoughts, angry thoughts are all fine as long as you express them vigorously and then act energetically to make your situation better.

Vitality can mean heart-gripping anguish, towering rage, nail-chewing anxiety, or rapturous delight. But above all, it means feelings.

Good attitudes don't come from inspiration, faith, passivity, or an absence of thoughts. All the good attitudes we've developed in a lifetime have come from decisions followed by action. When we were learning to brush our teeth, most of us had the attitude that it was a waste of time and one more thing that parents forced on us. After we practiced it a thousand times, our attitude changed and we began to think it was a pretty good idea. So it is with depression, that if we develop the habit of expressing it and then acting productively on it, our attitudes will change over time.

To deal effectively with depression, sad and helpless feelings need expression, not just a bland statement of emotion, but colorful, emphatic expression: descriptions of deep, wrenching sadness, overwhelming fear, or paralyzing hopelessness, expressions of doom that have vitality and life, tears, anger, mourning, whining. This needs to happen until our feelings begin to bore us, until we feel that we've used them up and we are spent. We need to talk about emotions, write about them, sing about them, cry about them, and generally give them life. Feel the feelings again and again until the sting is gone and you start to get distracted when you talk about them.

When you feel emotionally cleaned out and emptied, you need to make creative decisions about what is best for you and what will optimize your health chances.

After giving vent to emotions and applying judgment to the problem, you need to *do* what you have decided. Often when we choose a course of action, it can feel like the work is done, so that making a list of chores gives us a feeling of completion. But this is just a form of procrastination, so that we assume that things are done if we think about them. But you need to *do* the behavior after planning it, or you don't get the results, and thinking about doing behavior gives different results from actually doing it.

Dealing with feelings is important for good health generally and will make you feel happier and more able to get what you want in life. But when you have cancer, it is particularly important. You can't afford to use up your system's energy by repressing feelings or developing elaborate rituals so that you don't have to think about emotions. Cancer stirs up such strong feelings that if you don't deal with them effectively, they clog up the works, and with cancer, you need every part of you at maximum power.

If you think that you can deal with feelings by not letting them bother you, not paying any attention to them, or not giving in to them, try this experiment. Decide that for the next twenty-four hours, you will ignore all the feelings that tell you when you have to use the toilet. At the end of that period, analyze how well you used the hours, how effectively your day went, and how happy and comfortable you were. And be prepared to clean up a mess.

Developing Good Mental Housekeeping

So how do you develop good mental hygiene habits for taking care of everyday feelings and cancer feelings? Steven Greer at the Royal Marsden Hospital in London, a man with a great deal of compassion, has worked in the area of breast cancer for decades. He has been concerned with the mental anguish that women experience when they are diagnosed and treated for breast cancer. He has found that each patient copes with breast cancer in a manner uniquely her own.

Some breast cancer patients he observed are very strong and brave and accept their lot gracefully, while others "hit the ground running," ready to do battle in every direction for their own health. They may be angry, sad, or anxious, but they are, above all, busy and active. Recently, Greer published the results of a fifteen-year study of women's attitudes and breast cancer; he found that women with "fighting spirit," as he termed it, lived longer and had a better disease course than women who were more resigned.[13] In his view, the way that we see things determines how we react to them, and we learn our reactions over time, both from our own experiences and from what the culture teaches us.

For all of us, our mental closet is generally messy and contains lots of old, ill-fitting ideas and beliefs, as well as new things that we haven't unpacked and put away yet. There are also quite a few random associations, misconceptions, and bits of erroneous information that have been tossed in there. It's surprising that any of us get through our lives so efficiently with so much mental clutter, but we usually muddle through.

Greer says that we also have lots of sloppy mental patterns that are made up of automatic thoughts and distortions of what we see and hear. These affect our lives in many ways, and they get us into trouble. One of the most common troublesome thought patterns is what he calls *mind reading,* which is what we do when we figure we know what other people are thinking. Mind reading is reflected in the following:

"I know exactly what you're feeling."

"The doctor would think I was really vain if I asked about reconstruction."

The best illustration of mind reading comes from a couple I saw in my office who were in their eighties; they had been mind reading for sixty years of marriage. He knew that she liked the window shut when she slept, and so he left it shut when they were in bed, even though he loved fresh air. She knew he liked the window shut because he shut it every night, and so she never told him that she liked it open. They finally heard each other's thoughts directly and made a different arrangement. Now the window is open, and they both sleep better after sixty years of annoyance.

Often our thoughts are part of a continuous commentary on the day, and they may include many errors that give rise to attitudes that direct our behavior. But the mental commentary is so continuous that it is like background music that we rarely notice and never critique for accuracy. That's one of the reasons that talking about feelings out loud helps to correct them, because then our intellect gets to work and begins to make corrections. It's the same reason that authors do best when they read their work out loud, preferably with others listening. When we think only in isolation, without hearing ourselves clearly, we slip easily into the same habit of thinking. It's awfully hard to deal with something invisible and soundless, like our thoughts.

Greer found that with breast cancer patients habits of think-ing have a profound effect on how they feel and how they make choices in dealing with their illness. Let's see what happens when a woman has another thought habit, that of *labeling*. This means that when she thinks about things, she's in the habit of sum-marizing them with a name or class label. The woman next door is a *gossip*, the mayor is a *crook*, and the daughter's boy-friend is a *drip*. The labels are usually judgmental and negative; there is criticism in the words, and they sting if said aloud.

"I'm such a wimp," such a woman might conclude when she feels tearful during chemotherapy. Rather than looking openly at her feelings, she abruptly dismisses them as a failure in character and does not ask for the help that would lessen her ordeal.

These thought habits develop early in life and usually in the si-lence of our own minds, although we can also learn them from parents or brothers and sisters. When you were a girl, your mind was very busy trying to figure out how the world around you worked. There wasn't much information, and the assumptions you made could not have been based on careful and mature rea-soning, so the conclusions adopted were certain to be limited. Sometimes the information you got was wrong, drawn from other children who didn't know much.

But the mind is a relentless hypothesizer, constantly trying to figure out what causes what. Why do some kids like me and others don't? Why is Mom happy today when she was sad yesterday? Why do they let me have ice cream today when they wouldn't yesterday? On and on our thoughts go, drawing conclusions and formulating hypotheses. If we have had a lot of unhappy experi-ences in life, we may develop the mental habit of making negative predictions, such as "Nothing ever turns out right for me" or "It will all get messed up in the end."

If we say these things out loud when we first begin to think in these ways and test the logic of them, we get more efficient in our thinking. But often they remain unspoken in our minds.

The Cost of Sloppy Mental Habits

You might think that you would shy away from habitual gloomy conclusions like this, but the mind hates uncertainty and feels safer if it can predict accurately, even if it is predicting unhappy outcomes. These reasoning habits, if they work well enough or seem to, get ingrained and become part of our view of the world. You probably don't even realize that you have these habits. Most people don't because they usually don't stop to think about how they are thinking.

If you have breast cancer, these patterns become a problem, because they are likely to overload your system and stress you even further than the disease does. If you're in the habit of expecting the worst and making negative predictions by habit, for example, you may find yourself thinking, "Why bother with anything — I have cancer and I'll be dead soon anyway, no matter what the doctor says." It would be equally unrealistic to say, "I have cancer, but it's no problem and I'll soon get rid of it." This constitutes denial and serves to make a serious situation more difficult by minimizing it. Our thinking needs to include all information to make an accurate assessment of our situation. To think, "I have a serious disease that will take energy and effort to fight, and I have a good chance of reestablishing my health if I work at it" is realistic and useful.

Sometimes we're in the habit of screaming at ourselves internally, talking to ourselves in a way that is upsetting and unnerving, and we may occasionally explode to others:

"This is the most horrible thing that could happen to me!"

"I can't stand this! I can't deal with this!"

It is important to express aloud this sort of excessive reaction so that it can be refined and qualified and so that it does not internally paralyze you. When you talk over your feelings, you break up this sort of thinking, for example, by substituting:

"I certainly don't like what is happening to me!"

"I hate having to deal with something challenging!"

Talking about feelings saves you from constant alarm bells in your mind so that you can save your energy for real emergencies. In the first few weeks of having breast cancer, you may feel as if alarm bells go off with every new thought, but this is only the result of shock and trauma and the inclination to avoid expression of feelings.

You can cool down some of the internal screaming by voicing it and challenging your exaggerated conclusions. Is this really the worst thing on earth that could happen? Are there really no ways to deal with it at all? If we write down all of the most terrible aspects of what is occurring, and do so in lurid detail, describing how horrible things are, how dreadful these events are, how awful, how unfair, and how this is the worst that could happen to a person, our thinking changes. At some point we run down and begin to see the situation as one we dislike very much, but one that is, ultimately, manageable. This is where upsetting thoughts are most helpful, because they act as a laxative for the system. If we use them, they clear us out and help us reach a state of mind in which our good judgment can operate.

You've been sad or worried or annoyed at other times in your life, and you know how best to deal with these situations. But if instead of being sad or worried or annoyed you tell yourself you are as miserable as a person could be in life, or you are scared to death, or you are enraged, then these conceptualizations freeze all of the efficient responses you've learned in the past. When you express them out loud, your reasoning mind begins to cut them down to size.

"They're cutting off my health insurance at work. I'll end up in the streets, sick and cold and lost."

"They're not actually cutting off all my health insurance, but they are cutting down the benefits."

"This doesn't affect me right now, but if I need a lot of treatment, or a bone marrow transplant, they may not cover it."

"But I don't need that now. And what I do need, they still cover. But there is a larger co-payment. And I don't like that."

"I guess it's not actually so bad."

"Big deal."

Distorted responses based on powerful feelings can cause distorted thoughts rather than stirring you to productive action. What's more, without challenge, these thoughts get thought over and over again in the silence of your mind, and they then seem more and more true. To say them aloud tends to shrink them down to size and force you to straighten out your thinking.

When you're cleaning out your mental closet and sorting through your thinking habits, the following will be helpful:

1. Talk about your thoughts to other people and listen to what they say. You may not agree with their perspective, but then you probably won't agree totally with yourself either.

2. Do some individual psychotherapy with a trained counselor. Such people are trained to understand thinking and dysfunctional thought patterns that get in the way, and it will help to be in an arrangement where you regularly sit down and clean out your mental closet a bit at a time. The therapist that you work with in this way is not a doctor who is treating your sick psyche, but is rather a partner in helping you to tidy up your problem-solving thought patterns for maximum efficiency. This sort of therapy works on identifying your thinking tendencies and the beliefs they generate, and then testing them out and using the new insights gained. Remember, though, that most of us would prefer to *think* about doing this sort of work rather than actually *doing* it; you don't get the results unless you actually *do* it.

3. Check your thinking as you go through the day, and observe how you usually form conclusions. Are you in the habit, for example, of personalizing bad outcomes and assuming that if something went wrong, it's because you blew it? This shows up for parents when they assume that any problem or shortcoming in their children is attributable to something they did or did not do. Keep track of how you think about things, particularly your illness, and write down your thoughts at the times they occur. Take a look at the total of these thoughts and check out the mental climate in which you live. Is is a warm and happy place?

4. Practice including helpful instructions in your thought patterns, for example, reminding yourself that bad things happen to good people or noticing when you feel sad or worried or angry, and reassuring yourself that your healthy psyche is hard at work on this new challenge. Restate your excessive or illogical self-statements, so that instead of saying,

"That ache in my back must be the start of a new cancer that will spread and kill me."

you say,

"Human bodies sure do have lots of aches and pains, and I never noticed them so much before I had cancer."

Learned Liveliness

Once when my cousin was sixteen, she was dumped by her boy-friend, a black-haired charmer with devilish eyes that were always looking for new conquests.

"What's the point of it all?" she sobbed to our great-grandmother. "Why go through all this? You just die in the end anyhow."

Our great-grandmother, an energetic woman of ninety-four, beamed down at her and said gently: "Why, for all the adventures and the excitement, my dear."

Sometimes our thinking has great vitality, and it opens the way to fuller living and more vivid experience. At times, however, our thinking patterns needlessly drain off our energy. Steven Greer is interested in the habits of thought that generate our attitudes and beliefs about the world. Martin Seligman is also interested in our thinking, but his concern is more with the style of our thinking patterns.

Our view of the world, and our place in it, is always the result of the way we look at things, the beliefs we have that are not prov-able one way or another. Einstein said that the great question for modern science was whether the universe is friendly or not, and this is indeed the question that we all try to answer in our own thinking.

Seligman says that through many early experiences we develop a worldview, a set of overall expectations, that colors our thinking about any particular set of events. He has described this as our *explanatory style,* the way that we have of making sense of what is happening around us and to us. Our explanatory style determines how we react to challenges, how much energy, intelligence, creativity, and courage we bring to a problem. It has nothing to do with our feelings or emotions, however. It is a way of thinking, reasoning, and analyzing events and planning future behavior.

If our thinking style leads to more efficient decisions and productive behavior, then it is a real source of strength. If, on the other hand, it traumatizes us further and increases the stress load, then it needs changing.

When something happens to you like being diagnosed with breast cancer, you may see it in one of two ways. You may feel that breast cancer is bound to happen to a certain number of women each year and you had the misfortune to be one of them, or you may feel that it happened to you because of something that you did or didn't do, for example, not doing enough BSEs (breast self-examinations) or eating too much fat. When we explain events by our actions or our character rather than random happenings, this is an *internal* style.

If something negative happens to you, then for your own peace of mind you have to decide whether what is happening is a trend or a one-time event. You may feel that getting breast cancer is a piece of random bad luck and that you're usually luckier. Or you may feel that it is the beginning of a long chain of bad events, and that bad happenings are a *stable* part of your life.

The third part of your explanatory style involves whether you see bad events as just one part of your life or as more comprehensive. You may feel that having cancer is bad, but at least you don't have heart disease. Someone else may feel that having breast cancer means that her health is ruined, her life is ruined, and everything is ruined, which is a *global* perception of what is happening.

These three ways of thinking — seeing bad events as internally caused, as stable, and as having a global rather than a limited effect — make up what Dr. Seligman calls *pessimistic explanatory style*.

There is really no way to tell whether bad events are actually attributable to a person or enduring or all-encompassing. These are just opinions, and we know that most bad events are caused by a multitude of factors. If my son gets mad and punches me, for example, I can say:

"It's my fault for how I raised him." (internally caused)

"He will always treat me like this." (stable)

"This will ruin his whole life, and mine." (global)

But I could just as confidently say:

"He lost his temper." (not caused by me)

"He can probably learn better self-control." (so this won't happen again)

"This will be a problem in his relationships." (unless he takes up boxing)

Having a pessimistic style is likely to make you more unhappy when bad things happen, and it might even get you depressed or lethargic in seeking good solutions to problems. If you are in the habit of seeing misfortunes as your own fault, maybe because somebody always tells you they are, and as occurring forever and everywhere, it will be tough to whip up any enthusiasm for trying new solutions to problems. More importantly, such a habit can make you hide your feelings out of shame and emotionally lock yourself in. As it turns out, explanatory style has far-ranging effects on many aspects of our lives.

The Effects of Your Explanatory Style

In a research project that tried to sort out how pessimistic explanatory style affects a person's life, Seligman looked at health as one arena where thinking might have an impact. He found that when someone has pessimistic thinking habits as a young person, it is a good predictor of health problems in middle age.

There is some evidence that the immune system is weakened by pessimistic explanatory style, and there are other effects as well: It reinforces passivity because it assumes that bad events will continue regardless of what we do, and it lowers our faith in ourselves since we cause bad things to happen by our deficiencies, our omissions, or our character.

When college students with pessimistic explanatory style get colds, they are less likely to take measures that will clear up the cold quickly, such as getting rest, drinking fluids, and sleeping. Perhaps pessimistic style does its greatest damage in disconnecting us from those activities that require energy and initiative on our own behalf. We are much more likely to withdraw into ourselves and stoically endure.

Pessimistic style does not cause cancer, and optimistic thinking cannot cure cancer. But learned optimism leads to those habits of behavior and problem-solving that are more effective in maintaining and achieving good health. Optimistic thinking is also a generally happier way to spend one's days.

Explanatory style can take a few events and conclude that all events will turn out the same way, not so much because of the events, but because the person has been proven to be helpless and hopeless. This kind of logic shortcut is no different than deciding that all men are fickle because one is disappointing.

What happens physically when we feel hopeless and helpless? In animals, events perceived as uncontrollable lead to suppression of animal immune reactions and more tumor growth.[14] Does the same thing happen to people? At the University of Pennsylvania, Martin Seligman, Leslie Kamen-Siegel, and their colleagues looked at a group of elderly people, aged sixty-two to eighty-two, to see if explanatory style affects health.[15] The elderly folks were interviewed, and then their conversation was analyzed. Researchers classified their statements according to whether they personalized bad events, they felt they were global, or they seemed permanent.

Using blood tests, researchers then did a comprehensive profile of each person's immune function, making sure that the folks were healthy and had not had any recent life stresses. In order to clarify their results, they ruled out alcohol intake, sleep patterns, weight changes, age, health, and depression. Their findings were the same as those for animals. People who usually explain disappointments by blaming themselves and who see them as repeated and all-inclusive have lower immune measures.

How can you change mental habits so that there is more optimism and more opportunity for creativity and productive action? It won't work to pretend that everything is fine and to be determined to show only a happy face. Optimism is not idiocy, and neither is it denial or wishful thinking. It is merely a thought style that energizes our systems so that we do what we need and enjoy our days.

People with optimistic style have lots of unhappy times in their lives and they are not protected from injustice and misery, but these things don't do much damage, since the events are not seen as personally caused and so self-esteem stays together. In addition, these folks can be much more hopeful and have faith in the future because in their view bad things are only occasional and temporary. It's easier to forget about trouble if you see it as happening only in limited parts of your life.

Perhaps the major difference between optimists and others is that optimists are optimistic about *themselves*. When bad things happen, they don't feel like they are at fault or defeated, and that helps everyone. So how do you get to this point?

It will help if you test out your private thoughts and conclusions so that you can make a new determination about whether the universe is friendly to you and whether you consider bad things as random misfortunes that are temporary and limited in their impact.

Having Arguments inside Your Head

Think of your head as a courtroom where you are the judge hearing a dispute between two opposing sides. On the one side is the prosecutor, a person with pessimistic explanatory style, who is trying to prove his case about your cancer. His arguments consist of statements that are aimed at having you believe that you are the sole cause of all life's difficulties and that this will never change. He starts off with this:

> *"It's your own damn fault that you got cancer, because of the food you ate [or your stress level, or your genes, or your bad judgment, or your freckles, or whatever]."*

Now let's hear the defense attorney, a person of optimistic explanatory style, make her case in your defense:

> *"What evidence is there that cancer is caused by these things?"*

> *"Did you intend to give yourself cancer?"*

> *"Have you behaved less responsibly than other people in your situation?"*

> *"If it's your fault that you got cancer, does that mean that we are all guaranteed not to get cancer if we don't do these things?"*

Now the prosecutor goes on:

"The misery that you're experiencing with breast cancer will never end."

"This is the way that life will be, forever."

"You'll never again be able to enjoy life."

Now the defense attorney gets enthusiastic, because she loves a fight she can win:

"Where is the evidence that the trouble in your life is never-ending?"

"Are there breast cancer patients who enjoy life after treatment?"

"Do people without breast cancer always enjoy life?"

"People with breast cancer die, and so does everybody else, and we all live with mortality, don't we?"

"Are you totally helpless, a victim of this disease forever, or is this a disruption and an inconvenience that will go through harder and easier periods?"

The pessimistic prosecutor is looking haggard at this point, because he can't manage to maintain any of his positions, and so he goes for one last pitch:

"Breast cancer has far-reaching effects, and it will change everything in your life."

"It will undermine every pleasure and good moment."

"It will affect all of your relationships and change the way everybody reacts to you."

"It will ruin your relationships, destroy your pleasures, make you hate your body, and spoil the beauty of life."

Now the defense is positively gleeful because the prosecutor is doing so poorly:

*"It will change **everything**? You still have to pay the paper boy the same, right?"*

"Does milk at the grocery store cost the same as before?"

"Things change continuously, and no day is the same as the last, but is your disease really so important that it changes everything?"

"Lots of things in life don't change, for example, the risk of your being killed by a drunken driver."

"Cancer, like heart disease or diabetes, has its effects, mainly when you feel ill or have a disrupted schedule, but you can't blame everything on cancer, and it is impossible to attribute all changes to cancer."

Having courtroom arguments inside your head is a good way to change old thought patterns, since you will be considering both sides and making a reasonable decision. But it starts with opening up, airing all our feelings, and giving voice to the turbulence inside. For it is the energy of our feelings that makes our brains wrestle with new ideas.

Developing Fighting Spirit

Steven Greer has found that women whose attitude toward their breast cancer was one of fighting spirit, as opposed to denial or stoic acceptance, did better with their treatment and lived longer. But how does one develop this attitude? Much of it comes from the beliefs one adopts.

Our beliefs are always adopted and are sustained by our thinking. When I was a child, nobody thought that exercise was good for girls, but now we believe differently, and our actions support our belief. Changing our beliefs requires flexibility in our thoughts, so that we don't assume the explanation for things is always the same: I caused it, it will always be this way, and it ruins everything.

Fighting spirit involves attitudes that focus on life as being alive. It is concerned with maximizing our pleasure in *this day*, energetically going after those things that we treasure, and moving on from difficult problems once we have done our best to solve them. Cancer is not a career, and it cannot substitute for a life well lived. Mortality is a real issue for all of us, cancer or not, and not just an ugly rumor. We need to plan appropriately and act as though we had limited time on this earth, rather than drifting and procrastinating. Living life fully makes us more resilient, and our anxieties about sickness and death diminish as we get more active on our own behalf.

There are many ordinary areas of our lives that can be improved, and we often put off what we can change out of sheer laziness or cowardice. Cancer can be the spur to get us moving, and we may find that the fear of illness is often sufficient justification to make us do things we would not otherwise dare. You might, for example, refuse to do things you hate for a change. Or you might dare to tell a friend how much you care about her. In those moments when we are down and feel we have nothing to lose, we may acquire the strength to make changes we should have made long ago.

Developing the Action Habit

Intellect is always impressive, and many of us have come to see our mental lives as deeply meaningful. But intellectualizers often miss the pleasure and richness of other forms of experiences, and what seems like invigorating and powerful thinking and analyzing can be nothing more than a rigid and self-serving mental monologue.

After we've thought and thought, how do we move to action? The action habit is not always easy to develop, since culture encourages a great deal of passivity. Our sports are usually spectator sports, our homes are dominated by televisions and computers, where we sit for long periods. Our greatest pastime is eating, which is far from an active endeavor.

Life changes through behavior, action, and our energetic manipulation of the world around us. It is this that gets our blood flowing and our hearts beating and lets us know that we are truly alive. When were you last truly scared at trying something new? When did you feel enormous self-doubt as you tested your limits? Remember when you were a kid getting up the courage to dive off a diving board? Where do you find those experiences now?

When I first began to go to continuing education programs as a psychologist, I became aware of the terror that routine jet flights set off in me. My hands and back would sweat; I would feel sick to my stomach, dizzy, and flushed. Often I would mindlessly jabber to the person who had the misfortune to sit next to me on the plane as I tried to avoid noticing the awful noises of flight.

Thinking that I couldn't be more frightened than I already was, I impulsively signed up for flying lessons. In the cabin (fifty inches wide) of a small plane, I thought I learned the true meaning of terror when we first went up. But I also learned of the earth's extraordinary beauty as the expanse of green fields and houses flattened out below us. I could see schoolchildren getting aboard their bus from three thousand feet up in the sky, roads like ribbons, and kites above the trees. The sunlight gleamed on the wings, the sky was endlessly blue, and it became clear why sometimes pilots talk about flying like a religion.

It was when I made several bad errors all at once that flying had its full impact on me. While practicing routine wing stalls, I dropped the plane into a nose down/spin position, the most dangerous mistake for a pilot to make. For in this attitude, a small plane begins to autorotate, to plummet downward like a maple seed.

As my instructor fought to regain control of a now wildly spiraling plane, the sky and the land flashed past the windows, and we were trapped in a spinning box. But in the face of overwhelming fear, I suddenly understood that this was as bad as it gets. This was it. The thing that frightens us most. I realized that dying is just dying, however it happens. You may not want it to happen, but you can't live your life as though you can prevent it or avoid it in the end. It's just one of the givens we live with, and not the worst. As Erica Jong put it, the greatest risk is to take no risks at all.

(My instructor had a very different reaction. "Wow," he said, "acrobatics!" and for him it was a great adventure. It's true that a brave man dies once, and a coward dies many times.)

Strong intellect and insight can give the illusion of action, and it can feel like our lives are changing because our perspective is changing, but it is only action that truly and lastingly changes us. So any new insight must be supported with action to be valid and enduring. Many of us are in the habit of solving problems by thinking about them a lot and analyzing them to death rather than experimenting with doing something different. This is likely to be a habit that develops long before cancer appears.

You need routines and schedules to insure action that can occur, and you need to plan realistically for your own energy and health levels. To decide to join a new ski club the day after getting chemotherapy is not the best planning, although neither is putting it off until you settle all this cancer business.

Decision-making will be important as you try to sort out what is truly in your best interest and what are merely old habits. It will help to identify areas where you feel a sense of competence and to develop your skill in these areas. Self-esteem is greatly enhanced if others, preferably strangers, benefit from your talents. In thinking about what brightens your days, you might ask, what is the bravest thing I can do?

When we try to make changes in our lives, we often run into disapproval or resistance from those around us who are accustomed to having us behave in certain ways. Assertive skills are often easier to learn in those moments when we feel great fear or desperation, for we can use these uncomfortable feelings to motivate us. If we are serene, we may not feel the impetus or the energy to risk new behaviors.

Assertive behaviors are not aggressive, because they are not aimed at doing damage to others, but they are instead focused on helping you to speak clearly and act effectively on your own behalf; surely there is no one else who can effectively do it for you. Assertive action can be graceful, polite, and charming and can make it easier for others to deal with you because you are clear.

Imagine the situation where a cancer patient and her friend are trying to be sensitive to each other rather than trying to speak for their own needs:

"Do you need a ride to the hospital today?"

"Well, that's okay. I can manage. You're probably busy, and I can get a cab."

"I don't mind, really. Do you want me to take you?"

"It's too much trouble. Don't mess up your day. I'll be okay."

"I hate to think of you trying to get a cab. Really...."

"That's okay. Don't worry about it. I don't mind going alone."

And so forth. By contrast, here's how assertiveness looks:

"Do you need a ride to the hospital today?"

"Yes, I do. Thanks a lot. That will be a real help."

When you speak assertively, you get into the habit of starting sentences with I, as in "I want...", "I prefer...", and then listening for what the other person wants, and trying to find a common solution that will give each of you some of what you want. It will also help if you speak clearly and stand by your own judgment:

"I think it would be helpful to talk with a sex therapist about changes in our relationship."

Sometimes you may need to repeat your requests:

"Yes, I know he has a busy schedule, but I still think that I need to talk directly with the doctor."

When you concentrate on your own feelings, you don't get upset by others' criticism, because you keep your eye on your goal:

"You may be right that I'm too emotional, but nevertheless I still want you to listen to my thoughts on this."

After you have cleaned out your mental closet, thrown out the stuff that is broken, and tried out some of the things you got long ago, you need ways of speaking that will express your own judgments and needs clearly and effectively. In order to do that, you need to understand yourself in the new context of breast cancer patient. For this experience stirs up a range of feelings and reactions, and it will help if you understand the emotional currents that ebb and flow during this period. In the next chapter we will explore specific ways to deal effectively with your feelings and thus limit the trauma of breast cancer treatment

Chapter Seven

Limiting the Trauma
of Breast Cancer Treatment:
I. Understanding How You Feel

In earlier decades, hospital treatment was considerably less sensitive than it is now. One hospital used to end parent visiting hours by having a policeman announce closing time on the pediatric ward. A kindergarten boy who was due to have his tonsils removed had a particularly bad time with his unfamiliar surroundings, and his parents tried to distract him with new toys, games, and anything at all that would calm him down.

When visiting time ended, he was a small, explosive ball of misery, and so his parents left quickly and without ado. When a nurse came in to take his temperature, he shrieked and kicked and blasted away against his unfair treatment.

The nurse, a mother herself, came back to check on him when her shift ended. He was weeping into his pillow, and he screamed at her when she reached to comfort him. So she began to tell him about operations on tonsils, even though he kept his face to the wall. She told him about the doctors and the operating room, with all the machines, large knobs, buttons, and lights. She told him about the masks the doctors wore, and the special medicine that makes it feel like its all happening to the bed instead of to you. She told him about the small, very sharp knives they use, and how it doesn't bleed more than a little cut.

Then she told him about all the kids who left their sick tonsils there, and how they felt and what they said. How some were scared, and some were mischievous, and how all of them went home with their parents and went back to playing and having

178

fun. She explained that they all missed their Moms, but the Moms always came back in the morning.

He listened very carefully, and it soothed him, her voice filling in the whole picture. He liked her and he liked her name, but mostly he liked knowing that he was like the other kids. He felt normal, like things were going the way they were supposed to, that people knew what they were doing, and that it made sense. He felt important, and he could see that his part in all this wasn't really so scary, and he could handle it. Most of all, he liked that she kept him company and that it made a difference to her how he felt.

So powerful an experience was it for him that years later when he became a great surgeon, famous for his sensitivity to patients, it still shaped him, and he understood the strong need of a patient to understand her feelings. When Josephine Hennik, the nurse, came to him for a lumpectomy, he was able to return the kindness.

The Emotional Response to Breast Cancer Treatment

It's worth understanding the stressful effects of cancer treatment and working to reduce them. This accomplishes several things. First, it allows you to tolerate higher levels of medical treatment, and it enhances the effectiveness of whatever treatment you get. It also limits the effect of stress on your immune system, which you want to keep strong and effective. We know, for example, that students have better immune function after summer vacation than they do during final exams.[1] If we can make the external pressures easier to deal with, we can lessen the pressure on our your insides. Second, limiting the impact of treatment helps you be more comfortable and allows you to get on with your life. It also limits the potential for emotional damage to the system and prevents you from becoming a psychological invalid.

We all repress upsetting feelings at times, when our judgment tells us to stay cool. You may feel a strong urge to express your outrage to a police officer writing you a ticket, for example, but chances are that your good judgment will help you to respond thoughtfully.

When a woman deals with breast cancer, it is never from the context of a problem-free life, for every life has its tensions. It may seem that the emotions stirred by diagnosis overshadow everything else, but other areas of life begin to exert their pull again after the immediate trauma subsides.

If you have always ignored feelings about problems and difficulties, it may seem natural to do so now, but it is worth trying a new tack and speaking thoughts and feelings to others. Medical organizations are not usually equipped to focus on your psychological state, however, and you may not find much emotional support in medical treatment. Cancer treatment can have a powerful impact on women because of limited sensitivity to emotional reactions and life patterns, and it may appear at first that you're expected to be tough and stoic:

> "I felt like it was clear what I was supposed to do. Like I was supposed to sit there in the waiting room, 'til like whenever they got around to me, then be good and act like it was no problem if they couldn't find a vein, 'cause God forbid you should ever hurt a tech's feelings, and then never, I mean never ask these poor, busy angels of mercy for a glass of water. Like it was a privilege to get treatment at their _____ clinic."

Sometimes our response to insensitivity is anger. More damaging is the response of resignation and passivity. Cure and comfort are intertwined, and the one supports the other. The more that your psychological state is improved, the more it contributes to your health.

A strong psychological stance is also likely to help you make treatment decisions more intelligently. Although we wish all medical care were the same, there are differences in diagnosis, treatment, and communication among doctors and patients with the same disease.[2] The quality of medical care varies, even within the same hospital, and it is important to arrange for the best treatment. To be strong and active on your own behalf, relating well to others and making clear judgments, can only help in healing.

It can be a challenge to deal with the many relationships that develop in cancer treatment. You will probably feel very dependent on medical caregivers, and it may seem dangerous to incur their displeasure for fear that you will get less than the full treatment needed. There are real power differences between human beings in this setting, and it is important to understand your own power.

Cancer treatment limits your sense of control. When treatment decisions are discussed and your opinions are asked, you feel that you have more control. In lesser matters, for example, if you are left in the waiting room for long periods or if you are ignored by nursing staff when you need help, you may feel differently. It is easy to be angered or demeaned by these experiences when you feel vulnerable.

For women it may be harder to deal with medical systems that offer so little opportunity for connection. Doctors, nurses, and staff are often uncomfortable dealing with cancer and the emotion it generates in them as well as in you, and you may feel discouraged from talking about how you feel. Other women, for example, nurses, who might ordinarily be more emotionally sensitive, will be restricted by their roles and responsibilities and may be more detached than they would be outside their jobs. This may suggest that you are a different person because people treat you differently, but in fact it is the setting that is novel.

When one person shuts down emotionally, others may do the same, and it is tempting in these circumstances to withdraw and pretend that everything is fine. You may try to reassure your doctor and the staff that the treatment is fine, assuming that they don't want to hear if you have problems.

Instead, you could try acting alive, calling over a weekend if you feel bad, telling your doctor in great detail how you feel, inquiring about medications or rearrangements of treatment to help you feel better, and complaining about how it feels if it doesn't feel good. Although this may seem like an imposition, most medical professionals are concerned about patient welfare, and it is riskier to say nothing.

Treatment acquaintances: When a woman becomes involved in treatment, the range of contacts widens. Women are more responsive than men to interpersonal influences, so experiencing either contacts with people or isolation from people is likely to exert a powerful influence on a woman throughout cancer diagnosis and treatment. The receptionist who makes appointments by telephone, the billing clerk in admissions, the floor nurse, and the night shift nurse all have a strong impact on the course of treatment, and together these experiences make up a patchwork quilt that becomes a woman's emotional climate. Our responses to relationships are different when conditions are stressful, and one way we are likely to deal with stress is to try to connect with strangers and find people like ourselves.

We do this to gauge the normality of our reactions, feeling more comfortable if the experience of others matches ours. If others understand, it can relieve tension to talk over our experiences and gain understanding and support. Some research has shown that waiting for a threatening physical procedure is easier and less fearful when you are with others about to undergo the same procedure, although this is probably truer when the procedure stirs displeasure rather than anxiety.[3] For women undergoing mastectomy, lumpectomy, or chemotherapy, acquaintances and roommates randomly encountered can have an effect on a woman's mood. One major source of comfort for women waiting for medical procedures is contact with women who have already had the same procedures. It can be reassuring to talk with another person who has undergone the same treatment and emerged successfully, and it offers a mental image for the outcome of treatment.[4] In addition, it provides a source of information and clarification when medical personnel are busy or unresponsive.

The exact effect of sharing conversation before procedures depends a great deal on the personalities and needs of the women involved. For some, it may raise rather than lower anxiety levels.

Usually we feel better in stressful times if we can talk to other people. Women in particular are likely to use this approach to deal with emotional tension. It will work best, however, when both people in a conversation are not emotionally needy. When one woman is tense because of an impending procedure and the other is relieved at having already undergone it, decisions about who should get most attention and support are easily made. In most female relationships, there is a shifting of nurturing-support-attention based on prioritizing each person's needs; for example, if my daughter-in-law snapped at me but your son lost his job, then you get the spotlight.

In situations where both women are tense as they wait for the same procedure, there will not be any automatic way to decide who needs more of the relationship's support energy. Two women may feel a need to either compete for support or compete to be nurturing and find it harder to relax as a result.

The following will help you understand the range of feelings involved in various aspects of breast cancer treatments.

1. Diagnosis

A diagnosis of breast cancer usually comes as a shock, even if you were suspicious about a lump or some other sign. If you had diabetes or multiple sclerosis instead of breast cancer, the symptoms that had already appeared would have led to thoughts about possibilities. With breast cancer, there are so few symptoms that a patient may be completely surprised.

In 75 percent of cases, women themselves find malignant lumps,[5] but women often delay for a month or more before having them checked. This seems to be a combination of wishful thinking and avoidance. Some lumps do disappear during the monthly cycle, but it is wise to have all of them checked out.

Breast tumors are often identified by mammograms. Mammograms seem like a dependable way to see internal tissues because they give a clear picture of the breast, but they are far from foolproof. It has been estimated that more than 10 percent of breast cancers are missed by mammography, and the error level could be higher.[6] Breast cancer is not one disease, and it has at least twenty different types. The nature, size, and position of the tumor all affect its likelihood of showing up on a mammogram. Since there are great differences in the growth pace of different breast cancers, sometimes there is no sign of advancing cancer until it has reached substantial mass. It is estimated that mammography screening would need to be done several times each year to effectively reduce errors in diagnosis, but even so some tumors would never show up at all.

It is difficult to accept that a procedure of such importance can be of limited reliability, and the error margin may give the impression that mammograms are not worth the trouble they take. But this is not true.

Mammography, like any other process of human measurement, involves decisions about how to go about assessing human characteristics and then interpreting their meaning. No matter how much we may need certainty, the great range of diversity in people and their bodies leads to some level of error, and decisions must be made about how much measuring is to be done to achieve a particular result. When mammography is medically recommended, it is a useful procedure, even with its imperfections, and all women can benefit from this relatively low risk tool.

When Elaine was told that her mammogram looked suspicious, she described her two feelings as panic and guilty remorse. "If only I had done those monthly breast exams," she thought, "I'd never be in this position." In fact, a physical exam provided little indication of a problem because of the size and shape of her breasts. After her recovery from a lumpectomy, when her self-esteem and confidence returned, she was better able to understand the difficulties in making an accurate diagnosis.

It is advisable to examine breasts monthly for lumps, but it can be difficult for a woman to tell the difference between healthy lumpy breast tissue and malignancies. When there is great anxiety about breast cancer, a woman may superstitiously avoid touching her breasts to feel for lumps or she may find the whole experience too anguishing to undertake. In these circumstances, it is particularly helpful to speak aloud about feelings.

In our health-conscious society, the idea has developed that if a woman follows the rules about diet, exercise, stress, and medical exams, then she will be healthy. From this perspective, it may seem that a medical problem is a personal failure of self-control and will. To some extent, breast cancer seems to be an automatic risk of living in our culture. Some research has indicated that by the age of seventy-five, 6–10 percent of women will have clinically detectable breast cancer.[7]

Psychological distress levels are very high during the initial diagnosis and throughout the time following. During this period, a woman and her physician wait for the pathologist's report, which will give the exact details on the nature of her disease. This tells whether the cancer is spreading and whether it has entered the blood or lymphatic system. Noninvasive cancers are referred to as precancers, ductal carcinoma, or carcinoma in situ. The cells will also be staged, which describes the tumor size, nodal spread, and metastatic spread. Getting the pathology report can take several days and may be a tense period.

Women who have just received a diagnosis of primary breast cancer with a good prognosis are nonetheless likely to have many of the same feelings as someone who has just been told she has AIDS or a terminal illness, even though their illness is distinctly different in its prognosis.

Over the time immediately following the diagnosis, a woman is likely to feel confusion, fatigue, and tension, and there may be difficulties in ordinary activities. She may find it hard to concentrate or think clearly, and she may be less efficient or ineffective at normal pursuits.[8] In general, she is likely to feel overwhelmed.

How long this period lasts depends on many factors. Overall health, including stamina and body tone, will affect how a woman feels. Her mental health status is also important, as well as the number of emotional challenges in her life. When the patient has little or no social support, there may be continued emotional distress up to two years after the diagnosis.[9] It is worth limiting emotional distress as much as possible, for there is a good deal of work to be done in this time. Following closely upon the shock of diagnosis, a woman is suddenly confronted with a number of new issues and decisions that must be made. Many women feel inadequate and overwhelmed at their new position, and everybody seems to look to them for direction.

Decisions must rapidly be made about treatment choices, and since most people have little or no information about cancer, there is a great deal of education required. The meaning of diagnostic tests, disease stages, types of surgery, reconstruction options, radiation schedules, chemotherapy medicines, and so forth are all introduced in a period of a few days, and a woman's confusion and disorientation level rise as a result.

This all occurs against a background of profound emotional upset, as a woman finds that her life perspective changes and there is a sense of uncertainty and loss. Concerns about her survival, financial ability, occupational future, and social network all become issues as well. Not surprisingly, many women feel incapable of handling all this and in the weeks afterward may feel a strong disappointment with themselves, particularly if they have high expectations of themselves and ordinarily achieve at a high level.

2. Surgery

Ada was a woman who had lived most of her seventy-six years comfortably. And she was still comfortable, which was one of the problems she had when she was told she needed surgery for breast cancer. "But I don't feel sick," she protested. "I don't feel like I have a disease. How can you be sure?"

It is common for women to have a sense of unreality when breast cancer surgery is recommended, since often they feel well and have no symptoms of illness. It helps if you can look at the radiologist's x-rays and images so that you can get a better picture of what's occurring in your body. Even though surgeons are sometimes seen as difficult to approach, most will support a patient's request when it promises to enhance or support treatment.

Fears: When Joan was diagnosed with breast cancer, she immediately thought of her aunt, whose suffering with colon cancer Joan had witnessed as a child. She felt doomed to the same fate, even though after a lumpectomy and radiation, she returned to a healthy life.

The word "cancer" stirs up strong feelings, and the experience of surgery can give rise to additional fears. You may worry that your surgeon will find that the cancer has spread, that you are "full of cancer," or that the surgery will make you sicker. Previous aches and pains may take on an ominous significance as you begin to doubt your body and your sensations. The surgery consent form will stir a whole range of new anxieties, since it lists every conceivable problem that can occur. All of these worries are normal for women before breast cancer surgery, and they are eased a good deal by a relaxed conversation with your surgeon and your anesthetist prior to hospital entry. Don't hesitate to ask all of your questions and call back if you think of more.

Sometimes fears are set off by unfamiliar procedures, disrobing, or the feel of cold metal equipment. If you are in treatment for a recurrence, it may be doubly upsetting to be back in the same rooms where you had earlier treatments. It helps to remember that breast cancer is a chronic disease and that recurrences are not uncommon and are treatable. They are not the result of bad judgments or medical mistakes, but the nature of the disease. It may be hard to accept that there are no foolproof treatments and that good decisions can sometimes be followed by disappointing results.

Depression: You may find it hard to tell the difference between the great physical fatigue that women frequently feel after surgery and the emotional down that is depression. The fatigue comes as much from the anesthesia as from the surgery and is the result of your body's systems trying to resynchronize after they have been disrupted. If you are determined to be energetic and cheerful for your friends and family right after surgery, this will be a great strain on your body and emotions. You will heal faster if you let yourself be what you feel and draw on others for help.

When you wake up from surgery, you may feel cold, nauseous, or tearful, and this can be disappointing if you planned to be strong. The weeks after surgery are a time for gathering resources, not expending them, and so this is a time to rest and heal.

You'll probably notice a different life tempo after surgery, as compared to before, since all of the treatment decisions are now made, the initial information gathered, and things are much less pressured and demanding. You are more likely to be in a passive state, which is a real contrast to the activity that was required before when you had to find doctors, make appointments, have tests done, read, talk with relatives and friends, and make plans for hospitalization and treatment. It is easy to feel helpless and handicapped in the forced passivity of post-surgical recovery, which is fertile ground for depression. It will be more productive if you think of this as "down time" in which your major task is to rest and put your energy into following medical recommendations exactly.

In the year after mastectomy, depression is common, and most studies show that one-third to one-half of women are depressed.[10] Depression may show up as a low mood that doesn't change, anxiety, tension, self-consciousness with strangers, new fears and phobias, or worries about a return of the cancer. Aches, twinges, and soreness can lead to periods of anxiety and a sense of helplessness and can make you feel isolated from others, who can't really understand the experience and its aftermath.

If you have chemotherapy before or after surgery, your anxiety and depression are likely to be much stronger; studies have shown that even though these treatments boost the success of the surgery, they burden you emotionally so that there is more of a strain. It's important to keep in mind that when this happens, you're not disintegrating or losing your mind, but only responding as a healthy organism to powerful encroachments on your system.

In surgical treatment there is more at stake than just your physical well-being, although this is of paramount importance. By taking care of your emotional well-being as well, you will enhance the effectiveness of treatment and feel better too.

Gathering resources: About a third of breast cancer patients would like their doctor to make all the treatment decisions, but it is more common for a woman to use a team of specialists, including a primary physician [gynecologist or general practitioner], a pathologist, surgeon, radiation oncologist, medical oncologist, nurses, social worker, and psychotherapist. This team advises and the patient makes the treatment decisions. Oncology has evolved to a point where it is very difficult for one specialist to be expert in all of the related fields, and you should seek out the best practitioners available, no matter how simple or common your cancer. After all, it is not simple for you.

When you consult with medical caregivers, it is wise to have both a companion and a tape recorder with you, so that you can sort out your conclusions at your leisure. The friend may be helpful for interpreting the information, but more importantly this will help you relax and feel comfortable in tense situations. You may not critically *need* either of these, but this is no time for heroic endurance feats. Save your strength. Most patients recall very little of what is explained during an initial consultation visit.

Nursing staff may have more time than doctors to talk over medical facts and procedures, and so you may find yourself in more contact with these folks. It helps if they have special training in oncology, since most medical personnel avoid asking about feelings, fears, or depressions and will distance themselves if you bring them up. This is not because you have committed a *faux pas,* and it is very helpful and facilitates treatment for you to talk about these issues. Medical caregivers receive limited psychological training, so they avoid areas that they feel are outside their field.

If you are fearful or depressed and the feelings last, it will be helpful to talk with a therapist who is trained and experienced in working with cancer issues and can help you plan ways to deal with them. Research suggests that it is best to begin counseling early, before radiation begins, since this considerably eases the stress of the treatment. Since you want your body to work hard at fighting cancer and at healing, you need to clear away other demands and burdens, particularly those related to stress. Talking about fears and depressions reduces their intensity, helps you to relax, and frees you from the grip of solitary thoughts.

Psychological help may include cognitive therapy, which is aimed at developing new ways of thinking and reacting, and deconditioning to diminish side effects of chemotherapy. Most women who have treatment for breast cancer insist that they need no emotional help, but it is advisable to avail yourself of every weapon. Illness is not a time for self-denial or proving one's emotional strength. Concentrate on maximizing your physical strength by giving yourself every help there is. Later on, when you are out of medical treatment, you can demonstrate how strong and self-reliant you are, if you still feel the need.

Friends are a particularly important source of support, and this is a good time to let them be part of your experience by accepting their offers of help and companionship. They will need your guidance in how to be helpful, so that when they make suggestions, for example, of bringing food, you offer several possibilities. You must guide conversations so that friends know how to be helpful, depending on your needs at the time:

> *"Do you mind just listening to me rattle off all the things that make me scared [or angry or depressed]. It would help if I just had a sympathetic ear, and later I'll figure out what I'm going to do with my surgeon."*

or

> *"I just feel like crying [or cursing] and I just need somebody to hold my hand."*

It's a good idea to make a detailed written plan for your course of treatment as decisions get made. It should list medical decisions as well as decisions about action to take to deal with uncomfortable feelings such as fear or depression. Ask a friend to look it over and help you evaluate how well it will work.

Informed choices: Women feel differently about how much information they want when they have breast cancer, and you may feel that you want to know everything, or nothing. It is important to work with medical caregivers who can be responsive to your needs. Research suggests that most patients fare better and are more comfortable with more information.

Although there is still a great deal that is unknown about breast cancer, your doctor can explain the reasons for recommending one course of treatment over another. It is *always* wise to get a second opinion on a major medical procedure before it is begun, and most physicians recommend that you do so. If you feel you would be hurting your doctor's feelings and that he or she would not be grateful for the extra enlightenment, it is wise to reconsider your choice of physician, for your welfare must be everyone's primary concern.

The doctor who won't talk: The relationship that you have with your doctor has important consequences for treatment, and so you need to do all you can to make it work well. The choice of a doctor is important, since some doctors are more skilled in communication and in giving information and psychological support than others. How you handle interviews is also important, as you must hold up your end of the communication process. If you decide that it is unfair to burden medical caregivers with your emotions, be they sadness, worry, or anger, or if you fear that you will be seen as self-centered, unappreciative, or disturbed, then you may not clearly communicate what is happening to you.

You need to describe your feelings clearly and, when you find treatment difficult, to ask what help is available. One way to do this is to write brief questions, keep a copy, and give them to your medical caregiver before your visit. This allows both of you to address issues that concern you, as well as the routine questions. Sometimes physicians may be seen as insensitive when they focus on the technical aspects of your illness, but this can reflect as much concern for your welfare as a focus on your feelings. And there is room for both if you take the initiative and ask for help.

Keep in mind that if your doctor is male the communication styles described earlier will continue to be an obstacle, no matter how good everybody's intentions. If Deborah Tannen's conceptualization is accurate, that males use communication to establish dominance and females use it to make emotional connection, then it is best to limit your expectations of an interview with a male doctor.

If you find it difficult to converse with your doctor, make a list of your concerns, give him a copy before your next visit, and take a copy with you. After he has finished his comments, ask him to answer your questions.

Insisting on preferences: Surgery is a trying experience, and although it is often the best choice for breast cancer treatment, it is not without its drawbacks. To make it easier, you should think about what is most comfortable for you and then try to arrange it. Suffering is not a test of character, and this is no time to try to raise your self-esteem by impressing your friends with your stamina, cheerfulness, or stoicism. You have just so much energy, and it must be fully invested in improving your health.

There are many sources of stress in surgery, and although most of them will be discussed early in treatment, some may not be anticipated and may stir up discomfort. You may find, if you have a mastectomy, that you have numbness in your armpit or you have temporary fluid drains (plastic tubing implanted under the skin around the incision) or you have difficulty raising your arm.

If you feel very needy, you may become self-conscious and worried about stirring up others' disapproval. You may find it particularly difficult to accept the attentions and offers of friends or relatives. Allowing others to help you is important because it will help you to feel reconnected to the human race; it will soothe many of the rough spots and promote healing. Just as you need to be connected to others, they need to reestablish their connection with you, to reclaim you from this alien experience. You need to allow others some control in the face of your difficulty, which will cut down on trauma all around. The worst choice is to withdraw from others and handle the illness and its treatment alone.

You may feel that you lose some status or some independence by asking for help, but in the long run it is a good investment. It can feel risky and may require that you have some bit of faith in other women, but it is more risky to attempt self-sufficiency during this period. Dr. Sandra Levy at the University of Pittsburgh has found that when women breast cancer patients feel that they have a great deal of social support, their immune system becomes more active.[11] It is wise to talk over problems with medical caregivers and to make choices according to what will maximize healing. Some women choose to stay in the hospital until drains are removed and to obtain help with temporary inconveniences of surgical recovery. There may be many new bodily sensations; it is good to discuss them and to ask for help if they are uncomfortable. If there are difficulties in relaxing or sleeping, short-term medication may ease the adjustment and promote healing.

When radiation is offered in conjunction with surgery, imaging procedures will be performed right after surgery and may require some separation from visitors and patients. If you have radiation, you should plan for some solitary time and bring materials (books, tapes, pictures) to the hospital to keep you occupied.

Working for your own comfort helps the overall process of healing. One study has shown, for example, that when surgical patients have a room with a view of a natural setting, they have a shorter hospital stay and more positive nursing notes and require fewer pain relievers.[12]

If there are foods that are cheering or comforting, you should ask friends and relatives to bring them, after clearing this with the medical staff. Bathing supplies are a good idea, and you may need a friend to help you bathe. If medically approved, exercises that begin the first day after surgery can promote healing. Music tapes from people who love you, and anything else that will give your body all the support possible to do its healing work are all recommended.

During the time of waiting for the pathologist's report, which usually comes in one to three days after surgery, it is helpful to have companionship, to have someone with you when the report is discussed and to make a tape recording.

Feelings about mastectomy vs. lumpectomy: "Modified radical or total mastectomy with axillary dissection" is removal of the entire breast, underarm lymph nodes, lining over the chest muscles, and the minor pectoral muscles. "Lumpectomy," also called "partial mastectomy," "wide excision," "segmental mastectomy," or "quadrantectomy," is surgical removal of a breast tumor, along with immediately surrounding tissue. The size of the section removed is determined by the size and the location of the tumor. When women have an equal choice, about one-third choose mastectomy, and two-thirds choose lumpectomy.

The primary consideration in the choice of treatment is always a medical one, with the effective treatment of the tumor the most important factor. You may have strong preferences for a lumpectomy or other procedure, but your doctor is trained to put together all of the information and offer counsel on a decision. It is advisable to have two expert opinions so that you can compare perspectives. You also need to consider how you may feel with either procedure.

Research with women who have had these procedures shows that in the first six months after surgery, both mastectomy and lumpectomy patients feel less attractive and less feminine. But by fourteen months, women who have had lumpectomies are back at the same point as they were before surgery in their feelings about themselves. Women who have lumpectomies (which usually include radiation) are more likely to feel that they don't get enough emotional support, particularly if they are younger patients.

Women who have mastectomies, however, tend to have a more difficult time over the long run. They continue to have a sense of loss, to be self-conscious, and to have less confidence in their appearance. They are also more reluctant to talk about their illness, and their living habits are different: they dress differently, wear night clothes more often, and are less likely to undress in front of their husbands.

With either of these procedures, appearance is changed, to a greater or lesser extent, which means that removing bandages can be stressful for you. It will help to have a supportive companion with you when the bandages come off. If you have had pre-excision chemotherapy to reduce the size of the tumor before surgery, you may feel more depressed and sick, but the change in bodily appearance will be less.

When your body changes, you are likely to feel emotionally vulnerable; you may be tearful and self-conscious and feel yourself less feminine. If you have had ovaries removed or are taking a drug like Tamoxifen, which produces menopausal symptoms, you may feel as though you have aged suddenly. The adjustment to these changes is gradual, and you need to allow yourself lots of time for feeling strange.

Sexual identity: Although not technically genital organs, females breasts are very much a part of sexual functioning and of one's image as a sexual creature. The effect of mastectomy and lumpectomy on sexuality varies and depends heavily on sexual relationships before the diagnosis. In general, women who have lumpectomies are more comfortable with their body image and their sexual feelings after surgery.

Mastectomy patients are far more fearful of not being sexually attractive, although surveys of husbands indicate little change in their attraction to their wives after mastectomy. It may be that women become uncomfortable and lose faith in their husbands' reaction to them, leading to sexual withdrawal.

For women who are unattached at the time of mastectomy, the problems will be quite different. Concern about how another will react to the news of breast cancer and mastectomy and the fear of the effect of one's appearance may raise substantial anxiety.

But these are primarily issues of trust in a relationship, for fears about how another will respond to news that has little real impact on the other person is really fear about one's relative value in the relationship. Sharing private, sensitive information about ourselves is best done gradually when we have had the opportunity to measure the other person and the strength of the relationship.

Often sexual problems are not primarily sexual problems but rather intensified relationship problems that show up clearly in our physiological response. One index of sexual comfort in a relationship is how easily two people can discuss sex and their feelings about it.

Fears of recurrence: For many women, the enormous fear of cancer, particularly of terminal cancer, is the single most important factor in treatment decisions. Often women feel that if they take the toughest treatment, sacrifice will bring security, a "magic bargain" with fate.

In general, mastectomy patients and lumpectomy patients both fear recurrences, but there is *more* fear if a woman has received chemotherapy as part of either treatment, in part because chemotherapeutic treatment stirs powerful emotions in all directions. At eleven months after surgery lumpectomy patients are more afraid of recurrence than mastectomy patients, but this difference disappears at eighteen months.[13]

When a physician tells you that either choice has the same outlook and that there is no greater risk with either one, it can be hard to accept that the future is so unpredictable. And it stands to reason that if the breast is removed there can be no further breast cancer. But this is not necessarily true and involves a misconception about how breast cancer spreads.

Cancer of the breast is most worrisome when it spreads to the liver, lungs, or brain, for then it affects vital bodily processes and threatens life. The common belief is that cancer cells are spread to other parts of the body because the tumor in the breast begins to shed cells as it gets bigger. But the time when cells break off and begin to travel is usually long before any lump is discovered in the breast, so that when a lump is removed, the cells have either traveled or not traveled, and it is often difficult to tell which, unless tumors have developed and can be identified in other body parts. This is why the lymph nodes are important, because it is believed that cells travel in part through the lymphatic system.

When there is a recurrence of a breast tumor, it is not the cause of the cancer spreading to other parts of the body. The risk of the tumor spreading has to do with many factors. Tumors need to be removed early, but this is not a guarantee that there will be no spread of the cancer. Mastectomy patients have no risk of future breast cancers in the removed breast, although tumors may appear later at the site of excision, but they have the same risk of distant disease as lumpectomy patients.

Some types of treatment increase the risk of other diseases and can make your health seem far more fragile. Women who receive Tamoxifen, for example, have an increased risk of endometrial cancer and need regular gynecological exams for protection.

Reconstructive surgery: For many women, reconstructive surgery to replace a lost breast is important to psychological well-being, while for others, the surgery offers little. You will probably want to let some time go by while you consider this issue, although if you are firmly and clearly of the opinion that it will be helpful, it is worth considering it before a mastectomy, since your surgeon will want to consider the options early.

Breast reconstruction is done in many ways, often with a silicone or saline implant below the pectoralis muscle or with a TRAM-flap (Transverse Rectus Abdominus Myocutaneous), which involves the use of the abdominal muscle and fat tissue to recreate the breast shape. The result in these types of surgeries is varied, but it is helpful to anticipate accurately by looking at surgical photos to estimate your own personal results.

Breast reconstruction is a limited solution to some problems and will not make a drastic change in your life. Neither will it erase the experience of a diagnosis of breast cancer and a mastectomy. It can make a difference in the level of comfort you feel with your body. If it allows you to put more energy into pursuing your life goals, then it is worth exploring.

If you are trying to decide whether breast reconstruction is a good idea, it helps to think about how often the change in your breasts bothers you, whether it crosses your mind occasionally or is frequently on your mind, whether it makes you change your daily patterns or give up the things you enjoy or that are good for you.

You also need to separate your feelings from those close to you. Your husband or relatives may feel that reconstruction is unnecessary and may reassure you that it makes no difference to them, but you may still feel more comfortable having the procedure. On the other hand, you may assume that even though you do not want a reconstruction, it will make your relatives happier, and so you may choose to please others.

If you decide to have reconstruction, be aware that there are many fears that may crop up. Returning to the hospital for breast surgery will set off small alarm bells deep in your undifferentiating subconscious, which will jump to the conclusion that you are in trouble again. Prepare to be anxious and tense, even when there is no reason to be.

There may be fears that your body cannot stand any more surgical procedures. Talk with your surgeon to ascertain the risks here. You may also fear that any reconstruction will hide new tumors and that more cancer may develop. In part this is a penance view of cancer: if you appease the gods by suffering, no more bad things will happen, and if you become self-indulgent, you will be punished. Neither is true, and reconstruction is not self-indulgence.

Checklist of Things to Do to Make Surgery Easier:

1. Relax. Be aware that there is a limit to how much you can do to help yourself and that when you meet that limit, you must rest.

2. Be aware of strong needs for competence and control, which may lead you to refuse help and to isolate yourself. Make yourself as comfortable as possible. Ask friends for help and accept it. Don't make surgery a test of character. This is no time to prove your strength.

3. Keep watch for fears, and where information would help, ask questions. Talk with sensitive friends about those things that are upsetting.

4. Remember that severe fatigue is the most common result of surgery for breast cancer. In the months after surgery, watch for depression, particularly if there is chemotherapy, and seek help for it.

5. In all medical consultations, bring a friend and a tape recorder. Ask your physician first if he or she is comfortable with taping the session, and if not, ask for a follow-up visit or telephone call to clear up any questions that might arise as you later think over the session.

6. Remember that if there is a choice between mastectomy and lumpectomy, the medical considerations are always first, but that your own peace of mind is a close second.

3. Radiation and Chemotherapy

Radiation is generally used in combination with lumpectomy, but may be administered at other points as well. It is used less often in the United States than in other countries and can feel more aversive than other treatments. The noise of the radiation-delivering machines is intimidating to some women and may heighten their reactions.

Emotional reactions to a course of radiation include apprehension, tension, anxiety, and depression. Sometimes women become socially withdrawn during this period, partially because of fatigue and emotional preoccupation. Severe fatigue, particularly toward the end of the sequence, is a particular problem and may mimic or feed depression.

Psychotherapy is useful at many points in the cancer experience, but it is particularly useful with radiation treatments. Some research has shown that when supportive psychotherapy is started before radiation treatments begin, it reduces the side effects, including anorexia, fatigue, and nausea.[14]

Chemotherapy involves the administration of drugs, orally or intravenously, that interfere with cell reproduction; it is given in cycles, usually in a variety of combinations depending on the type and stage of cancer and the health needs of the patient. The side effects of these medications vary but usually include nausea, vomiting, hair loss, and emotional mood swings. The drugs that attack the cancer cells also affect other body areas that produce fast-growing cells, including hair, the gastrointestinal tract, and bone marrow, which is why there is hair loss, nausea, and decreased immune response. There may also be mouth sores, weight gain, and diarrhea. Eating may be distasteful, but good nutrition will help to ease the emotional reaction. Some of the medicines used in pharmacological treatment affect the hormone balance of the body. For example, Tamoxifen produces more mood swings and hot flashes.

Sometimes women believe that they can stop side effects through will power and that if they think correctly, they will have no difficulty with chemotherapy. Although there are many things that a woman can do that have the potential of boosting chemotherapy and reducing the side effects, they have more to do with taking proper care of yourself rather than feats of mental control. Each human body reacts in its own manner, and there is no way to force responses of one sort or another. Individual characteristics have an important effect on reactions, so that a woman who becomes nauseous from anxiety will probably have more difficulty in this area regardless of her frame of mind.

Some women feel that powerful side effects indicate that the drugs are working and destroying cancer cells. If there are few side effects, a woman may feel anxious and frightened that the medications were too weak or administered incorrectly. Side effects, however, are not an indication of how well the medication is working.

Chemotherapy makes the psychological adjustment to the situation more difficult, and when women of equal health status are compared, women in chemotherapy have more psychological difficulty. Even though they are receiving more treatment and so should feel more protected, the women who receive chemotherapy often feel more tension about recurrence, more anxiety and depression, and more feelings of being angry and overwhelmed.[15] Additionally, they may feel more fatigued.

It is difficult to feel emotionally balanced during this period, as you try to deal simultaneously with the shock of diagnosis, the decision-making required, and the physical experience of treatment. It may be an upsetting experience as the body registers its anxiety and exhaustion at these experiences.

The end of treatment, which is usually looked forward to with great anticipation, means an important change, and can be a difficult time. The security of the medical routine and contact with medical personnel disappears, and a woman is no longer in an active health routine. She returns to her old schedule, perhaps a job or household responsibilities, but these are likely to feel different than before, and she may be edgy or anxious. Relationships with friends and family change without treatment to focus on, but it is hard to return to all the old and now diminished concerns. Others may find it hard to establish comfortable patterns of relating, since to focus on a woman after treatment might remind her of her illness but to treat her like anyone else may seem insensitive.

Often a woman's thoughts are dominated by a fear of recurrence, and the more she tries not to think about this, the more it will be in her thoughts. Minor physical complaints may frighten and preoccupy her for days as she tries to make peace with a body that seems to have betrayed her. This will produce no effect on her health, but it may isolate her from others and make her feel alienated and melancholy.

Sometimes there is great sadness that the earlier carefree days before diagnosis are forever gone and that nothing will be the same again. Physical discomforts of any sort will be a reminder of this, and a common cold or the flu may be a truly depressing experience during this period. Fatigue, headaches, pain, shortness of breath, or nausea will all lead to thoughts of cancer and the possibility of a recurrence or spread.[16] Visits to the doctor or hospitals can be particularly unpleasant experiences at first, even when there is no objective reason for concern. It will help a great deal in this time to have women to share with who have made the transition and fared well.

Part of the difficulty of adjustment after chemotherapy occurs because ongoing treatment gives a sense of magical protection, as though the cancer is fully under scrutiny and control. When this ends and a woman is alone, out of a medical setting, she may feel very vulnerable and not strong enough to continue the protection herself. It is easy to forget that the only reason she survived that far is through the sturdiness of her own immune system; without it, she would perish immediately.

How does the treatment period affect relationships with family and friends? In one study 23 percent of women said that there was increased distress in their marital and family relationships.[17] This is not surprising, since chemotherapy involves major disruptions in the routines of a household and the patterns of families.

It is easy to assume that disruption and distress signify that things are going badly, but this is not necessarily accurate. If breast cancer produces traumatic experiences and upsetting feelings, then healthy relationships will offer ways to cope with these and will register the turmoil. This may explain why in one study disruptions in the sexual relationships of spouses were related to *increased* sexual satisfaction.[18] Perhaps those relationships that were not disrupted had little vitality or flexibility.

4. Autologous Bone Marrow Transplants (ABMT)

This procedure is used when there is a poor prognosis or the patient's disease is recurrent or resistant cancer that has not shown improvement with other methods. Usually a woman is hospitalized for a lengthy period and administered very high doses of chemotherapy, along with antibiotics. Following this procedure, which knocks out her immune system and leaves her highly vulnerable to infection, she is given chemicals to revive her immune system or her own preserved bone marrow is reimplanted to revive production of the bone marrow immune cell factory.

The procedure may involve six weeks of medical treatment, often at a cancer center far from home, and for much of the time there may be extremely restricted visiting by family and friends. The cost is very high, often over $100,000, and is frequently not covered by insurance.

ABMT is too new to evaluate in terms of its long-term medical effectiveness, and it will be decades before its impact can be assessed. As of this writing it looks like a promising procedure.

Emotionally, the cost of the autologous bone marrow transplants is very high. Considering all of the information about the importance of social support during trauma, ABMT represents the most severe social support deprivation: removal from all familiar surroundings and nearly complete isolation from loved ones. Disruption of routines, contact with unfamiliar medical personnel, and the loss of all of those things that build self-esteem and personal stamina are serious problems. It is not clear how these changes tie in with the success of the procedure, but it is doubtful that they can aid it.

The cost of the treatment causes a crisis for most women. To decide between a risky medical procedure and the financial needs of one's family is an impossible choice. The procedure is so expensive that for many women there is no possibility of financing it, and the woman and family may feel a sense of failure at being unable to provide the medical treatment. The financial decision can come to seem like a measure of a woman's worth.

Use of this procedure also suggests a kind of urgency, that it is the only real or good treatment, and that without it there is nothing that can be done. Additionally, the treatment, because it is such an ordeal, can seem to be the rite that guarantees cure. Because of its dramatic nature and the threat it poses to survival, the risk seems to enhance the procedure's value. A woman may feel that if she can cope with this trial, then she is entitled to regain her health. In fact, it is more of the same kind of routine chemotherapy administered under different conditions. It is a promising treatment, but not magical and not guaranteed.

The treatment has produced increasing controversy, but not regarding its clinical effectiveness. The dispute, represented in several court cases, involves whether insurers can be required to pay for new breast cancer treatments.

Although ABMTs are familiar to the American public, they are sometimes described as experimental and therefore are not covered under usual health insurance. The courts have increasingly taken a dim view of what appears to be a rather opportunistic fiscal restraint on the part of insurers and have sometimes awarded heavy punitive damages where ABMT claims have been denied.

This sequence of events is most unfortunate, since it adds worry, work, and distraction when serenity and support are most needed. Although legal action is sometimes the wisest choice in these matters, it is advisable also to draw on all friends and acquaintances for help.

5. Recurrences

With all of the talk about the war on cancer and curing cancer, it is easy to forget that breast cancer, like diabetes and heart disease, is a chronic illness, one that tends to recur again and again. Because breast cancer is described as curable, it is easy to feel that if the first treatment didn't cure it, it must be too strong for medicine. But breast cancer requires continued treatment and care and is controllable for lengthy periods. Our all-or-nothing orientation feeds feelings of panic and doom when there is a recurrence.

When breast cancer is discovered, it already involves more than the breasts; what is important is not getting every cancer cell but the overall strength of a woman's resistance and the type of cancer that she confronts. Most women with breast cancer will deal with recurrences at some point in their lives.

But because cancer is so mysterious, it is easy to personalize the outcomes. A recurrence can seem to indicate that a woman didn't do all she should have, for example, diet, exercise, think the right thoughts. These fears are painful at the time of diagnosis and will be more painful in recurrences.

Sometimes women make magical and secret bargains with fate regarding their cancer. When Jody was finished with treatment, she felt that she had been through a trial by fire and had learned her lesson. She decided to eat perfectly right, exercise on a rigid schedule, and so forth. Consequently, two years later, when she developed cancer in the opposite breast, she was doubly upset, because she felt that she had truly been cheated; she had kept her part of the bargain but had been denied a fair outcome.

Emotionally, we react to trauma in predictable ways. Most of us can scrape together enough of a response to one trauma to manage, but if we are hit another time in the same place, we are liable to feel overwhelmed and disabled. It is also easy to feel that there is no hope if a woman is not given a completely clean bill of health. If there is any cancer, she may feel that there is no possibility of normal living.

Recurrences can raise great doubt about earlier treatment decisions, as though they indicate a bad choice. When people review their decisions in hindsight, they often conclude that they should have anticipated all information and consequences that later turned up, when in fact this is impossible.

All medical procedures have a predictable failure rate; some percentage of the time they will not work. After lumpectomy, for example, there is a 20 percent local recurrence rate, and sometimes this occurs long after the surgery. There is no risk in preserving the breast where this is medically advised[19] but it may feel that if there is a recurrence, the original decision was a bad one.

Breast cancer involves a broad range of emotional reactions, and women dealing with the disease may often feel considerable emotional turmoil. This will be greatly helped by frequently discussing your internal reactions with others who understand. The following chapter describes techniques that can help make you more comfortable and enhance the effectiveness of treatment.

Chapter Eight

Limiting the Trauma
of Breast Cancer Treatment:
II. Boosting Chemotherapy

In early adolescence all women face a choice: whether to be active or passive. From many directions comes the message that relationships are more available if women are docile, sweet, agreeable, accommodating.

The bouncing vitality and spirit of adventure in girls gives way to the socially sensitive, easily embarrassed twelve-year-old. Girls learn to become silent about their genuine feelings, to act the way that others need them to be, and to ignore their internal voice. This seems to be the safest way to hang on to belonging.

Does anybody want us if we speak what we feel and say what we see? If we are daring and adventurous, do we give up our femininity? When you are dealing with breast cancer, it can seem that your feminine nature is under assault and that you need to be more rigidly female to compensate for the damage to or loss of a breast.

There are techniques that make a difference in breast cancer. You will need daring and energy to learn them, but they are worth being yourself for.

Most people who are diagnosed with cancer know somebody who has had treatment for it in one form or another. Often the stories remembered are dramatic and colorful. For many of us, these recollections are our total educational experience in cancer treatment, and they can cause anxiety, fear, and dread.

The reaction to chemotherapy is heavily affected by our perceptions and expectations and by our general health. Sometimes people believe that taking a positive attitude is necessary for treatment to work. In one study, when women were asked how having cancer affected them, 79 percent said that it had at least one positive consequence. This was in contrast to their family members, who were more likely to see the experience as completely negative.[1]

A great deal of a woman's reaction depends on how much the cancer interferes with normal living and how many changes she must make. Her worry and upset about treatment are likely to rise in proportion to these disruptions. One researcher suggests that the best way to predict the turmoil a woman will feel from chemotherapy is to count the number of side effects that she experiences.[2]

Our emotions are greatly affected by our physical comfort, and anxiety goes with discomfort as fear goes with pain. People react in many ways to chemotherapy, depending upon the medications used, the frequency and intensity of treatment, their overall health, and other factors.

To make sure that treatment for breast cancer has its maximum effect, it is important to reduce side effects as much as possible. This allows the body to function normally with all its systems, taking in oxygen and nutrients, making internal cellular repairs, eliminating wastes, and generating new healthy tissue. Chemotherapy works best on a human body that is healthy and strong with all organs functioning well.

When there is too powerful a reaction to chemotherapy, it interferes with all of these processes. If there is a great deal of vomiting, for example, the effectiveness of the medication can be reduced because of the other factors affecting the body. A woman may develop anorexia and fail to take in enough nutrition for body sustenance, she may become dehydrated, thus limiting the effectiveness of body processes, or she may develop a metabolic imbalance and have difficulty with normal daily activities.

Some techniques can make a difference in how a woman gets through breast cancer treatment. These techniques are not intended as self-help methods. They must be learned as part of a relationship with a trained helper and practiced with companionship. Breast cancer treatment is no time for going it alone.

Good cancer treatment requires connection with other people. You need to listen carefully, ask questions, use a tape recorder, call back with more questions when a doctor or nurse explains treatment. You need to talk to friends, relatives, therapists, and acquaintances and learn to speak clearly about what you need. It will help to find out about helpers within medicine as well, for example, the patient advocates employed by some hospitals to help patients.

Complete Treatment

Cancer is one of the most treatable of the chronic diseases and can usually be slowed or arrested so that normal life continues. In order for this to happen, however, medical treatment has to work at its best. And to do this, it needs psychological backup and human connections.

Even with the established effectiveness of the methods used in this chapter, most cancer patients will not use them and so will limit the good impact of their medical treatment. When cancer patients have instruction, help, and companionship, they are far more likely to use psychology, although a substantial proportion still refuse. In one study, for example, when patients were offered a way of avoiding nausea and vomiting from chemotherapy by learning a technique that had no side effects and was free, 25 percent of them refused it.[3]

This is a problem for medical treatment in general, since patients often refuse treatment or use it in a way that limits its effectiveness. In routine medical care, of 750 million new prescriptions written each year, 520 million are used only partially or not at all.[4] Recommendations for cancer treatment usually stir up more aversive reactions than other illness treatments, and so patients may not follow them well enough for them to have their intended effect.

There is also a good deal of reluctance to use all of the recommended cancer treatments and resources. In one study of youthful cancer patients, 40–60 percent failed to take their prescribed medication as indicated.[5] In a separate study, when glaucoma patients were given eye drops and told that they must use them three times each day to prevent blindness, 58 percent of the patients didn't use them often enough to be effective. At the point of losing their vision and becoming legally blind, they showed only a small improvement in following instructions.[6]

There are many reasons why this occurs, and much attention has been given to factors that affect how patients follow instructions. Sometimes directions are too complicated, or not explained well, or fail to include adequate information. Patients may be elderly, too ill, or too upset to follow instructions.

The relationship with medical caregivers is very important in this regard and has a great impact on how patients respond to the specifics of recommendations. The emotional climate of cancer treatment affects our body's response as well as our emotions, and the level of social support available from medical caregivers can be used to predict natural killer cell activity levels. This relationship between medical caregiver and patient has an important impact on how well a human body can utilize cancer treatment.[7]

Because it is traumatic to deal with cancer, normal ways of asking questions and making choices may be temporarily impaired during adjustment to the shock of diagnosis. Oncology is a complex clinical science and not easily understood without medical training.

Communicating complex information is a tricky process. When researchers asked patients about what they had been told after leaving a doctor's office, more than half of the instructions given them could not be accurately recalled.[8] Medical information is confusing and unfamiliar to most people, and although doctors may believe that they speak clearly, patients do not always hear clearly. In all of us, the tendency to edit what we hear, to block out whatever is threatening or unpleasant, is a natural inclination.

Even though medical caregivers may strive to give clear information, in one study, two-thirds of patients forgot their diagnosis and treatment explanations, and one half forgot instructions immediately after receiving them.[9] Although it may seem that patients ignore or resist medical advice, they are more likely affected by confusion about what has been communicated.

Some doctors try to reduce patients' confusion by laying out their explanations and instructions in print and sending these home with the patient. The rationale is that after the patients have had a chance to relax, they may then be ready to absorb more information. In one study, however, it was found that between 21 percent and 51 percent of patients don't read the materials given to them.[10] (Most of us have this type of informational reading material lying around the house; we plan to get to it "one of these days.")

Perhaps when we are in the patient role, we see our participation in the healing process as essentially passive. Sometimes patients disagree with treatment instructions and form their own judgment about whether it is worthwhile to follow the prescribed plan. Disagreement, though, isn't usually voiced to medical people, and seeking another opinion is not routine. More commonly, patients use those parts of treatment that make sense to them and ignore the others. They rarely communicate their decision to the medical team.

When treatments are ineffective or troublesome, this is not always reported back to medical caregivers, nor is help sought if treatment is uncomfortable or disruptive of daily living. Patients may assume that a doctor or nurse doesn't care about the effects of treatment or that patients should be stoic and not complain, but in either case patients may give misleading feedback by not complaining.

Sometimes failure to comply with medical instructions may be a form of self-denial about the seriousness of one's condition and a way to demonstrate one's own power in the face of frightening information. Since there are usually no immediate consequences, it can seem that the patient has overcome the condition, for the moment at least.

An additional reason for nonadherence to medical instructions has to do with how people feel about being submissive. Entering the medical system as a cancer patient can leave you feeling powerless over what is happening to you. You are required to endure tests and procedures or risk your health if you refuse them. In such a high-anxiety setting, others can appear to have enormous power. In one study of breast cancer patients, 75 percent of women believed that the decision to use chemotherapy was made solely by their doctor and that they had no say in it.[11] It can feel to a patient like she has no power at all over health when she is confronted with modern science and its implements.

In this situation, most people need to exert some minimal degree of control over events. One way to do so can be to discard what seems unimportant or trivial. Patients may sometimes follow major instructions, taking medicines and coming for treatments, but ignore the details. In this way, a patient regains some power and self-esteem in a system that seems to require passivity and surrender. It can also feel reassuring if we can defiantly flout the folks in power and assert, "I don't really need that."

But limiting treatment for cancer doesn't optimize chances for health, regardless of the reason or the gratifications. To minimize the effectiveness of cancer treatment gives you the trauma of treatment without the same good results. As long as you have to have treatment, why not do it all? Since it can be difficult or unpleasant, why not go whole hog and get the complete treatment, so that there is nothing left out and no loose ends? To do everything to maximize the effects of surgery, chemotherapy, and radiation is far more satisfying, no matter the temporary difficulty or inconvenience.

Psychological support for medical treatment can make a big difference in how fully you use treatment and how alive you feel during the process. To use psychological techniques doesn't mean that there is a psychological problem at the outset. This is a different use of psychology, for here it is used to boost medical treatment in emotionally healthy people instead of treating psychological disorders.

Side Effects of Chemotherapy

All medical conditions include emotional as well as physical aspects, and it is impossible to separate the two. When treatment utilizes both the physical and psychological systems of the patient, the outcomes are enhanced.

Chemotherapy is a good example of the power that results from combining medical and psychological treatments. When Hans Eysenck and Ronald Grossarth-Maticek in London used individual psychotherapy with breast cancer patients, the results of their chemotherapy were different from those in routine oncology.

The chemotherapy clearly helped breast cancer patients, but it had a substantially stronger effect when it was combined with psychotherapy. The process of emotionally connecting and sharing feelings apparently boosted the physical impact of the chemotherapeutic medications. But there was another, more surprising result. In routine chemotherapy treatment, the level of white blood cells often drops because the anticancer medications affect the bone marrow, and this can complicate treatment by reducing a patient's resistance to infection. In the Eysenck research, white blood cell counts *rose* with psychotherapy, helping patients to tolerate more powerful treatments.

Why this should occur is difficult to explain in the context of our working assumptions about the human body, although it parallels the results of Fawzy Fawzy at UCLA and Sandra Levy at Pittsburgh. The process of relating to others translates to changes at the cellular level of the immune system.

The side effects of chemotherapy, including a drop in lymphocyte levels, seem to be a result of both psychological and medical factors. The side effects that are most disturbing to patients are the nausea and vomiting, for these can produce just plain misery.

Some types of human reactions become conditioned to outside cues, so that each time the same cue appears, the same reaction occurs. Remember my dog's reaction of salivation to the food bowl and the grocery bags? This is a conditioned response, and one that involves a link between something on the outside and a reaction on the inside.

The drugs used in chemotherapy are powerful ones, and they affect all tissues in the body, not only the cancer cells. They particularly affect the fast-growing cells of the body, including the stomach and intestines, with resulting nausea and vomiting. These reactions occur one to two hours after receiving the drug and can last for several days.

These reactions tend to get stronger with more chemotherapy treatments, as the effect of the medications increases. Usually in the first treatment or so, there is little or no discomfort, and so patients may not utilize preventive techniques against side effects. Chemotherapy includes a long list of drugs, some of them more upsetting to the system than others.

Conditioning

Interestingly enough, the drugs used in breast cancer treatment don't have as strong a potential to produce nausea and vomiting as patients' reactions might suggest. In other types of cancer, chemotherapy agents are used that produce far more nausea. Human systems respond to cues, and many of our biological responses have become trained to environmental signals, as I learned as a pet owner. When my dog had diarrhea, I became increasingly nauseated each time I cleaned up, and I had a difficult time getting through each episode as it continued.

One day one of the neighborhood boys played a trick on me and left some rubber look-alike material on the kitchen counter, and my stomach reacted as though it were the original, with all of the muscle contractions and heaving. This wasn't a psychological reaction and it wasn't a psychosomatic disturbance, and you wouldn't say it was all in my head. Instead, it was what is called classical conditioning. My gastrointestinal reactions didn't change much after I learned that my system had been fooled, and it still made me ill to see the look-alike.

In the same way, part of the reaction to chemotherapy has to do with conditioning and cues, which combine with our internal sensations to produce a powerful effect. The medications themselves are irritating to the system, but this is increased greatly by the conditioning that elicits nauseous responses.

The reactions of our bodies, the queasiness and heaving, become associated with the sights, smells, and thoughts of the place and circumstances where we get chemotherapy. It may be the sight of a syringe, the odor of alcohol, the wallpaper in a room, or even a day on a calendar that serve as cues, but the body responds. You don't have to feel sick the first time that you see these things for the reaction to be connected. In lab animals, even if they don't get sick until hours after treatment, the connection becomes established between nausea and the setting at the time of receiving the drug.[12]

One factor that speeds up the conditioning process and makes the reactions stronger is anxiety during the process. When there is a high level of arousal, for example, when we are very tense, the association between cues and nausea is made more quickly. Anxiety is invariably a part of treatment for breast cancer, and it is a healthy human reaction to the complex challenge of the illness. But the higher the anxiety level, the greater the likelihood of nausea and vomiting. This becomes complicated, however, because for some people, nausea and vomiting are also a *reaction* to high anxiety, and so it gets hard to tell what part of the nausea is due to pharmacology, to conditioning, or to anxiety.

There is some relationship between chemotherapy side effects and a woman's coping style, and it appears that women who tend to be open and direct in dealing with problems have less difficulty with side effects than women who are more inhibited.[13] This is likely to be because the more effective you are at solving problems, the less anxiety you will have.

It is difficult but not impossible to break up a conditioned reaction once it has developed, so dealing with conditioned reactions to chemotherapy is most effective when it occurs early in treatment, before responses get established.

There are always creative people who can use adversity to their advantage. Louise was a woman who had struggled with nutrition and weight throughout her life, and she was constantly depressed at her inability to eat a balanced diet. She came from a large European family that encouraged the enjoyment of food, in particular the irresistible pastries and cookies that her family produced in great numbers.

When she needed to have chemotherapy, she decided to use side effects to her advantage. She was able to limit her nauseous reactions by using psychological techniques, but she allowed enough reaction so that she could work on conditioning her appetite. When she came to the chemotherapy treatment, she brought with her the pastries and cookies that had always tempted her, as well as the high fat, nonnutritional items that she had been unable to avoid.

She found that when her appetite returned, it was only for the healthy food items, the fruits, vegetables, and nutritious grains rather than the sweets, which now nauseated her. Her excellent coping style also reduced her anxiety in the situation, and gave her a sense of achievement that she had, as she said, "turned a lemon into lemonade."

The best illustration of conditioning is the nausea and vomiting that can develop *before* receiving a round of chemical treatment. From 25 to 35 percent of women have nausea and sometimes vomiting prior to their treatment, which may occur on the way to the treatment or while they are at home. This tends to increase as the number of chemotherapy treatments increases and may be worse than the actual effect of the drug itself.

For a woman dealing with the difficulties of breast cancer, this can seem like an unfair burden. While most people will accept the inconvenience and discomfort of chemotherapy for cancer because it seems to increase their chances for health, anticipatory reactions are hard to accept. For some patients, it can even feel like a sign of weakness or cowardice. In fact, it is only the conditioning process at work.

People are not exactly like dogs in the way that their reactions become conditioned to outside cues. Their emotions and thoughts are always involved, and these tend to vary widely. Those cancer patients most vulnerable to developing nausea and vomiting before chemotherapy treatments have certain personality characteristics in common, suggesting that the conditioning process may occur differently for them.

These women, about one in every four breast cancer patients, appear on psychological assessment as generally more imaginative, with a wider range of physical sensations and reactions to all of their experiences, not only chemotherapy. They also appear to have more flexible thinking processes, as they are able to meditate and recall dreams more frequently. These greater capacities may paradoxically trap the patient in forming conditioned reactions where other less sensitive patients would not. This capacity can also lead patients to think a good deal about upcoming chemotherapy experiences and to begin to anticipate external cues and their internal reactions on the basis of prior learning. The ability to recall and visualize part of the treatment may set off physical responses.

Physical reactions to chemotherapy drugs tend to be stronger in people who are already physically aroused and tense, easily leading to the muscle reactions that are part of nausea and vomiting.[14] These two together, an active mind and an active body, set the stage for the development of reactions before treatment which in effect administer treatment in advance, albeit in fantasy.

Using Professionals:
When Self-Help Is Not Helpful

In the following pages, a number of psychological techniques are discussed for easing the stress of breast cancer treatment. Many of them are familiar and have been written about in the press and described in detail in self-help books. They include four variations of the same technique, including progressive muscle relaxation, hypnosis, systematic desensitization, and biofeedback, and all involve deep muscle relaxation and cognitive restructuring. Why are they not frequently used in cancer treatment? The answer has to do with the great value this society attaches to independence and self-reliance.

When I was a child, an uncle of mine, a dentist, and a very frugal man as well, used to drill his own teeth and do his own dental work. He would buzz away inside his mouth, fill his cavities, and even do extractions. It was fascinating to watch him. He used a series of mirrors, which he positioned using screws and vises and tape. Then he would twist and turn to try to get the light just right. When it was uncomfortable, he would stop for a minute; he would sweat but he would stick to it. He was a person of remarkable determination, constant dental problems, and a minimally attractive smile.

One day I had a flash of insight, and I understood that his teeth looked okay to *him* because he could never get outside his own perception to see what they looked like to the rest of the world. In fact, he had never taken himself very seriously at all; he had trivialized his own needs and exulted in the money he saved by doing his own dental work.

The failure to take seriously the comfort of cancer patients is a much more powerful issue, and as a society we have given far too little attention to patient ease. Although medical treatment and procedures are prescribed and administered by trained professionals, psychological techniques for easing cancer discomfort are left to the patient to figure out for herself.

There is clear evidence that these techniques work poorly, if at all, when they are self-administered. When relaxation, for example, is taught and guided by a trained therapist, the outcome is quite different from when a patient tries to learn it from a book.[15] What's more, a therapist must be present when these techniques are used during cancer treatment, at least for the first chemotherapy sessions, in order for them to be effective.

Patients often struggle valiantly with books that describe how easy it is to learn and administer self-help, or perhaps they buy an audiotape and listen to it. But it can be a disheartening experience to learn that you can't master something described as so easy. The research that compares self-administered relaxation and therapist-directed help shows the two to be quite different, with the former a weak substitute for the latter.[16]

When patients try to use relaxation methods alone, they are significantly less powerful. There is less concentration and involvement in the process and more distraction; often a patient falls asleep. When a state of hypnosis is achieved, for example, it is more likely to be superficial and fluctuating than deep and useful. Trying to read a self-help book at the same time that you monitor a procedure, particularly one that involves an altered state of consciousness, is impossible.

Using audiotapes offers little more than working alone to learn these techniques, since there are the same difficulties with self-monitoring and making decisions about treatment. The results are not as good as when you work with a trained therapist to learn these techniques, although using tapes can be a part of the learning and practicing.[17] It is unfortunate that so many useful tools have been misrepresented as "self-help" when their potency depends on help from others. They would more appropriately be called "other help."

Although relaxation techniques are generally benign, they have enormous potential power. This was brought home to me when I was watching a therapist in hypnosis training present a hypnotic image to a child. Consisting of a lovely grassy meadow, with cows and flowers, the scene presented was pastoral and serene. But it affected the boy quite differently. It set off an asthmatic response as though the boy's respiratory system were actually confronted with the cues, and he went into respiratory arrest. Fortunately, help was immediately available to reverse the chain of associations and return him to healthy breathing. Using hypnosis without adequate training and supervision is risky, and rarely are the naive prepared for untoward reactions.[18]

In planning treatment for cancer, it is best to look at the long-term picture. Breast cancer is a serious illness, and the treatment is difficult. There needs to be careful attention to a woman's needs and an integrated treatment plan, which includes the best available medical treatments and whatever can boost and support them. All of the procedures described here work best when they are part of a medical treatment plan and are administered by a trained therapist.

The following is a description of relaxation techniques that use many of the same processes and are based on similar assumptions. Do not practice them or use them on your own. They need to be administered by a trained therapist familiar with their usage and results and also intimately familiar with your needs and your experience.

Most therapists will require a period of time to become familiar with your needs and circumstances before deciding which of these techniques will be most effective. Following an initial teaching experience, there will be a period of guided practice in which you learn to use them smoothly and effectively.

The four techniques, progressive muscle relaxation, hypnosis, systematic desensitization, and biofeedback, all have common elements. Each begins with a deliberate reduction of tension in the musculature and uses mental activity to foster this.

All four are effective in reducing the side effects of chemotherapy for various reasons. Because they reduce muscular tension, they lessen the upset in the gastrointestinal tract, and deep muscle relaxation in the digestive tract is particularly useful in reducing the contractions that precede vomiting. Antinausea medications mentioned earlier generally produce a physical relaxation similar to these techniques, although they too can cause side effects.

Relaxing the body also helps to lessen the sensations of anxiety, which always involve some level of physical tension. By making a planned change in your reactions, you are likely to feel more powerful and effective in dealing with physical challenges.

These techniques also have the inadvertent effect of shielding the patient from the associations that make for stronger conditioning of cues for nausea and vomiting. Patients generally focus inwardly during relaxation procedures, and they are less likely to strengthen connections between side effects and cues.

There is likely to be a mood elevation with these techniques, since they remove the sense of helplessness that comes from passivity. All of these techniques require activity and focus by patients, and so they are likely to enhance self-esteem.

1. Progressive Muscle Relaxation

Try to picture how it feels when you are the most tense and feeling the greatest internal tightness. Frequently this shows up as rapid, shallow breathing, a feeling that you can't get a deep breath, a rapid, pounding heartbeat, and perhaps dizziness or nausea. When these sensations are artificially induced in people, they assume that they must be very anxious, because they have all of the physical sensations of anxiety. When you change these sensations, you then change the interpretation of the experience.

Imagine for a moment that you met a man, and your heart began to beat fast, you felt lightheaded and trembled, and you felt a rush of energy. If this happened several times when you were with him you might begin to wonder if you had romantic feelings for him, or if you were infatuated. Now imagine that your doctor tells you that the medicine she has been prescribing for you may make you feel energetic and lightheaded and give you a fast pulse. Does the romance disappear? Probably. Our body signals often set off the experience of certain emotions, like love or anxiety.

Deep muscle relaxation is more than just taking it easy. It requires regular practice and brings about powerful changes inside the body. The heart rate slows down, as does breathing, which also becomes deeper. Blood pressure drops, as does metabolic rate and oxygen consumption, and there is a marked change in muscle tension. Activity in the brain also changes, with notable differences in thinking patterns and alpha wave activity.

When relaxation is used repeatedly over a period of time, its effects extend into the rest of the time when you are not practicing. There is an overall decrease in body tension level and a change in mood and thoughts. But like any skill, muscle relaxation is developed by repeated practice, and the more practice, the more powerful the effects.

There are several ways to teach progressive muscle relaxation, depending on your physical needs, emotional preferences, and learning style. All approaches, however, involve sequential concentration on groups of muscles and paced breathing, and these are controlled by our two nervous systems.

It is the sympathetic nervous system that produces our fight or flight response to threatening situations. Our heart races, our muscles tighten, sugar is pumped into the blood, our emotions are stirred, and our reactions speed up. We are ready for action at this point. When this reaction cools down, it isn't because it just drains away. It is another body system, the parasympathetic nervous system, that takes over and returns us to normal functioning. It is this system that the relaxation response accesses and tries to get into action.[19]

Most people who learn about muscle relaxation don't practice it and abandon it in disappointment, similar to most people who take piano lessons. One way to gauge how much you need to use muscle relaxation is to look at how easy it is to find time to practice, since the more you need it, the harder it becomes to find time to learn it. When life is very fast-paced and demanding, it can make you tense and offer little opportunity to practice relaxation. A policy decision is usually required to change the way you use your time.

It is also hard to apply enough self-control to practice relaxation regularly, and at the beginning it can feel that it makes little difference or cannot contribute to your well-being. But like with piano lessons, it is wise to avoid evaluating the effects until after you've been at it for awhile, six months at least.

There is good reason to believe this technique can make a positive contribution to your health. When progressive muscle relaxation training is used before beginning chemotherapy and during the first five treatments, there is a clear change in the side effects. In one study, by the fifth session of chemotherapy only 10 percent of patients using relaxation had nausea after undergoing chemotherapy.[20] In the control group, where there was no relaxation training, 54 percent of the patients were nauseous by the fifth treatment, and anxious and upset as well.

Relaxation training changes the way the body responds to chemotherapy. In a study where patients were given relaxation training just before and then during chemotherapy, they had clear positive changes in reduced anxiety and depression, less nausea and vomiting, and a lower pulse rate and blood pressure. These patients also had less nausea at home over the thirty-six hours following the chemotherapy treatment. In contrast, in a control group in which a therapist spent time only in talking to the patient, there was no improvement in side effects[21] and the patients had all the typical reactions.

Patients are likely to reduce nausea and vomiting due to chemotherapy by 50 percent if they use progressive muscle relaxation, but, just as importantly, they are likely to take in more nutrients in the forty-eight hours following treatment.[22] This is one more way to support the body's return to health and to boost all the body systems in utilizing medical treatment.

There are other effects of progressive muscle relaxation that are not well understood, but that continue to occur. The practice seems to have an effect on the immune system, so that immune responses change.

When researchers taught relaxation training to the geriatric residents of four nursing homes in Columbus, Ohio, they found an improvement in their immune measures, including their natural killer cell activity levels. The relaxed inpatients were also less distressed than residents who had no training, or who had only social contact, but the effect depended on the frequency of relaxation practice.[23] The more practice, the greater the response.

2. Hypnosis

In the history of psychology, stories are told about the early years of Freud, when he was first exploring ways to help people with emotional and physical problems. At that time in Vienna, hypnosis was very much in use, and Freud used it too. That was, until the day that a young woman whom he had hypnotized, not very effectively it seems, threw her arms around him in the middle of a therapy session, deeply embarrassing this rather proper Victorian doctor. As a result, Freud forbade the use of hypnosis in psychoanalysis, claiming that it released dangerous passions.

Since that time, hypnosis has been among the curiosities of psychology. There are no good explanations for the effects that reliably appear when it is used by trained therapists, and understanding seems to evade both those who come from a medical background and those who focus on the cognitive aspects.

An example of one of the milder but nonetheless puzzling effects is the use of hypnosis to treat warts. This is generally not effective unless the therapist has thorough training in hypnosis, but when this is the case, the results are perplexing.

In one study, patients who had warts on both sides of the body were treated by a hypnotic trance in which instructions were given so that warts would disappear on one side of the body only. The instructions involved changing the blood flow to the affected area, and so cutting off nourishment for the warts. Of the fourteen patients who received these instructions, nine of them were cured of their warts on the treated side only.[24]

There is no current theory that can offer an explanation for why this effect is produced in the body from something that occurs only in the mind. But there are many areas where hypnosis produces a physical change. It is possible, for example, to produce allergic skin reactions by using a trance. When people are given the hypnotic suggestion to respond allergically to conflict or to heat, the characteristic weal formations that appear in allergy can be seen on the hypnotized person.[25]

The results are impressive when hypnosis is used to reduce chemotherapy's side effects. Hypnotic trance had first been used to control pain, but an incidental benefit was that it also turned off nausea. There might still have been nauseous sensations, but these were controllable by the patients.

It was interesting to see the impact of the technique. When patients felt nauseous, if they had substantial previous practice with hypnosis, they could, in the midst of vomiting, focus on a visual point in the room and go into a trance. This would stop the vomiting. If they were interrupted, they would immediately begin vomiting again, but they could regain control by going back into a trance.[26]

The use of focus points will seem familiar to women who have used techniques like LaMaze or Bradley for assisted childbirth. Through practice and support from others, women learn to focus their attention and energy to maximize the body's efforts in labor and delivery.

Hypnosis has a powerful effect on the nausea and vomiting that appear before and after chemotherapy. When it is used prior to and during injections, there is no anticipatory vomiting, but when hypnotic training sessions are missed, the nausea and vomiting return. When training is reinstituted, the side effects again disappear. Interestingly enough, notwithstanding these clear benefits, in one study 25 percent of patients refused to accept training in the use of hypnosis.[27]

There are other advantages to using hypnosis during cancer treatment. It reduces the tension and upset of procedures, the sense of time in the hospital is reduced, and there is less fatigue from treatment. Nurses report that medications are administered more smoothly and that it is simpler to find a vein with a patient in trance because of the change in blood flow that accompanies the trance state.

When hypnosis is used to support surgical treatment, there is less pain and distress, so that fewer medications are necessary, recovery time is faster, and there is less time under anesthesia with fewer blood transfusions required.[28]

David Spiegel's group psychotherapy treatment for breast cancer patients used a hypnosis exercise that focused on a specific theme each week. The trance was used at the end of each weekly group session. Patients were left with a sense of restfulness and completion and encouraged to continue the hypnotic practice at home.

How does hypnosis work? There is no clear way to explain its effects by reference to standard communication, for hypnosis works outside this process. We have all experienced trance, perhaps during a long car ride, while sitting in church, or while watching television. Some describe the experience as a person's becoming independent of present time and space coordinates.[29]

Hypnosis is based on the brain's limited capacity to process information and its shifting to other tracks when the major routes cannot operate. Often in hypnotic trance the therapist talks to other parts of the brain, rather than the one that is most familiar to us. It is these other parts that operate independently of our awareness, making us blush, for example, or giving us dreams.

Hypnosis is best described by Milton Erickson's explanation to a woman dealing with pain. When he told her he would remove her pain and she would feel no discomfort she was doubtful, and asked him how he could do this, since it had not been medically possible. "If that door were to burst open right now," he said, "and you looked over and saw a great big tiger licking its chops hungrily and staring at only you, how much pain do you think you'd feel?" Later, when people asked her what had helped her get rid of her discomfort, they were mystified when she said that she had a tiger under her bed and she just listened to it purr.[30]

What actually happens in hypnosis is complex, and the experience can be like being in another world, because it is using parts of the brain that are not directly assessed. Trance work rarely focuses on only one physical reaction, for example, controlling nausea and vomiting, and it usually influences mood states and general life satisfaction.

There are many ways to structure trances; one of the most innovative is an approach described by Moshe Torem.[31] This is particularly useful for those experiences that stir up feelings of helplessness and hopelessness and generally begins with an open discussion between patient and therapist about how the patient would like to be more comfortable, confident, and healthy.

After this a trance is induced in which the patient mentally imagines herself in a future time when she has solved the problems that now are troubling her. She is encouraged to feel the sense of pleasure and pride in having achieved a resolution of the problems and to examine those parts of herself that were most useful in reaching this state.

She is helped to picture all of the visual, auditory, and other sensations that would be involved in the experience. As the patient pictures herself in the future time, she is asked to examine what she did to solve the problems and what she learned as a result.

All of these experiences are saved and internalized as she is brought back to the present time in her thinking. The insights that develop are preserved and operate subconsciously to motivate behavior and mood in the present. To strengthen the experience after she leaves the session, she is asked to write an essay about her experience.

This innovative and enriching exercise is clearly not possible without the guidance and planning of an experienced therapist, but in such a setting it can be extremely effective in helping a patient dealing with breast cancer to more effectively use all modes of treatment.

3. Systematic Desensitization

Another member of the class of relaxation techniques involves counterconditioning, or reversing reactions that have been conditioned. Originally this technique developed to help people to deal with phobias, those automatic fearful reactions to animals or insects or other things.

Systematic desensitization involves teaching people the relaxation response and then gradually exposing them to increasingly upsetting experiences so that the patient can adjust to each. Although this was at first successful in reducing fears, it was cumbersome to arrange encounters with dogs, horses, spiders, or whatever set off the phobia, so imagination was used instead.

We often try to countercondition our own reflexive reactions, although we are probably not very organized in our attempts to do so. When, for example, young people first try cigarettes or whiskey, they have strong physical sensations. Over time, they change these negative reactions to positive ones by repeatedly introducing the item in small doses.

In treatment for chemotherapy reactions, patients are first taught relaxation, with a good deal of practice so that they thoroughly master the technique. Following this, a list (or hierarchy) is developed that arranges experiences in order of increasing upset. With reactions to breast cancer chemotherapy, the list might look like this:

- Parking car in hospital lot

- blood drawn

- hearing of white blood cell count

- waiting in the waiting room

- Carol the nurse appears

- "We're ready for you"

- Smell of alcohol

- Sight of syringe

- Pricking sensation

- Finding a vein

- Stomach heaves

This list serves as a route for reducing anxiety by sequentially changing the body's reaction to each level. After initially getting into a trance or relaxed state you first begin to imagine parking the car in the hospital lot. Since this is likely to stir some queasy feelings, you spend time reestablishing the relaxed state, and regaining your internal balance. It may take five or six separate exposures to each item before you begin to notice a change in your response and feelings. Your body will operate at its own pace, and you need to give it time.

When this is done you move on through the list. It is important to take the list slowly, giving yourself plenty of time to adjust to each item. You may also find it necessary to revise the list, if you find there are other things that should be included. It is rarely possible to cover more than three or four levels of the list in one sitting. Even so, you will require repeated practice to condition the new internal response.

When this procedure is used under trained hands with patients, the results are good, with a reduction in the side effects of treatment.[32]

4. Biofeedback

Human beings are forever trying to figure out what causes what: Why don't people like me? What made it snow so much this winter? and How come I'm not rich and famous? Biofeedback is one of the relaxation procedures that utilizes this interest and helps people to become aware of the unique pattern of responses that the body makes to certain situations.

When we were psychology students, we were required to spend time working in the laboratory supervising experiments. One of the longest running involved showing undergraduate men pictures of females to see which ones would stir physical responses. We would measure their pulse, blood pressure, and electrical skin responses and then show them how the various pictures had affected them. The reactions of these young, energetic males were predictable: they responded physically to pictures of attractive young females, and their pulse, blood pressure, and electrical skin response all rose when they looked at these pictures.

Life in a psychology laboratory has its slow periods, and during one of them a fiendish graduate student cooked up a variation on the standard experiment. She substituted pictures of motherly, middle-aged women for a few of the attractive young females. She then rewired the biofeedback machinery so that the readings shown to the young men registered physiological arousal to the new pictures of the more seasoned women. Some of the young men looked puzzled as they left the laboratory, but the female faculty reported more friendly behavior and an increase in courtesy that week in their male undergraduates.

When it is used in clinical treatment, biofeedback measures are reported on meters that keep the patient informed about what is occurring in her body. This may involve pulse, blood pressure, galvanic skin response, or other indicators, but they all are actual changes in the body.

Through listening to or watching these readings, a person can experiment with various ways to change the results. Galvanic skin response, which is a measure of the electrical conductivity of the skin, is usually measured by electrodes that lie on top of the skin and report changes with a beeping sound.

A high beep means that there is more tension in the system, and a low beep means that the person is more relaxed. When people use these devices, they usually try to change the reading by jiggling the electrodes, holding their breath, or something else. At some point they notice that something they did made a change, and so they try to do it again.

Eventually, after much practice, people are usually able to produce changed results in the physiological readings as they learn to calm the system. This can be applied to chemotherapy for breast cancer, since the patient can reduce the overall tension in the system and change the body's conditioned reactions.

In effect, biofeedback controls the physical underpinnings of anxiety and so affects the body's response to circumstances that produce anxiety. The stuttering, heart rate, and perspiration that are characteristic of upset can be reduced, and so the subjective sensation of upset is also reduced.

Biofeedback is clearly useful, and when compared to group therapy for anxiety, it does better at controlling arousal and mood disturbances. Short-term structured group treatment did not seem to be as effective as the individual practice in reducing individual distress.[33] Sometimes biofeedback is used to prepare patients for hypnosis, since it develops the skills necessary for controlling physical reactions so that they can get on to mental exercises.[34]

Some researchers have seen a parallel between biofeedback, in which body responses are modified to achieve a goal with a machine, and the playing of video games. When cancer researchers used video games to reduce the side effects of chemotherapy, nausea, and vomiting, they found them useful. They particularly helped anticipatory nausea, although they were not useful in reducing anxiety.[35]

Most of these techniques involve greatly intensified distraction, so that attention is structured and focused in ways different from usual. More common, milder forms of distraction, such as watching movies and having someone read to you, are also useful as supplemental aids.

The psychological techniques described in this chapter offer great opportunities for changing the experience of chemotherapy and maximizing its impact. But there is no magic here, only instruction by trained helpers and repeated practice.

Chapter Nine

Women Connected

This book is an attempt to help women draw on their own wisdom to enhance health and boost breast cancer treatment. The research described in the preceding chapters demonstrates that women have enormous capability to change the course of their health and illness. Although biology is primary, it is never more than a starting point. That women know many things within themselves, truths that the larger society ignores, can serve them as a source of power.

It will change in the future, this approach of looking for answers outside of ourselves, finding new chemicals to inject into the body, raising the levels of this and lowering the levels of that. For two million years on this earth, humans have survived primarily by recourse to their own inner resources. With all the miracles of modern science, a human life span is still virtually unchanged from biblical days. Perhaps it is time to be more humble about our intellectual discoveries and look instead to our species learning and gender leanings for enlightenment.

If we look carefully at our lives, we can see these forces at work everywhere. How else do we avoid serious illness for so many decades of our lives? The intricate interplay of heart, soul, and brain constitutes a balanced system that we need only to support with all of our female inclinations. In this way, we strengthen the body and help it do what it needs to do.

Breast cancer is a far more widespread problem than the culture accepts. The figure often cited, that 182,000 women each year are diagnosed with breast cancer, doesn't give any sense of the scope of the problem. Currently, 1.6 million women in the United States have been diagnosed with breast cancer, and since 1980 450,000 have died of it. (In the same time period, 194,000 died of AIDS.) The number of women who have undiagnosed breast cancer is impossible to tell, although the research is surprising. In random autopsies of adult women, 25 percent had invasive breast carcinoma or premalignant lesions.[1]

The assumption can be made that some women have breast cancer, but they have no symptoms or decline in health, and they will live out their lives with no awareness of the disease.

This does not mean that regular checkups and exams are unnecessary. These are essential in determining whether there is a disease process at work and in applying active treatment when there is.

Regular screening and exams make it possible in most cases to initiate medical treatments while the disease is limited, and the impact of surgery, chemotherapy, and radiation can have the strongest effect when it is detected early.

Although breast cancer is a disease that is present more often than we realize, it may be possible to use our energy to create life patterns that enhance the body's ability to control malignant growth and spread.

Breast cancer research has traditionally been concerned with prediction and prevention, and while a great deal of useful information has thus been produced, the overall rate of breast cancer among American women has not been reduced. In addition to screening and prevention, attention needs to be paid to slowing the course of the disease.

Whether breast cancer can be prevented may not be as useful a question as whether the course of the illness can be slowed. If women can live a normal life span with a controlled chronic illness, perhaps such a life can be accepted as a reasonable alternative to complete cure.

For many women breast cancer appears to be cured after routine treatment, and so they retire as breast cancer patients, with no further work. Most cancer authorities support the assumption that breast cancer is cured if there are no recurrences five years after diagnosis, but this is not an accurate conclusion, and it leads women to ignore their own resources and judgment.

If a woman is diagnosed with breast cancer, there is an 80 percent chance of a recurrence at some point in her life. It is impossible to determine when or whether a recurrence will happen, and many women live for decades with no symptoms of illness.

Women who are cured after treatment by the five-year defini-
tion do not return to normal risk categories, and they have a risk
of mortality from breast cancer fifteen times higher than women
who have not had breast cancer. The talk of cure often leads
women to believe that they can be healthiest by avoiding thoughts
of breast cancer, when they could instead be active on their own
behalf.

It is more fruitful to think of the disease as a chronic condition that requires constant attention, one that is responsive to
the emotional climate in which we live. Medical treatment is the
beginning of recovery, and supplementing it with psychological
treatment increases the likelihood of good health. Fortunately,
using psychological techniques enhances life as well as health.

Some women like Marylu have a strong sense of their own
needs and are guided by an inner voice that moves them to seek or
create the best context for their own health. Combined with good
medical care and good luck, this offers the possibility of long remissions in breast cancer. In order to make this possible for more
women, they need to have easy access to all of the most useful
information in the field.

If a psychologist gets breast cancer, she has an advantage, since
she knows where to look and how to read what she finds. She
knows of the great research laboratories at Ohio State, the University of Pittsburgh, and Miami and can follow the trends and
developments. Although the research may not be uniform in its
findings, there's enough information to guide her choices. The
purpose of this book is to share that information with as many
women as possible.

Much of the research reported in this volume is preliminary,
and the results will require many replications before they can be
accepted as scientific givens. Some of the findings may even fail to
find confirmation in future research, but the overall trend of the
data is clear, and no science can ever stand or fall based on the
findings of one study.

Breast cancer has not been a dominant concern of American
medicine, partly because it is considered by many to be a curable
disease and partly because it is only a woman's ailment. This is
reflected in the funding made available for breast cancer. In the
funding year beginning in October 1994, there was a dramatic increase in monies for breast cancer research, with an increase of

33.5 percent over the previous year, but that is still very skimpy funding for this major disease.

In this year of high research funding, breast cancer research will get $262,900,000, compared to the $15,000,000,000 for the National Aeronautics and Space Administration.[2] Most of the breast cancer research money will go to research that looks at chemical treatments aimed at stimulating the immune system and destroying malignant cells. Only a tiny fraction of funds will go to research aimed at identifying psychological influences and treatments that can boost medical treatment, even though these factors currently show great promise.

The impetus for using psychological techniques and information must come from women dealing with breast cancer, for they have most at stake and are in the best position to evaluate the utility of the information. What's more, they are women and need to speak for a woman's unique needs.

The Power of Women's Connections

David Spiegel's work represents a major turn in the road for cancer research; it demonstrates conclusively that psychological forces can change the course of a physical ailment in its most powerful stages. It is doubly significant because it examines not only psychological forces, but specifically the power of women's relating to affect the course of disease. Women's proclivity for making connections — for relating to others in a way that shares confidences, offers mutual support, helps relaxation, and gives practical help — appears to change the way that biology unwinds.

This is a revolutionary development and a major advance in cancer treatment. Not only does help come from a new quarter for treating cancer, but it is relatively cheap and easy help. In group psychotherapy, there are no disturbing side effects and no disruption of life; if anything, psychological treatments help people do better in other aspects of their lives as well. The cost alone should make it appealing to a health care system trying to reform itself.

At the same time that David Spiegel was trying to help women with breast cancer by bringing them together and helping them to forge powerful bonds of relationship, another researcher was looking at women's relationships in a new way.

In 1982 Carol Gilligan published *In a Different Voice: Psychological Theory and Women's Development,* which was an outgrowth of the Harvard Project on Women's Psychology and Girls' Development. The project is a feminist collaborative research effort and looks at the forces affecting women's psychological development.[3]

In a number of writings, Gilligan presents a view of women's development as distinguished from men's growth. She sees females as more oriented to relating to others from an early age as a way to develop. It is difficult if not impossible for them to grow outside of a context of relations with others. Connections with others provide a structure within which a woman can build personality organization. Through connecting to others a woman develops an image of herself, as well as vitality and strength.

The results of the Spiegel study and Gilligan's research give strong support to the idea that women's connections have a powerful effect on female immune function, not in some theoretical or abstract way, but in helping women's bodies deal with disease progression. The ways that women related in group psychotherapy allowed the release of strong and traumatic feelings, the sharing of intimate and personal reactions, and the offering of help to others.

In this way, women could limit the effect of the illness and deal with other aspects of their lives. They could also find a sense of personal worth through the acceptance of their feelings and reactions by others in the group. One's own voice was accepted, and connections were preserved.

Speaking with your own voice may also directly change the experience of dealing with breast cancer, aside from all the psychological complexities. One way that cancer patients disconnect from their insides is to try to ignore pain when they feel it. There is great resistance to "giving in" to cancer pain, and half of cancer patients are reluctant to report pain to medical caregivers, even though it can be adequately controlled 90 percent of the time.[4]

Complaints about pain may seem to cast a patient in a bad light, as a whiner or wimp, a baby who can't stand what everybody else seemingly can. Complaining may also seem like a repudiation of a physician's capability, proving that the doctor doesn't know what he or she doing. And sometimes doctors do take offense. Said one, "This medicine is supposed to work. It works for everybody else...."

One fear that comes from traumatic experiences is that unless we are very good, we may be abandoned. If a patient complains too much, she may fear that her doctor will refer her to a specialist, to get rid of her, and this does occasionally happen.

Sometimes complaints about pain seem to inconvenience other family members; there may be more doctor visits required and the additional expense of more prescriptions. The pain may seem to ruin the experience of family time together, so that the patient feels obligated to ignore inner sensations and instead acknowledge what others want her to feel.

All of these reactions relegate pain reporting to the trash heap so that it cannot be used as a rudder by which to steer a course, an inner voice that offers help and good guidance. We need to listen to the inner signals that remind us that something hurts. Pain is best controlled in cancer treatment, since it limits tolerance for treatment and interferes with other bodily functions, like eating and sleeping.

The immune system is not improved by more stress in the system, and pain causes more tension and upset. Some of this is physical tension, since discomfort prevents relaxation and throws the body off balance, and some of it is emotional, for pain always gives rise to some anxiety and depression.

When we silence the inner signals of pain because we fear others' reactions and believe that we will fare better by being ideal patients, we are destroying that which makes us unique. We give up a part of ourselves needlessly in the belief that we cannot have our connections and speak forthrightly about what we experience internally. Instead we may find ourselves talking about our "wonderful" doctor or our "wonderful" family because we need to believe that we are gaining something by our stoicism.

Cancer as a Breakdown of Physiological Connection

The concept of community is a central idea in women's psychological functioning and provides the framework against which women generate their own individuality. It is also central to the body's healthy functioning, since all parts of the body must work in unity. The organs and tissues of the body are all supremely interdependent, and they are in constant communication with one another so that each can operate effectively.

One way to conceive of cancer is that malignant cells are autonomous and disrupt the interdependency of tissues in the body. The healthy body's systems are all connected and operate in balance, modulating each other's reactions and functions. In appetite, for example, the digestive system, central nervous system, and sensory system all interrelate and affect each other, so that when you smell hamburgers cooking at dinnertime, you develop stomach sensations.

Cancer cells ignore the moderating influences of other body systems and grow and spread without response to the rest of the body. They disrupt the body's integration by interfering with normal processes and avoiding physical controls. They are not responsive to the routine restraints that affect division, so that tumor suppressor genes usually don't limit cancer cells (although sometimes they do). They do not respond to the immune cells, which keep the body in balance, and they fail to anchor themselves by cell surface receptors, so that they travel throughout the body.

How do normal cells become cancerous? There is apparently no single change that leads to the development of a cancerous growth, but instead genetic changes move a normal cell step by step to becoming malignant. Neither is this process unstoppable. Some forces in the body provoke growth and others restrict it, but there is a gradual movement toward malignancy when these forces break down.

The emergence of cancerous cells involves a disruption of the connection of cells to their surrounding cells and to the organ system of which they are a part. Instead of maintaining a balance of function, cancer cells are parasitic, draining off energy and offering nothing in return. The cancer cells' growth rate ceases to be determined, as in healthy tissue, by the needs of the cells around them. Instead division is the result of the cells' own forces, with no connection to surrounding tissue.

In its extreme, the cancer cell becomes immortal, no longer limited, like normal cells, by the natural forces that govern the cellular community. In the laboratory culture, the cancer cell can continue to divide endlessly, unrestrained by surrounding influences. Similarly, cancer cells can grow without anchorage, which other cells need, and do not need direct contact with a solid base. In the process of becoming malignant, normal cells lose their specific characteristics and function, so that they no longer do any of the two hundred or so types of jobs that human cells perform.

Their energy is no longer devoted to the task that was their lot and instead is absorbed by endless self-aggrandizement. The unity and integration that constitute an organ system are destroyed, and the cancer cells grow at their own pace without reference to the welfare of the larger body. Mutuality is replaced by independence, integration becomes chaos, and internal balance is lost.

This is a description of the biology of cancer, not its psychology, but the terms used are similar, and it appears that there are, coincidentally, similar processes. Cancer is a disease of cellular autonomy and loss of connection in which cellular community is destroyed. It is only within the well-organized and internally connected body that each cell can best function and perform its unique task. When cells lose their connection to the larger system, they also lose their uniqueness and the ability to self-regulate. Does the same thing happen to women in American culture?

Gender Health Differences

Women and men differ greatly in their physical vulnerabilities. Most medical research has examined male characteristics and then generalized the findings to females, assuming that the two were the same. This is not in fact true, and when gender differences are examined, different conclusions must be drawn.

Women live longer than men, with an average life span of 78.3 years to men's 71.3, and the way that women and men live in these years differs. In their physical health, women tend to have more chronic diseases than men, although when men get sick, their illness is more frequently lethal. Women's diseases are often connected with reproductive organs, and they suffer from more autoimmune diseases as well, diseases in which the body's defenses turn back on themselves, for example, multiple sclerosis, rheumatoid arthritis, and systemic lupus.

In every age group, however, there is greater female survival, even though women have more illnesses than men. Both genders suffer from cardiovascular disease and various forms of cancer, but as a rule women have better outcomes.

In mental health as well, there are clear gender differences. Decades ago it was thought that females were more prone to psychological disorders, but with the influx of women into the various therapy professions, this view has changed. Both genders suffer from stress and from the emotional afflictions that cause disability.

Men are most subject to those disorders that involve withdrawal and alienation from others. Suicide, substance abuse, and antisocial personality disorders all involve rifts in the relationship of a man with his emotional context, with others in his life, and with the broader community. They are responses that involve profound damage to the individual in terms of his health, relationships, and membership in society. But taking one's life, abusing alcohol or drugs, or committing criminal acts also involve a profound rejection of others in one's life. Men's psychological disorders most often involve the breaking of relational ties to others.

Women's psychological disorders have more to do with destructive attempts to change themselves to fit into relationships. The major women's disorders — depression, phobia, panic disorder, and obsessive compulsive disorder — are a response to one's feelings, usually unacceptable feelings of anger and anxiety, that have the potential of disrupting connections with others. In their attempt to reach some compromise between the voice within and the need for connection, women sometimes strangle the internal voice, which results in emotional reverberations throughout the system.

There are many theories to explain why men and women differ in general health statistics. At one time it was thought that men suffered far more stress than women, which would explain the high rates of cardiovascular illnesses and other illnesses with a direct stress causation. It has since been accepted that although both genders experience substantial stress, their perception of stress is different.

Men and women also have different perceptions of what is needed to live well and the difficulties involved in reaching the good life. Although both seek relationships, their ways of dealing with conflict and separation are quite different.

There are also differences in communication patterns that are determined by values. Women are far more likely to report distress and to give voice to upsets, at least to other women, and are less likely to see this as a sign of inadequacy or defeat. For men, discussing distress is felt differently. Paradoxically, merely voicing distress reduces it, so that when women complain, they may appear more distressed, but they are in fact lowering internal tension.

There are real biological differences in how males and females respond to challenging life experiences, a result of the different reactivity of the male and female central nervous systems. In cardiovascular response, men and women differ, although they both register emotions in these systems. Men show changes in blood pressure during emotional experiences, but women more often show changes in heart rate.

The release of some stress hormones, such as catecholamines, is higher in men in acute stress, but the sex hormones, estrogen, progesterone, and testosterone, have different effects on how the stress hormones are released. To complicate matters further in looking at the interplay of bodily systems, immune cells have receptors for sex hormones, so that the release of estrogen, for example, is registered in the immune system.

The emotional context in which men and women live is perhaps the most significant difference, particularly in looking at health outcomes. The Alameda County health study discussed in chapter 5 found that having fewer social and community ties was related to increased mortality, and that the people with the fewest connections were most likely to die early. Across all the research in this area, the same result emerges: low levels of social support are predictive of early death. This appears to be because low social-support levels or a cold emotional climate lead to increased sympathetic medullary activity, which increases blood pressure, heart rate, and circulating levels of stress hormones.

It is apparent that female relational patterns are different from male patterns. Women tend to have more friends than men, they confide more often, talk over problems, seek companionship, and join in one another's life events. Women are more often involved in the welfare of the community and caring for other individuals. They offer help, both in relationships and in occupations such as nurse and teacher.

Women reduce stress for others, perhaps the way a friendly dog in the corner does for children. In one study having a supportive companion reduced reactions to stress-inducing events in a laboratory setting.[5] The appeal in this culture of having a "woman in the kitchen" may be less culinary or power-related and more a cue for conditioned relaxation.

Women often get more support from their friends and from their children than men do. Their traditional role generally involves social network maintenance needs, like writing thank-you notes, sending cards, making condolence calls, planning social events, and so forth. Getting social support is really one-half of a reciprocal interchange that keeps women active. The way that women get social support is to give it, and the experience of caring for others involves great expenditures of emotional energy and time.

Women tend to build social networks and create a warm emotional context for themselves out of habit, cultural expectations, and need, but this setting can serve as a powerful resource when a woman becomes ill. It seems that it can also serve to limit the progression of illness.

Type A personality, which includes irritability, a sense of time urgency, and low self-esteem, is connected with increased cardiovascular risk, so that there is a higher incidence of heart attack and stroke in people who manifest an excess of these characteristics. People with this personality type seem to be affected by social context, so that a Type A unmarried man with little social support would have a greatly increased risk of a heart attack or stroke. In comparison, a Type A woman with high social support does not have increased risk.[6]

When asked about how men and women affected each other's health, David Spiegel commented ruefully that women benefited most from relationships with other women, while men benefited most from marriage, and that it does people's health good to be involved with women but does little for their health to be involved with men.[7]

Why is it beneficial to health to be involved in relationships with women? The data is mixed and suggests that a woman's typical behavior offers a means of emotional connection, and hence less general life stress. These behavior patterns result from traditional expectations of men and women, but rarely offer women all the opportunities for relating that they need. In traditional marital relationships, where the husband is the provider and the wife is the homemaker, women have poorer physical health, lower self-esteem, and less satisfaction than in relationships where there is role equivalence and flexibility in husbands' and wives' behavior.[8]

But this is not the only way that men and women can combine in forming unions. Often, particularly among younger couples, there is a more equal view of the need for each spouse to contribute. Nonetheless, whether both spouses work or one stays home, women do about the same amount of work, that is, 80 percent of household and childcare work.[9] It may seem to women that a change in household responsibilities would reduce stress, but social connection outside the marriage is likely to be a more promising source of strength.

Several studies have shown that men and women are affected quite differently by marriage. Women experience more dissatisfaction and psychological distress, perhaps because of different expectations. In one study, men rated their marital communication, sexual relationship, and relations with parents as good, while their wives rated these as problematic.[10]

The consequences of acting as a husband or a wife are quite different, according to the research, even though there is no uniform agreement on what these roles involve. Husbands are physically healthier and have fewer psychological problems than bachelors, and they achieve greater job success as well. For women, the opposite is true: there are more physical and mental problems and less job success for wives than for single women.[11]

The different consequences of marriage for husbands and wives may be the result of a perceived imbalance in emotional expression. In one study of aging couples, men reported giving less support to their wives than they received as they got older.[12] But men seem to depend on women for their needs to share secrets, have friends, and be helped, while women look to their friends.[13]

In traditional marriages a husband's role included that of provider and breadwinner, while a wife served other functions and met her emotional needs with a range of relationships. During the earlier part of this century, when there was less mobility, marriage usually expanded a woman's primary family to include her husband's family. Women generally married a man in the same locale, and so continued to relate to her family and friends but took on his as well. She also founded her own household and began to relate in the community as an adult among equals. These new circumstances offered the opportunity for a much wider social network, including neighbors, and for the development of more connections and relationships.

With the economic and occupational changes of the latter part of this century, it is less common that women remain in the places where they were born, and therefore often their entire social network must be created anew. Frequently this is impossible if a woman works during the day; she may never come to know her neighbors at all, in part because these women may also be working. With the occupational changes also come residential changes, and it is not unheard of for a rapidly advancing man to move his family once every few years to a new city, forcing the repeated abandonment of a woman's connections.

In these circumstances the opportunity for women to connect diminishes, even though the basic format of marriage does not. The old connections that sprang from relatives and in-laws living close by, children at home, and neighbors around during the day are all generally unavailable. Instead, a woman has primarily her work acquaintances to relate to, as long as she is not moved from one geographical location to another.

Because the chance for interpersonal connections has been so sharply limited for women, marriage comes to take on a far bigger burden in satisfying women's relational needs. It is easy to feel great relationship dissatisfaction and blame it on marriage when it properly has to do with the lack of women's relationships. Most men, no matter how responsive, cannot replace the need for women to connect with women.

Marriage is often targeted as the major opportunity for a woman to relate to others. Women have been counseled to avoid letting children or friendships interfere with this primary tie and to examine themselves relentlessly to consider which of their flaws, or their husbands', might be an obstacle to full satisfaction in marriage.

The extraordinary number of women's periodicals that publish material to help women improve their marital performance gives a sense of the emotional riches that seem potentially available in marriage. But what happens in those times when women find that marriage, even a good marriage, does not give the sense of fullness and completion that they seek?

Under these conditions many women still their voice and quiet their need, sensing that their requirements are too much for marriage and finding no other outlet for them. But denial of feeling doesn't change the nature of the need. When women are asked to rate their needs for a happy life, having friends rates second only to health in importance.[14]

For some women, homosexual relationships offer an opportunity for emotional balance, with each of these unions created uniquely from the needs and styles of the women involved. Sometimes this produces a deeply satisfying relationship that transcends the bounds of traditional male/female marriages, and sometimes it produces a parody of the husband-wife roles.

The same need, that of women to speak clearly and with their own voice, is an issue in lesbian relationships, and these are not inherently insulated from a woman's vulnerability to pathological niceness. Saving others from our feelings is often seen as an integral part of femininity.

For women living in a homosexual lifestyle, a particular concern is the disruption in social support that can come when a lesbian woman becomes a breast cancer patient. In a situation where she has little power or control, a woman may find her medical treatment dominated by heterosexual expectations. She will be asked for her husband's insurance information, sexual relations will be discussed in a heterosexual framework, and female companions will be accorded less standing than male partners.

In addition, a homosexual woman will be exposed to scrutiny of her private life and patterns at a time when she is least able to speak confidently for her own needs. She will be in the position of making many new acquaintances, and the need to deal with gender preference issues may be too demanding at a time when health concerns dominate.

Breast cancer diagnosis is a serious life event and will typically bring a woman into increased contact with family members. If there has been emotional turmoil over her homosexuality, this will be reactivated, and there may even be angry expressions at the woman for getting sick.

In the psychological thinking of the past few decades, a major change occurred when psychologists began to look at the context of people's lives. It came to be understood that we are deeply influenced by the folks we live with regardless of gender preference and that when we are anxious or depressed, this is partially the result of the way that our family system deals with conflict, challenge, and growth.

The assumption of family therapy, however, has been that the family is the main context for people; but it is not the sole source of psychological support. For women, friendships are particularly important, since they offer significant emotional satisfaction and also protection for health.

What happens when a woman's primary emotional context becomes the medical system in which women have traditionally been subservient to males? Although this is rapidly changing, for many women the context will be a powerful influence on their behavior, and they will be strongly compelled to defer to male authority figures. For male or female physicians, accustomed to the hierarchical power structure of medicine in which the male doctor is in control and the female patient behaves, this will be comfortable. For women who choose to speak clearly of their own perspectives and requirements and who reach for emotional connections with medical caregivers, this may be a disquieting experience.

All the research reviewed here emphasizes the power of human contact as essential to health and healing. Pennebaker's work on sharing confidences, Levy's findings on the effects of social support on natural killer cell activity levels, Kiecolt-Glaser's work on loneliness, and Spiegel's findings on the awesome power of women's connections all point to the significance of the emotional context in which we live. Apparently we are biologically different when we belong to human relationships.

What does this suggest about the use of self-help techniques for mental or physical needs? This vast array of practices that enhance human well-being has made a powerful contribution to the human race. Through reading books or using audiotapes or videotapes, people have educated themselves to the value of various health practices and have improved their lives and health care as well.

The problem with self-help techniques is that they stress autonomy, self-reliance, independence, and individuation. All of the best research on health, and certainly on breast cancer, indicates that healing is powerfully supported by human contact and connection. To encourage people to withdraw into themselves and bypass the potential for human connections does not seem in the best service to health.

We know that social support is not only conducive to healing, but that it is soothing and reduces stress, helping the body to better utilize treatment. Self-help techniques handicap the self rather than help, for they deprive it of that most important resource, a caring other.

In relating to others, women find their voice and speak from their feelings and judgment with real vitality. When they relate only to themselves and try to help themselves in isolation, their thinking operates less well, feelings reinforce themselves, and there is more stress on the system.

Social support is a lifelong source of protection from ill health and premature death, but it is not only in receiving that the benefit comes. It is also in the giving that women gain strength, for their self-esteem, sense of personal power, and identity all benefit.

Have you ever watched girls of nine and ten, the way that they move with freedom and assurance? They are energetic and fearless, and there is a sense of vitality and brightness that is delightful to watch. This is the essence of fighting spirit, the energetic and ardent response to a challenge, which is so promising in dealing with breast cancer.

This fits the spirit of women who know joy, as described in Levy's work, or women who have an optimistic explanatory style, as described in Seligman's work; it is a clear contrast to those who are hopeless and helpless and have difficulty dealing with negative feelings and relating to others. All women have the capacity for these responses; they are most apparent in these early years, before women come up against what Carol Gilligan calls the wall of Western culture, when they lose faith in their inner voice as women.

The verve and vitality of youth may seem reckless and irresponsible, but it is primarily an understanding that risk is part of life and that there is enough strength to take chances. Prepubertal girls have dreams, images that form as they first look out on the world as adolescents and get their first broad view of adult life and its possibilities. In this moment, a belief is formed about what constitutes a life well lived, a life worth living, and for each girl, still mostly a child but nonetheless with a unique personality, there is a vision that will predominate throughout her life.

In adult therapy it is often necessary for women to return to this period and recover the early dreams and impressions to discover their deepest needs and yearnings. What women find in these recollections is often remarkably useful as adults, for the basic form of the personality changes little in the years after puberty. When I was a child of ten, I wanted very much to be a brain surgeon so I could understand how the brain works. Although I became a psychologist, it fulfilled the same dream.

Taking chances, daring things untried but promising, is often the way that we expand our faith in ourselves and our vision of our possibilities. When we face challenges with courage, we invariably feel stronger and more pleased with ourselves. Being careful rarely brings such gains.

This does not mean that life should be lived carelessly or without due regard for safety. Fastening seat belts and eating one's vegetables will always constitute a wise course. In the same vein, following medical recommendations for breast cancer treatment is mature judgment. But this is only the beginning, and the rest needs to come from within, as women listen to what they need and experiment boldly with ways to obtain it.

As women learn what is expected of them in the adult culture, it can mean the abandonment of the great spirit of adventure that characterizes girls. The fun of exploring and experimenting is replaced by more sedate pursuits, and women learn to take good care of others who will have adventures, rather than having them themselves. Risk-taking becomes associated with striking out on our own and leaving others behind, even though there are many ways to take risks in service of happiness and stay connected.

For some, taking risks endangers support from those we love or it may risk their disapproval. In addition, self-esteem may drop if we criticize ourselves for decisions that end poorly. Paradoxically, the lack of habitual and responsible risk-taking is often the basis for endless obsessing over decision-making.

When they evaluate their lives, most people will consider whether they took enough chances in service of what they wanted and will regret the risks avoided, not those that ended poorly. It is the roads not taken that haunt us and make us wish we had had more courage. Preserving security, or what is the illusion of security, can be extremely risky.

Epilogue

Marylu and I were having coffee this fine morning, the buds just beginning to show on the forsythia. She had been talking about the farm and how good the animals felt to get out on to the fresh grass again. She was planning to put in roses this year, up against the barn where the sun was warm and welcoming.

"How's your book coming?" she asked. "Last time I talked to you, you were having a hard time getting anybody to look at the manuscript. Any luck yet?"

"Not yet," I said.

"You can't ever give up, you know," she said with a wink. "If you just keep going, you can do it. Trust me."

Notes

Chapter One: Marylu's Battle

1. L. LeShan and R. E. Worthington, "Loss of Cathexis as a Common Psychodynamic Characteristic of Cancer Patients: An Attempt at Statistical Validation of a Clinical Hypothesis," *Psychological Reports* 2 (1956): 183.

2. D. Spiegel, J. R. Bloom, H. C. Kraemer, and E. Gottheil, "Effect of Psychosocial Treatment on Survival of Patients with Metastatic Breast Cancer," *The Lancet* (October 14, 1989): 888–91.

3. T. Beardsley, "Trends in Cancer Epidemiology: A War Not Won," *Scientific American* (January 1994): 135.

4. From J. Holland and J. Rowland, *Handbook of Psychooncology: Care of the Patient with Cancer* (New York: Oxford University Press, 1990).

5. Beardsley, "Trends in Cancer Epidemiology," 135.

6. Ibid., 130.

7. Ibid., 135.

8. R. A. Hahn, "Profound Bilateral Blindness and the Incidence of Breast Cancer," *Epidemiology* 2 (1991): 208–10.

9. C. C. Hsieh and D. Trichopoulos, "Breast Size, Handedness and Breast Cancer Risk," *European Journal of Cancer* 27, no. 2 (1991): 131–35.

10. B. Hillner and T. Smith, "Efficacy and Cost. Effectiveness of Autologous Bone Marrow Transplantation in Metastatic Breast Cancer: Estimates Using Decision Analysis While Awaiting Clinical Trial Results," *JAMA: The Journal of the American Medical Association* 267, no. 15 (1992): 2055.

11. American Psychiatric Association, *Diagnostic and Statistical Manual of Mental Disorders,* 3d ed. rev. (Washington, D.C.: American Psychiatric Association, 1987).

12. S. M. Levy, J. Lee, C. Bagley, and M. Lippman, "Survival Hazards Analysis in First Recurrent Breast Cancer Patients: Seven-Year Follow-Up," *Psychosomatic Medicine* 50 (1988): 520–28.

Chapter Two: The Power inside Us

1. D. M. Ewin, "Hypnotherapy for Warts: 41 Consecutive Cases with 33 Cures," *American Journal of Clinical Hypnosis* 35, no. 1 (July 1992): 1–10.

2. L. E. Moore and J. Z. Kaplan, "Hypnotically Accelerated Burn Wound Healing," *American Journal of Clinical Hypnosis* 26, no. 1 (July 1983): 16–19.

3. S. Ferraro, "The Anguished Politics of Breast Cancer," *New York Times Magazine,* August 15, 1993.

4. Mortimer B. Zuckerman, *U.S. News & World Report,* November 23, 1992, 104.

5. D. Plotkin and F. Blankenberg, "Breast Cancer — Biology and Malpractice," *American Journal of Clinical Oncology* 14, no. 3 (1991): 254–66.

6. T. Beardsley, "Trends in Cancer Epidemiology: A War Not Won," *Scientific American* (January 1994): 138.

7. J. R. Harris, S. Hellman, G. P. Cnellos, and B. Fisher, "Cancer of the Breast" in *Cancer: Principles and Practice of Oncology,* ed. V. T. DeVita, S. Hellman, and S. Rosenberg (New York: J. B. Lippincott, 1985).

8. Plotkin and Blankenberg, "Breast Cancer — Biology and Malpractice," 254–66.

9. D. V. Fournier, U. Schiller, H. Jundermann, U. Legler, and M. Bauer, "Natural Growth Rate in 300 Primary Breast Carcinomas and Correlation to Hormone Factors," *Annals of the New York Academy of Science* 464 (1986): 563–65.

10. Ibid.

11. Ibid.

12. E. M. Greenspan, *The Breast Cancer Epidemic in the United States* (New York: Chemotherapy Foundation, 1990).

13. This material is reported by Dr. Leopoldo Carlos Cancio of the 82d Airborne Division, United States Army, in "Stress and Trance in Freefall Parachuting: A Pilot Study," in the *American Journal of Clinical Hypnosis* 33, no. 4 (April 1991): 225–34.

14. T. Kuhn, *The Structure of Scientific Revolutions* (Chicago: University of Chicago Press, 1970).

15. B. H. Fox, "Current Theory of Psychogenic Effects on Cancer Incidence and Prognosis," *Journal of Psychosocial Oncology* 1, no. 1 (1993): 17–31.

Chapter Three: Immune Cells and Emotions

1. I. Shimakowara, M. Imamura, N. Yamanaka, Y. Ishii, and K. Kikuchi, "Identification of Lymphocyte Subpopulations in Human Breast Cancer Tissue and Its Significance," *Cancer* 49 (1982): 1456–64.

2. J. Blalock, "The Immune System as a Sensory Organ," *Journal of Immunology* 132 (1984): 1067–70.

3. T. B. Herbert and S. Cohen, "Stress and Immunity in Humans: A Meta-analytic Review," *Psychosomatic Medicine* 55 (1994): 364–79.

4. B. F. Skinner, *Beyond Freedom and Dignity* (New York: Alfred A. Knopf, 1971).

5. H. Benson, *The Relaxation Response* (New York: Avon, 1976).

6. J. K. Kiecolt-Glaser, R. Glaser, E. Strain, et al., "Modulation of Cellular Immunity in Medical Students," *Journal of Behavioral Medicine* 9 (1986): 5–21.

7. L. M. Verbrugge, "Marital Status and Health," *Journal of Marriage and Family* 41 (1979): 267–85.

8. S. J. Schleifer, S. E. Keller, M. Camerino, J. C. Thornton, and M. Stein, "Suppression of Lymphocyte Function following Bereavement," *JAMA: The Journal of the American Medical Association* 250 (1983): 274–377.

9. J. K. Kiecolt-Glaser, S. Kennedy, S. Malkoff, L. Fisher, C. E. Speicher, and R. Glaser, "Marital Discord and Immunity in Males," *Psychosomatic Medicine* 50 (1988): 213–29.

10. W. McKinnon, C. S. Weisse, C. P. Reynolds, C. A. Bowles, and A. Baum, "Chronic Stress, Leukocyte Subpopulations and Humoral Response to Latent Viruses," *Health Psychology* 8 (1989): 389–402.

11. S. Levy, R. Herberman, M. Lippman, and T. d'Angelo, "Correlation of Stress Factors with Sustained Depression of Natural Killer Cell Activity and Predicted Prognosis in Patients with Breast Cancer," *Journal of Clinical Oncology* 5 (1987): 348–53.

12. L. D. Jamner, G. E. Schwartz, and H. Leigh, "The Relationship between Repressive and Defensive Coping Styles and Monocyte, Eosinophile, and Serum Glucose Levels: Support for the Opioid Peptide Hypothesis of Repression," *Psychosomatic Medicine* 50 (1988): 567–75.

13. Mogens R. Jensen, "Psychobiological Factors Predicting the Course of Breast Cancer," *Journal of Personality* 55 (1987): 317–42.

14. J. Pennebaker, W. C. Hughes, and R. C. O'Heeron, "The Psychophysiology of Confession: Linking Inhibitory and Psychosomatic Processes," *Journal of Personality and Social Psychology* 52 (1987): 781–93.

15. L. Berkowitz, *Advances in Experimental Social Psychology* 22 (New York: Academic Press, 1989).

16. H. Williams, "The Effect of Thought Vocalization on Sleep Latency," unpublished master's thesis, Southern Methodist University, 1987.

17. See, for example, N. Tarrier and P. Maguire, "Treatment of Psychological Distress following Mastectomy: An Initial Report," *Behavior Research and Therapy* 22 (1984): 81–84; A. D. Weisman and J. W. Worden, "The Existential Plight in Cancer: Significance of the First 100 Days," *International Journal of Psychiatric Medicine* 7 (1976): 1–12.

18. R. Grossarth-Maticek and H. J. Eysenck, "Creative Novation Behavior Therapy as a Prophylactic Treatment for Cancer and Coronary Heart Disease: Part 1 — Description of Treatment," *Behaviour Research and Therapy* 29, no. 1 (1989): 1–16.

19. See, for example, M. Watson, S. Greer, L. Rowden, C. Gorman, et al., "Relationships between Emotional Control, Adjustment to Cancer and Depression and Anxiety in Breast Cancer Patients," *Psychological Medicine* 21, no. 1 (February 1991): 51–57, or M. Watson, S. Greer, J. Pruyn, and B. Van den Borne, "Locus of Control and Adjustment to Cancer," *Psychological Reports* 66, no. 1 (February 1990): 39–48.

20. L. Temoshok and H. Dreher, *The Type C Connection: The Mind-Body Link to Cancer and Your Health* (New York: Penguin Books, 1992).

21. For a more extensive study of coping styles, see E. Heim, E. F. Augustiny, L. Schaffner, and L. Valach, "Coping with Breast Cancer over Time and Situation," *Journal of Psychosomatic Research* 37 (1993): 523–42.

22. S. Greer, S. Mooney, and J. Baruch, "Evaluation of Adjuvant Psychological Therapy for Clinically Referred Cancer Patients," *British Journal of Cancer* 63 (1991): 257–60.

23. S. Greer, T. Morris, K. W. Pettingale, and J. L. Haybittle, "Psychological Response to Breast Cancer and 15-Year Outcome," *The Lancet* 335 (January 6, 1990): 49–50.

24. R. Grossarth-Maticek and H. J. Eysenck, "Length of Survival and Lymphocyte Percentage in Women with Mammary Cancer as a Function of Psychotherapy," *Psychological Reports* 65 (1989): 315–21.

25. For a complete description of the current research in the Heidelberg Prospective Intervention Study, see R. Grossarth-Maticek and H. J. Eysenck, "Creative Novation Behaviour Therapy as a Prophylactic Treatment for Cancer and Coronary Heart Disease: Part 1 — Description of Treatment," and "Part 2 — Effects of Treatment, in *Behavioral Research and Therapy* 29, no. 1 (1991): 1–31. For a detailed critique of this research, see the series of articles published in *Psychological Inquiry* 2, no. 3 (1991): 221–32. See also R. J. DiClemente and L. Temoshok, "Psychological Adjustments to Having Cutaneous Malignant Melanoma as a Predictor of Follow-up Clinical Status," *Psychosomatic Medicine* 47 (1985): 81.

Chapter Four: Women's Conversations and Cancer Cells

1. See, for example, Irving Yalom, *The Theory and Practice of Group Psychotherapy* (New York: Basic Books, 1975).

2. D. Spiegel, *Living beyond Limits: New Hope and Help for Facing Life-Threatening Illness* (New York: Random House, 1993), 80.

3. O. C. Simonton, S. Matthews-Simonton, and T. G. Sparks, "Psychological Intervention in the Treatment of Cancer," *Psychosomatics* 21 (1980): 226–33.

4. For a full report of his work, see I. F. Fawzy, N. W. Cousins, N. W. Fawzy, M. Kemeny, R. Elashoff, and D. Morton, "A Structured Intervention for Cancer Patients, I: Changes over Time in Methods of Coping and Affective Disturbance," *Archives of General Psychiatry* 47 (August 1990): 720–25.

5. I. F. Fawzy, N. W. Fawzy, C. S. Hyun, R. Elashoff, D. Guthrie, J. Fahey, and D. Morton, "Malignant Melanoma: Effects of Early Structured Psychiatric Intervention, Coping and Affective State on Recurrence and Survival Six Years Later," *Archives of General Psychiatry* (September 1993).

6. I. F. Fawzy, M. E. Kemeny, N. W. Fawzy, R. Elashoff, D. Morton, N. Cousins, and J. L. Fahey, "A Structured Psychiatric Intervention for Can-

cer Patients, II: Changes over Time in Immunological Measures," *Archives of General Psychiatry* 47 (August 1990): 729–35.

7. For full reports on these studies, see R. Grossarth-Maticek and H. J. Eysenck, "Creative Novation Behaviour Therapy as a Prophylactic Treatment for Cancer and Coronary Heart Disease: Part I — Description of Treatment," *Behavior Research and Therapy* 29, no. 1 (1991): 1–16, and H. J. Eysenck and R. Grossarth-Maticek, "Creative Novation Behaviour Therapy as a Prophylactic Treatment for Cancer and Coronary Heart Disease: Part II — Effects of Treatment," *Behaviour Research and Therapy* 29, no. 1 (1991): 17–31.

8. S. E. Taylor, R. L. Falke, S. J. Shoptaw, et al., "Social Support, Support Groups and the Cancer Patient," *Journal of Consulting and Clinical Psychology* 54 (1986): 608–15.

9. C. Gilligan, *In a Different Voice: Psychological Theory and Women's Development* (Cambridge, Mass.: Harvard University Press, 1982).

10. Richard E. Renneker, "Cancer and Psychotherapy," in J. G. Goldberg, *Psychotherapeutic Treatment of Cancer Patients* (New York: The Free Press, 1981).

11. H. Morganstern, G. A. Gellert, S. D. Walter, A. M. Ostfeld, and B. S. Siegel, "The Impact of a Psychosocial Support Program on Survival with Breast Cancer: The Importance of Selection Bias in Program Evaluation," *Journal of Chronic Disability* 37, no. 4 (1984): 273–82.

12. U.S. Army Medical Department, *Neuropsychiatry in World War II*, vol. 2, *Overseas Theaters* (Washington, D.C.: U.S. Government Printing Office, 1973), 995.

13. Stanley Schachter, *The Psychology of Affiliation* (Stanford: Stanford University Press, 1959).

14. I. Martinson and S. Anderson, "Male and Female Response to Stress, in D. Kjervik and I. Martinson, eds., *Women in Stress: A Nursing Perspective* (New York: Appleton Century Crofts, 1979), 89–95.

15. Albert Ellis, *How to Live with a Neurotic at Home and at Work* (No. Hollywood, Calif.: Wilshire Book Company, 1957).

16. Ivan P. Pavlov, *Lectures on Conditioned Reflexes*, trans. W. H. Gantt (New York: International Publishers, 1928).

17. For a full discussion of rituals, see the excellent work by E. Imber-Black, J. Roberts, and R. Whiting, *Rituals in Families and Family Therapy* (New York: W. W. Norton, 1988).

18. E. Goffman, *Stigma: Notes on the Management of a Spoiled Identity* (Englewood Cliffs, N.J.: Prentice-Hall, 1963).

19. B. Gunnar, "Social and Psychological Problems in Patients with Chronic Cardiac Illness," *American Heart Journal* 58 (1959): 414–17.

20. D. Tannen, *You Just Don't Understand* (New York: Ballantine Books, 1990).

21. Ibid.

22. J. Pennebaker and R. O'Heeron, "Confiding in Others and Illness Rates among Spouses of Suicide and Accidental Death Victims," *Journal of Abnormal Psychology* 93 (1984): 473–76.

23. M. Ueno, "The So-called Coition Death," *Japanese Journal of Legal Medicine* 17 (1963): 330.

24. J. Pennebaker and J. Sussman, "Disclosure of Traumas and Psychosomatic Processes," in *Social Science and Medicine* 26 (1988): 327–32.

25. N. Waxler-Morrison, T. G. Hislop, B. Mears, and L. Kan, "Effects of Social Relationships on Survival for Women with Breast Cancer: A Prospective Study," *Social Science and Medicine* 33, no. 2 (1991): 177–83.

26. J. Lynch, *The Broken Heart* (New York: Basic Books, 1977).

27. J. Calabrese, M. Kling, M. and P. Gold, "Alterations in Immunocompetence during Stress, Bereavement, and Depression," *American Journal of Psychiatry* 144 (1987): 1123–34.

Chapter Five: Relationships and Breast Cancer

1. J. S. House, K. R. Landis, and D. Umberson, "Social Relationships and Health," *Science* 241 (1988): 540–45.

2. K. Ell, R. Nishimoto, L. Mediansky, J. Mantell, and M. Hamovitch, "Social Relations, Social Support and Survival among Patients with Cancer," *Journal of Psychosomatic Medicine* (1993): 531–41.

3. K. A. Jarvinen, "Can Ward Rounds Be a Danger to Patients with Myocardial Infarction?" *British Medical Journal* 1 (1955): 318–20.

4. L. F. Berkman and S. L. Syme, "Social Networks, Host Resistance and Mortality: A Nine-Year Follow-Up Study of Alameda County Residents," *American Journal of Epidemiology* 109, no. 2 (1979): 186–204.

5. D. Funch and J. Marshall, "The Role of Stress, Social Support and Age in Survival from Breast Cancer," *Journal of Psychosomatic Research* 27 (1983): 77–83.

6. R. Mermelstein, S. Cohen, E. Lichtenstein, T. Kamarck, and J. S. Baer, "Social Support and Smoking Cessation and Maintenance," *Journal of Consulting and Clinical Psychology* 54 (1986): 447–53.

7. R. Fleming, A. Baum, M. M. Girriel, and R. J. Gatchel, "Mediating Influences of Social Support on Stress at the Three Mile Island," *Journal of Human Stress* 8 (1982): 14–22.

8. J. K. Kiecolt-Glaser, J. K. Garner, C. E. Speicher, G. Penn, and R. Glaser, "Psychosocial Modifiers of Immunocompetence in Medical Students, *Psychosomatic Medicine* 46 (1984): 7–14.

9. J. K. Kiecolt-Glaser, D. Ricker, J. George, G. Messick, C. E. Speicher, W. Garner, W. and R. Glaser, "Urinary Cortisol Levels, Cellular Immunocompetency and Loneliness in Psychiatric Inpatients," *Psychosomatic Medicine* 46 (1984): 15–24.

10. J. E. Brody, "Maintaining Relationships for the Sake of Your Health," *New York Times*, February 5, 1992, C12.

11. J. K. Kiecolt, J. K. Glaser, R. Glaser, D. Williger, J. Stout, G. Messick, S. Sheppard, D. Ricker, S. Romisher, W. Briner, G. Bonnell, and R. I.

Donnerberg, "Psychosocial Enhancement of Immunocompetence in a Geriatric Population," *Health Psychology* 4 (1985): 25–41.

12. S. Levy, R. B. Herberman, T. Whiteside, K. Sanzo, J. Lee, and J. Kirkwood, "Perceived Social Support and Tumor Estrogen/Progesterone Receptor Status as Predictors of Natural Killer Cell Activity in Breast Cancer Patients," *Psychosomatic Medicine* 52 (1990): 73–85.

13. H. Harlow, "The Nature of Love," *American Psychologist* 13 (1958): 673.

14. G. L. Enger, "Sudden and Rapid Death during Psychological Stress: Folklore or Folk Wisdom," *Annals of Internal Medicine* 74 (1971): 771–82.

15. T. H. Holmes and R. H. Rahe, "The Social Readjustment Rating Scale," *Journal of Psychosomatic Research* 11 (1968): 213.

16. G. W. Brown, M. N. Bliroldhaim, and I. Harris, "Social Class and Psychiatric Disturbance among Women in an Urban Population," *Sociology* 9 (1975): 223–54.

17. C. Dunkel-Schetter, "Social Support and Cancer: Findings Based on Patient Interviews and Their Implications," *Journal of Social Issues* 40 (1984): 77–98.

18. D. Reiss, S. Gonzales, and H. N. Kramer, "Family Process, Chronic Illness and Death: On the Weakness of Strong Bonds," *Archives of General Psychiatry* 43 (1986): 795–804.

19. C. Tavris and C. Wade, *The Longest War: Sex Differences in Perspective*, 2d ed. (San Diego: Harcourt Brace, Jovanovich, 1984).

20. N. Waxler-Morrison, T. G. Hislop, B. Mears, and L. Kan, "Effects of Social Relationship on Survival for Women with Breast Cancer: A Prospective Study," *Social Science and Medicine* 33 (1991): 177–83.

21. W. A. Satariano and N. E. Ragheb, "Living Arrangements and Problems with Daily Tasks for Older Women with Breast Cancer," in K. W. Schaie, D. Blazer, and J. S. House, *Aging, Health Behaviors and Health Outcomes* (Hillsdale, N.J.: Lawrence Erlbaum Associates, 1992), 101–19.

22. H. Peters-Golden, "Breast Cancer: Varied Perceptions of Social Support in the Illness Experience," *Social Science and Medicine* 16 (1982): 483–91.

23. Satariano and Ragheb, "Living Arrangements and Problems with Daily Tasks for Older Women with Breast Cancer," 101–19.

24. L. Verbrugge and J. Madans, "Social Role and Health Trends of American Women," *Melbank Memorial Fund Quarterly Health and Society* (Fall 1985): 63.

25. A. V. Neale, B. Tilley, and S. Vernon, "Marital Status Delay in Seeking Treatment and Survival from Breast Cancer," *Social Science and Medicine* 23 (1986): 305–13; and also, J. S. Goodwin, W. C. Hunt, C. R. Key, and J. M. Samet, "The Effect of Marital Status on Stage, Treatment and Survival of Cancer Patient," *JAMA: Journal of the American Medical Association* 258 (1987): 3120–25.

26. Waxler-Morrison, Hislop, Mears, and Kan, "Effects of Social Relationship on Survival for Women with Breast Cancer," 177–83.

27. Ell, Nishimoto, Mediansky, Mantell, and Hamovitch, "Social Relations, Social Support and Survival among Patients with Cancer," 531–41.

28. R. R. Lichtman and S. E. Taylor, "Close Relationships and the Female Cancer Patient," in B. L. Anderson, *Women with Cancer: Psychological Perspectives* (New York: Springer Verlag, 1986).

29. S. Levy, R. Herberman, M. Lippman, and T. d'Angelo, "Correlation of Stress Factors with Sustained Depression of Natural Killer Cell Activity and Predicted Prognosis in Patients with Breast Cancer," *Journal of Clinical Oncology* 5 (1987): 348–53; A. D. Weisman and J. W. Worden, "Psychosocial Analysis of Cancer Deaths," *Omega* 6, no. 1 (1975): 61–75.

30. J. K. Kiecolt-Glaser, L. Fisher, P. Ogrocki, J. C. Stout, C. F. Speicher, and R. Glaser, "Marital Quality, Marital Disruption and Immune Function," *Psychosomatic Medicine* 49 (1987): 13–34.

31. W. R. Gove, "Sex Differences in Epidemiology of Mental Illness: Evidence and Explanations," in F. Gomberg and V. Franks, eds., *Gender and Disordered Behavior* (New York: Brunner Mazel, 1979), and also, W. R. Gove, and J. F. Tudor, "Adult Sex Roles and Mental Illness," *American Journal of Sociology* 78 (1973): 812–35.

32. J. Lynch, *The Broken Heart* (New York: Basic Books, 1977).

33. E. H. Carmen, N. F. Russo, and J. B. Miller, "Inequality and Mental Health," *American Journal of Psychiatry* 10 (1981): 1319–30.

34. N. F. Russo and S. B. Sobel, "Sex Differences in the Utilization of Mental Health Facilities," *Professional Psychology* 12 (1981): 7–19.

35. T. C. Antonucci and H. Akiyana, "An Examination of Sex Differences on the Disease Process," in L. L. Carstensen and J. M. Neale, eds., *Mechanisms of Psychological Influence on Physical Health, with Special Attention to the Elderly* (New York: Plenum Press, 1987).

36. A. D. Vinokur and D. Vinokur-Kaplan, "In Sickness and in Health, Patterns of Social Support and Undermining in Older Married Couples," *Journal of Aging and Health* (May 1990): 215–41.

37. R. W. Levenson and J. M. Gottman, "Physiological and Affective Predictors of Change in Relationship Satisfaction," *Journal of Personality and Social Psychology* 49 (1985): 85–94.

38. B. Bloom, S. Asher, and S. White, "Marital Disruption as a Stressor: A Review and Analysis," *Psychological Bulletin* 85 (1978): 867–94.

39. Kiecolt-Glaser, Fisher, Ogrocki, Stout, Speicher, and R. Glaser, "Marital Quality, Marital Disruption and Immune Function," 13–34.

40. J. K. Kiecolt-Glaser, S. Kennedy, S. Malkoff, L. Fisher, C. E. Speicher, and R. Glaser, "Marital Discord and Immunity in Males," *Psychosomatic Medicine* 50 (1988): 213–29.

41. Lichtman and Taylor, "Close Relationships and the Female Cancer Patient."

42. T. M. Knobf, "Physical and Psychologic Distress Associated with Adjuvant Chemotherapy in Women with Breast Cancer," *Journal of Clinical Oncology* 4 (1986): 678–84.

43. R. F. Klein, A. Dean, and M. D. Bogdonoff, "The Impact of Illness upon the Spouse," *Journal of Chronic Disease* 20 (1967): 241–48.

44. D. K. Wellisch, K. R. Jamison, and R. O. Pasnau, "Psychosocial Aspects

of Mastectomy, II: The Man's Perspective," *American Journal of Psychiatry* 135, no. 5 (May 1978): 543–46.

45. Knobf, "Physical and Psychologic Distress Associated with Adjuvant Chemotherapy in Women with Breast Cancer," 678–84.

46. J. W. Hannum, J. Giese-Davis, K. Harding, and A. K. Hatfield, "Effects of Individual and Marital Variables on Coping with Cancer," *Journal of Psychosocial Oncology* 9, no. 2 (1991): 1–20.

47. Lichtman and Taylor, "Close Relationships and the Female Cancer Patient."

48. L. A. Peplau and S. L. Gordon, "Women and Men in Love: Gender Differences in Close Heterosexual Relationships," in V. E. O'Leary, R. K. Unger, and J. Wallston, eds., *Women, Gender and Social Psychology* (Hillsdale, N.J.: Erlbaum, 1985).

49. Philip Blumstein and Pepper Schwartz, *American Couples: Money, Work, and Sex* (New York: William Morrow, 1984).

50. Lichtman and Taylor, "Close Relationships and the Female Cancer Patient."

51. Peplau and Gordon, "Women and Men in Love."

52. T. G. Hislop, N. Waxler, A. Coldman, J. M. Elwood, and L. Kan, "The Prognostic Significance of Psychosocial Factors in Women with Breast Cancer," *Journal of Chronic Disability* 40 (1987): 729–35.

53. A. M. Rosenfeld, G. Caplon, and A. Yaroslavsky, "Adaptation of Children of Parents Suffering from Cancer: A Preliminary Study of a New Field for Primary Prevention Research," *Journal of Primary Prevention* 3 (1983): 244–50.

54. J. M. Hyland, E. S. Novotny, and L. Coyne, "Coping with Difficult-to-Treat Cancer Patients," *Bulletin of the Menninger Clinic* 48 (1984): 329–41.

55. R. Coleman, M. Greenblatt, and H. Solomon, "Physiological Evidence of Rapport during Psychotherapeutic Interviews," *Diseases of the Nervous System* 17 (1956): 71–77.

56. S. Nealing and H. Winefield, "Social Support and Recovery after Surgery from Breast Cancer: Frequency and Correlates of Supportive Behaviors by Family, Friends and Surgeon," *Social Science Medicine* 27 (1988): 385–92.

57. Waxler-Morrison, Hislop, Mears, and Kan, "Effects of Social Relationship on Survival for Women with Breast Cancer," 177–83.

58. C. Gilligan, *In a Different Voice: Psychological Theory and Women's Development* (Cambridge, Mass.: Harvard University Press, 1982).

59. A. Beck and A. H. Thatcher, *Between Pets and People* (New York: G. P. Putnam, 1983).

60. E. Friedmann et al., "Animal Companions and One-Year Survival of Patients after Discharge from a Coronary Care Unit," *Public Health Reports* 95, no. 4 (1980): 307–12.

61. F. K. Graham and R. K. Clifton, "Heart Rate Changes as a Component of the Orienting Response," *Psychological Bulletin* 65 (1966): 305–20, and E. N. Sokolov, *Perception and the Conditioned Reflex* trans. Stefan W. Waydenfeld (New York: Macmillan, 1963).

Chapter Six:
Acting Alive: Thoughts and Feelings

1. L. Jamner, G. E. Schwartz, and H. Leigh, "The Relationship between Repressive and Defensive Coping Styles and Monocyte, Eosinophile and Serum Glucose Levels: Support for the Opioid Peptide Hypothesis of Repression," *Psychosomatic Medicine* 50 (1988): 567–75.

2. A. L. Stanton and P. R. Snider, "Coping with a Breast Cancer Diagnosis: A Prospective Study," *Health Psychology* 12, no. 1 (1993): 16–23.

3. A. Kronful and J. D. House, "Depression, Cortisol and Immune Function," *Lancet* 1 (1984): 1026–27.

4. J. K. Kiecolt-Glaser, R. Stephens, P. Lipetz, C. E. Speicher, and R. Glaser, "Distress and DNA Repair in Human Lymphocytes," *Journal of Behavioral Medicine* 8 (1985): 311–20.

5. J. Calabrese, M. Kling, and P. Gold, "Alterations in Immunocompetence during Stress, Bereavement and Depression," *American Journal of Psychiatry* 144 (1987): 1123–34.

6. M. Kemeny, J. Reed, S. Taylor, and J. Fahey, "Personal Relationships as Moderators of Immune and Endocrine Function: Fatalism and Bereavement as Predictors of Immune Changes in HIV," paper presented at the American Psychological Association 101st Annual Convention, August 20, 1993, Toronto, Ontario, Canada.

7. M. A. Visintainer, and R. Casey, "Adjustment and Outcome in Melanoma Patients," paper presented at the meeting of the American Psychological Association, Toronto, Canada, 1984.

8. A. Ellis, *How to Master Your Fear of Flying* (New York: Institute for Rational Living, 1972).

9. R. S. Lazarus and S. Folkman, *Stress, Appraisal and Coping* (New York: Springer Publishing, 1984); also, M. A. Visintainer, and M. E. P. Seligman, "Tumor Rejection and Early Experience of Uncontrollable Shock in the Rat," unpublished paper, University of Pennsylvania, 1981.

10. M. Seligman, *Learned Optimism* (New York: Pocket Books, 1990).

11. E. J. Langer, and J. Rodin, "The Effects of Choice and Enhanced Personal Responsibility for the Aged: A Field Experiment in an Institutional Setting," *Journal of Personality and Social Psychology* 34 (1976): 191–98.

12. S. Levy and B. Wise, "Psychosocial Risk Factors and Cancer Progression," in C. L. Cooper, *Stress and Breast Cancer* (New York: Wiley, 1988). Also M. E. P. Seligman, *Learned Optimism* (New York: Simon & Schuster, 1990).

13. S. Greer, T. Morris, K. W. Pettingale, and J. L. Haybittle, "Psychological Response to Cancer and 15-Year Outcome," *The Lancet* (January 6, 1990): 49–50.

14. M. A. Visintainer, J. R. Volpicelli, and M. E. P. Seligman, "Tumor Rejection in Rats," *Science* 216 (1982): 437–39.

15. L. Kamen-Siegel, J. Rodin, M. E. P. Seligman, and J. Dwyer, "Explana-

tory Style and Cell-mediated Immunity in Elderly Men and Women," *Health Psychology* 10 (1991): 229–35.

Chapter Seven:
Limiting the Trauma of Breast Cancer Treatment:
I. Understanding How You Feel

1. R. Glaser, J. K. Kiecolt-Glaser, J. C. Stout, K. L. Tarr, C. E. Speicher, and J. E. Holliday, "Stress-Related Impairments in Cellular Immunity," *Psychiatry Research* 16 (1985): 233–39.

2. R. Duff and A. Hollingshead, *Sickness and Society* (New York: Harper & Row, 1968).

3. D. M. Amoroso and R. H. Walters, "Effects of Anxiety and Socially Mediated Anxiety Reduction on Paired Associate Learning," *Journal of Personality and Social Psychology* 11 (1969): 388–96.

4. James A. Kulik, Philip J. Moore, and Heike I. M. Mahler, "Stress and Affiliation: Hospital Roommate Effects on Preoperative Anxiety and Social Interaction," *Health Psychology* 12 (1993): 118–24.

5. Y. Hirshaut and P. I. Pressman, *Breast Cancer: The Complete Guide* (New York: Bantam Books, 1992).

6. L. J. Maholney, B. Bird, and H. M. Cooke, "Annual Clinical Examination: The Best Available Screening Test for Breast Cancer," *New England Journal of Medicine* 301 (1979): 315–16.

7. P. Skrabanek, "False Premises and False Promises of Breast Cancer Screening," *The Lancet* (August 10, 1985): 316.

8. F. I. Fawzy, M. E. Kemeny, N. W. Fawzy, R. Elashoff, D. Morton, N. Cousins, and J. L. Fahey, "A Structured Psychiatric Intervention for Cancer Patients, II: Changes over Time in Immunological Measures," *Archives of General Psychiatry* 47 (August 1990): 729–35.

9. M. L. S. Vachon, "A Comparison of the Impact of Breast Cancer and Bereavement: Personality, Social Support and Adaptation," in S. Hobfel, ed., *Stress, Social Support and Women* (New York: Hemisphere, 1984), 187–204.

10. J. Hughes, "Emotional Reactions to the Diagnosis and Treatment of Early Breast Cancer," *Journal of Psychological Research* 26 (1982): 277–83, and also K. R. Jamison, D. K. Wellisch, and R. O. Pasnau, "Psychosocial Aspects of Mastectomy: The Woman's Perspective," *American Journal of Psychology* 135 (1978): 432–36.

11. S. Levy, R. B. Herberman, T. Whiteside, K. Sanzo, J. Lee, and J. Kirkwood, "Perceived Social Support and Tumor Estrogen/Progesterone Receptor Status as Predictors of Natural Killer Cell Activity in Breast Cancer Patients," *Psychosomatic Medicine* 52 (1990): 73–85.

12. R. S. Ulrich, "View through a Window May Influence Recovery from Surgery," *Science* 224 (April 27, 1984): 420–21.

13. P. Maguire, "The Psychological Consequences of the Surgical Treatment

of Cancer of the Breast," in L. M. Nyhus and C. Judge, *Surgery Annual* 22 (1990): 77–91.

14. B. F. Forester, D. S. Kornfeld, and J. L. Fleiss, "Psychotherapy during Radiotherapy: Effects on Emotional and Physical Distress," *American Journal of Psychiatry* 142, no. 1 (January 1985): 22–27.

15. P. A. Ganz, M. L. Polinsky, C. A. Schag, and R. L. Heinrich, "Rehabilitation of Patients with Primary Breast Cancer: Assessing the Impact of Adjuvant Therapy," in H. J. Senn, *Recent Results in Cancer Research: Adjuvant Therapy of Primary Breast Cancer* (New York: Springer Verlag, 1989), 115.

16. D. V. Easterling and H. Leventhal, "Contribution of Concrete Cognition to Emotion: Neutral Symptoms as Elicitors of Worry about Cancer," *Journal of Applied Psychology* 74, no. 5 (1989): 787–96.

17. B. E. Meyerowitz, I. K. Watkins, and F. C. Sparks, "Psychosocial Implications of Adjuvant Chemotherapy: A Two-Year Follow-Up," *Cancer* (October 15, 1983): 1541–45.

18. Ibid.

19. Allen Lichter, "Lumpectomy and Radiation: Improving the Outcome," *Journal of Clinical Oncology* 10, no. 3 (1992): 349–51. Also A. P. Locker, I. O. Ellis, D. A. L. Morgan, "Factors Influencing Local Recurrences after Excision and Radiotherapy for Primary Breast Cancer," *British Journal of Science* 76 (1989): 890–94.

Chapter Eight:
Limiting the Trauma of Breast Cancer Treatment:
II. Boosting Chemotherapy

1. F. K. Hamera and F. C. Shontz, "Perceived Positive and Negative Effects of Life-Threatening Illness," *Journal of Psychosomatic Research* 22 (1978): 419–24.

2. H. Leventhal, D. V. Easterling, H. L. Coons, C. M. Luchterhand, and R. R. Love, "Adaptation to Chemotherapy Treatments," in B. Anderson, ed., *Women with Cancer: Psychological Perspectives* (New York: Springer Verlag, 1986).

3. W. H. Redd and M. A. Andrykowski, "Behavioral Intervention in Cancer Treatment: Controlling Aversion Reactions to Chemotherapy," *Journal of Consulting and Clinical Psychology* 50 (1982): 1018–29.

4. L. W. Buckalew and R. E. Sallis, "Patient Compliance and Medication Prescription," *Journal of Clinical Psychology* 42 (1986): 49–53.

5. C. K. Tebbi, K. M. Cummings, M. A. Zevon, L. Smith, M. Richards, and J. Mallon, "Compliance of Pediatric and Adolescent Cancer Patients," *Cancer* 58 (1986): 1179–84.

6. P. Vincent, "Factors Influencing Noncompliance: A Theoretical Approach," *Nursing Research* 20 (1971): 509–16.

7. S. Levy, R. B. Herberman, T. Whiteside, K. Sanzo, J. Lee, and J. Kirkwood, "Perceived Social Support and Tumor Estrogen/Progesterone Receptor

Status as Predictors of Natural Killer Cell Activity in Breast Cancer Patients," *Psychosomatic Medicine* 52 (1990): 73–85.

8. P. Ley and M. S. Spelman, *Communicating with the Patient* (London: Staples Press, 1965).

9. J. M. Dunbar and W. S. Agras, "Compliance with Medical Instructions," in J. M. Ferguson and C. B. Taylor, eds., *Comprehensive Handbook of Behavioral Medicine*, vol. 3 (New York: Spectrum, 1980).

10. R. E. Glasgow, L. Schefer, and H. K. O'Neill, "Self-Help Books and Amount of Therapist Contact in Smoking Cessation Programs," *Journal of Consulting and Clinical Psychology* 49 (1981): 659–67.

11. Leventhal et al., "Adaptation to Chemotherapy Treatments."

12. Redd and Andrykowski, "Behavioral Intervention in Cancer Treatment," 1018–29.

13. E. M. Altmaier, W. E. Ross, and K. Moore, "A Pilot Investigation of the Psychologic Function of Patients with Anticipatory Vomiting," *Cancer* 49 (1982): 201–4.

14. G. B. Challis and H. J. Stam, "A Longitudinal Study of the Development of Anticipatory Nausea and Vomiting in Cancer Chemotherapy Patients: The Role of Absorption and Autonomic Perception," *Health Psychology* 11 (1992): 181–89.

15. P. M. Black and G. M. Morrow, "Anticipatory Nausea and Emesis: Behavioral Interventions," in Maggie Watson, ed., *Cancer Patient Care: Psychosocial Treatment Methods* (Cambridge, Eng.: Cambridge University Press, 1991), 45–73.

16. W. H. Redd, P. H. Rosenberger, and C. S. Hendler, "Controlling Chemotherapy Side Effects," *American Journal of Clinical Hypnosis* 25 (1983): 161–72.

17. D. C. Hammond, C. Hasking-Bartsch, C. W. Grant, and M. McGhee, "Comparison of Self-Directed and Tape-Assisted Self-Hypnosis," *American Journal of Clinical Hypnosis* 31 (1988): 129–37.

18. See for example, S. Finkelstein, "Adverse Effects after Exposure to Lay Hypnosis in a Group Setting: A Case Report," *American Journal of Clinical Hypnosis* 32 (1989): 107–9.

19. For a full discussion and explanation, see Herbert Benson's works, such as *The Relaxation Response* (New York: Avon, 1976).

20. T. G. Burish, M. P. Carey, M. G. Krozely, and F. A. Greco, "Conditioned Side Effects Induced by Cancer Chemotherapy: Prevention through Behavioral Treatment," *Journal of Consulting and Clinical Psychology* 55 (1987): 42–48.

21. T. G. Burish and J. N. Lyles, "Effectiveness of Relaxation Training in Reducing Adverse Reactions to Cancer Chemotherapy," *Journal of Behavioral Medicine* 4 (1981): 65–78.

22. P. H. Cotanch, "Relaxation Techniques as Antiemetic Therapy," in J. Laszlo, ed., *Antiemetics and Cancer Chemotherapy* (Baltimore: Williams & Wilkins, 1983).

23. J. K. Kiecolt-Glaser, R. Glaser, D. Williger, J. Stout, G. Messick, S. Sheppard, D. Ricker, S. C. Romisher, W. Briner, G. Bonnell, and R. Donnerberg,

"Psychosocial Enhancement of Immunocompetence in a Geriatric Population," *Health Psychology* 4 (1985): 25-41.

24. A. H. C. Sinclair-Gieben, "Evaluation and Treatment of Warts by Hypnosis," *Lancet* 2 (1959): 480. See also T. A. Clawson and R. H. Swade, "The Hypnotic Control of Blood Flow and Pain: The Cure of Warts and the Potential for the Use of Hypnosis in the Treatment of Cancer," *American Journal of Clinical Hypnosis* 17, no. 3 (1975): 160-69.

25. H. Hall, "Hypnosis and the Immune System," *American Journal of Clinical Hypnosis* 25 (1983): 92-103.

26. W. H. Redd, P. H. Rosenberger, and C. S. Hendler, "Controlling Chemotherapy Side Effects," *American Journal of Clinical Hypnosis* 25 (1983): 161-72.

27. W. H. Redd, G. V. Andresen, and R. Y. Minagawa, "Hypnotic Control of Anticipatory Emesis in Patients Receiving Cancer Chemotherapy," *Journal of Consulting and Clinical Psychology* 50 (1982): 14-19.

28. R. P. Blankfield, "Suggestion, Relaxation and Hypnosis as Adjuncts in the Care of Surgery Patients: A Review of the Literature," *American Journal of Clinical Hypnosis* 33 (1991): 172-86.

29. J. Grinder and R. Bandler, *Trance-formations: Neurolinguistic Programming and the Structure of Hypnosis* (Moab, Utah: Real People Press, 1981), 53.

30. Ibid., 190.

31. M. Torem, "'Back from the Future': A Powerful Age Progression Technique," *American Journal of Clinical Hypnosis* 35 (1992): 81-88.

32. G. R. Morrow and C. Morrel, "Behavioral Treatment for the Anticipatory Nausea and Vomiting Induced by Cancer Chemotherapy," *New England Journal of Medicine* 307 (1982): 1476-80.

33. R. E. Townsend, J. F. House, and D. A. Addario, "Comparison of EMG Feedback and Progressive Muscle Relaxation Training in Anxiety Neuroses," *American Journal of Psychiatry* 132 (1975): 598-601.

34. N. P. Spanos and L. D. Bertrand, "EMG Biofeedback-Attained Relaxation and Hypnotic Susceptibility: Is There a Relationship?" *American Journal of Clinical Hypnosis* 27 (1985): 219-25.

35. W. H. Redd, P. B. Jacobsen, M. Die-Trill, H. Dermatis, M. McEvoy, and J. Holland, "Cognitive/Attentional Distraction in the Control of Conditioned Nausea in Pediatric Cancer Patients Receiving Chemotherapy," *Journal of Consulting and Clinical Psychology* 55 (1987): 391-95.

Chapter Nine: Women Connected

1. M. Nielson, J. Jensen, and J. Andersen, "Precancerous and Cancerous Breast Lesions during Lifetime and at Autopsy," *Cancer* 54 (1984): 612-15.

2. G. Kolata, "Weighing Spending on Breast Cancer," in *New York Times,* October 19, 1993, and "Budget Is Mixed for Behavioral Sciences," *The Psycho-*

logical Science Agenda of the American Psychological Association (July/August 1993): 3.

3. The research described in this section is reported in a number of writings from the Harvard Project on Women's Psychology and Girls' Development, including C. Gilligan, *In a Different Voice: Psychological Theory and Women's Development* (Cambridge, Mass.: Harvard University Press, 1982), and C. Gilligan, A. G. Rogers, and D. L. Tolman, *Women, Girls and Psychotherapy: Reframing Resistance* (New York: Haworth Press, 1991).

4. J. E. Brody, "Personal Health," *New York Times*, March 16, 1994, C12.

5. T. W. Kamarck, S. B. Manuck, and J. R. Jennings, "Social Support Reduces Cardiovascular Reactivity to Behavioral Challenge: A Laboratory Model," paper presented at the meeting of the Society of Behavioral Medicine, San Francisco, April 1989.

6. J. A. Blumenthal, M. M. Burg, J. Barefoot, R. B. Williams, T. Haney, and G. Zimet, "Social Support, Type A Behavior and Coronary Artery Disease," *Psychosomatic Medicine* 49 (1987): 331–39.

7. D. Spiegel, "Can Psychotherapy Prolong Cancer Survival?" *Psychosomatic Medicine* 31, no. 4 (Fall 1990).

8. J. Avis, "The Politics of Functional Family Therapy: A Feminist Critique," *Journal of Marital and Family Therapy* 11 (1985): 127–38.

9. G. K. Baruch, L. Biener, and R. C. Barnett, "Women and Gender in Research on Work and Family Stress," *American Psychologist* 42 (1987): 130–36.

10. D. Goleman, "Two Views of Marriage Explored: His and Hers," *New York Times*, April 1, 1986, C1, 3.

11. M. McGoldrick, "The Joining of Families through Marriage: The New Couple," in B. Carter and M. McGoldrick, eds., *The Changing Family Life Cycle* (New York: Gardner Press, 1988).

12. L. M. Verbrugge, "Marital Status and Health," *Journal of Marriage and Family* 41 (1979): 267–85.

13. T. C. Antonucci and H. Ayikama, "An Examination of Sex Differences in Social Support in Mid- and Late Life," *Sex Roles* 17 (1987): 737–49.

14. B. M. Schydlowsky, "Friendships among Women in Midlife," unpublished doctoral dissertation, University of Michigan, microfilm, 1983.

Technical Terms

Axillary node status: presence or absence of malignant cells in the underarm lymph nodes.

Antiemetic: medication given to prevent or relieve nausea or vomiting.

Catecholamines: stress hormones.

Breast self-examination: a monthly procedure used by women to examine their breasts for foreign tissue.

Clinical hypnosis: trance induction used in psychological and medical procedures.

Cognitive: having to do with logic, thinking, reasoning, and memory.

Estrogen receptor status: the responsiveness of malignant tissue to treatment by hormone therapy.

Helper cells: T-lymphocytes that stimulate the action of natural killer cells.

In situ: tumor in its original place without having spread from a previous site.

Lymphocytes: white blood cells in the immune system.

Lymphoid: pertaining to the lymph system.

Lyse: to destroy a cell by damaging its outer membrane.

Lumpectomy: surgical procedure in which cancerous tissue is removed from the breast, with limited change to healthy breast tissue.

Mastectomy: surgical removal of all or part of the breast.

Metastatic breast cancer: breast cancer that has spread to other parts of the body through the lymphatic system or the bloodstream.

Natural killer cells: Killer T-lymphocytes that are stimulated to attack by chemical signals sent out by abnormal cells.

Neuropeptides: chemical messengers containing amino acids.

Nucleotides: a class of chemical messengers.

Primary breast cancer: Stage I breast cancer; the mildest and most common form of breast cancer.

Psychotropic: a group of medications that influence mood and emotion.

Recurrence: Reappearance of cancer at the same or nearby sites.

Relaxation response: an exercise that releases muscle tension and achieves overall body relaxation.

Suppressor cells: T-lymphocytes that act as a brake on the natural killer cells.

T-lymphocytes: white blood cells that attach to abnormal cells and then release chemicals known as lymphokines, which help them destroy tumor cells.